STILL A DREAM

STILL A DREAM
THE CHANGING STATUS
OF BLACKS SINCE 1960

SAR A. LEVITAN

WILLIAM B. JOHNSTON

ROBERT TAGGART

Harvard University Press
Cambridge, Massachusetts, and London, England

PREFACE

A decade has passed since Martin Luther King voiced his dream that "one day this nation will rise up and live out the true meaning of its creed: 'We hold these truths to be self-evident, that all men are created equal.'" Although this dream remains more a goal than a reality, and while some would question whether adequate progress has been made in its quest, there can be no question that massive changes have occurred for the nation's 24 million blacks. In the home, on the job, at the polls, and in the classroom, they have made substantial advances. No one familiar with the insufferable conditions of the not-so-distant past can doubt that blacks are much better off today than they were a decade ago. But improvement has been uneven and some dimensions may even have deteriorated. Although there is disagreement about the meaning and causes of rising dependency, crime, and family break-up, these developments are cause for concern. It is difficult to sort out the positive from the negative and to weigh the benefits of progress against the costs of intensifying or continuing social problems.

This task is complicated by the diversity of change. In social matters, developments on one front cannot be fully understood without knowledge of the whole. Yet the interrelationships among family patterns, education, income, employment, health, housing, and other factors are never straightforward. The insights to be gained from a more comprehensive perspective are sometimes obscured by the maze of additional information. The pieces to the puzzle are constantly

v

changing, so that the picture is more a kaleidoscope than a lasting tableau.

The task of interpretation is compounded by data deficiencies. The major information sources are data collected by the federal establishment. At times, the concepts derived to measure conditions among the majority are of limited applicability in assessing the status of blacks. Data on crime, health, housing, labor market conditions, and almost any other factor are subject to bias and uncertainty when focused on the black population. Even the most basic statistic—the head-count of blacks—is questionable, since there are hundreds of thousands of blacks who are missed by census takers. On the other hand, anecdotal and limited case study information tends to be selective and a poor basis for generalization. In this, as in every case, statistics are no substitute for judgment, but judgment is often impossible without statistics.

Another problem, of course, is the normative element in any assessment. In every dimension of analysis, there is evidence of both advances and setbacks. Modest changes in the order or tone of presentation can determine whether the reader perceives a bottle half filled with progress or one half empty due to limited gains.

Given all these impediments, it may seem heroic to try to assess the changing economic and social status of blacks and the related policy issues. What new insights or perspectives can be achieved?

The answer is that there is still a lot to be learned. Much of the data provided by the 1970 census, which is the major benchmark for assessing change, has not been analyzed. Other information has been published but not pulled together and systematically analyzed. A variety of specialized studies concerning more specific aspects of black economic and social status have often received limited attention. Clearly, there is a great deal of information which has not been fully utilized.

The purpose of this study is to review and synthesize this information. There is no attempt to derive or interpret any grand scheme. The more modest goal is to assess the information as objectively as possible and to try to determine interrelationships and implications. The purpose is to provide an informational foundation rather than a comprehensive interpretation and understanding of the problems and progress of blacks.

Yet even with this more limited aim of organizing and synthesizing available data, the impediments to objective and realistic analysis have to be admitted. Some would argue that only blacks can understand and write incisively about black conditions. None of the authors are black and they can claim no intimate knowledge of the black community. Every piece of evidence which is utilized can and should be subjected to careful scrutiny.

However, to a large extent, the facts speak for themselves. After allowances for judgmental bias, limited experience, and statistical uncertainties, the evidence in most cases is consistent and, if not unequivocal, at least suggestive. Some facts may perhaps be altered or supplemented in the future or interpreted differently, but any theory dealing with the changing status of blacks must either build on these data or present more persuasive evidence.

Social and economic status is difficult to define, and individuals may differ concerning the relative importance of various factors. This study will focus on the following critical dimensions.

1. *Income*. Money is of central importance in a society where the consumer is sovereign and where public services and facilities are relatively scarce. Money may not buy everything, but income is probably the major determinant of well-being.

2. *Employment*. Earnings are the primary source of income, and work is a major activity for most adults. Job satisfaction affects overall well-being, while occupational positions and earnings are important determinants of individual status and prestige.

3. *Education*. A diploma is more and more frequently a prerequisite to employment in better paying, higher status, and more satisfying jobs. In its own right, education affects values and outlooks, and is another factor in determining class standing and future prospects.

4. *Marital and family patterns*. The stability and compatibility of the family unit affects the well-being of the partners, and more crucially, the development of their offspring. The family is still the basic mechanism through which economic and social status is transmitted from one generation to the next.

5. *Health*. Sound health is important for the enjoyment of life and its absence can affect earning capacity, education, family patterns, and more. Problems elsewhere may also affect health; for instance,

low income may mean a deficient diet which can result in health problems.

6. *Housing*. Adequate housing is also vital. Life in an overcrowded, deteriorated home can be a source of misery and a handicap to development. A home's location is a determinant of access to schools and jobs. Its quality is a prestige factor as well as a source of enjoyment. And its cost affects how much is left over for other less essential needs.

7. *Power and control*. The good life is not just a matter of comfort; there are also more intangible requirements such as self-fulfillment and self-determination. Having a voice in unions, on the job, in business and government, and in shaping community life are important to most people.

While there are other factors which might be considered in assessing social and economic status, well-being can be largely measured relative to these seven dimensions. Current conditions, and changes and rates of change in these dimensions, generally determine whether conditions for blacks are intolerable, favorable, or merely acceptable.

The purpose of studying change is to determine how it can be redirected, if necessary, and how trends of improvement can be accelerated. Public policy has played a pervasive role in effecting socioeconomic changes, and government intervention strategies must be analyzed to determine their impact on blacks as well as the most effective approach or combination of approaches for the future. The following broad areas of public policy deserve scrutiny.

1. *Transfer payments*. A range of programs were implemented or expanded in the 1960s to transfer income from more affluent taxpayers to those with greater needs, including a disproportionate number of blacks. Transfer payments may be an "earned right" based partially or wholly on past contributions, or they may be based on need alone.

2. *In-kind aid*. Rather than supplementing income directly, government funds can be used to provide or pay for specified goods and services. Assistance can be targeted for what society believes to be especially critical problems. Where existing institutions do not effectively serve those with limited income, new delivery mechanisms can be created or sustained.

3. *Human resource development*. An alternative to providing cash

and in-kind aid is to increase the capacity of individuals to make it on their own. To the extent that low earnings and poverty are related to limited education and skills or the lack of credentials, these impediments can be corrected through education and manpower programs, increasing self-sufficiency over the long run.

4. *Eliminating discrimination.* The impact of human resource development will be reduced if those assisted do not have an equal chance to prove themselves. A necessary supplementary approach is to change the rules of the game to provide equal opportunity in housing, education, employment, and all other areas. Pressure can be exerted through the courts, by jawboning, or with the leverage of government dollars.

5. *Building institutions.* After years of discrimination, blacks lack many of the institutions needed to compete on equal terms in today's society. While individuals can gain from improvement in skills and education, their sustained progress also depends on pressures from black owned and black run organizations which can support their interests.

6. *Considering black needs in the formulation of public policy.* Blacks are disproportionately affected by many government actions. Monetary and fiscal policies, minimum wage laws, military requirements, and legal and correctional policies have impacts on blacks which may conflict with or bolster efforts to achieve equality.

Though analysis from each of these perspectives may leave gaps, together they form a detailed composite picture. Whatever the shortcomings of this assessment, there is no doubt that such a synthesis is timely. Suffering from an "informational overload" as well as an anxiety over the rapid pace of change, society in general and public policymakers in particular have tended to neglect black interests in the early 1970s. There is evidence to suggest that the pace of improvement has slackened as a result, and that the neglect has not been entirely benign. If Martin Luther King's dream is to be realized, efforts to achieve racial equality must be vigorously renewed. This recommitment must begin with an understanding of how far we have come and the distance still to be traveled.

A number of knowledgeable readers reviewed earlier drafts of this manuscript. Without implicating them in the results, we are indebted to the following for critical and helpful comments: Hamilton Bryce, Joint Center for Political Studies; Charles V. Hamilton, Columbia University; Mario Obledo, Mexican American Legal Defense and Education Fund; Madelon D. Stent, Urban Education; Harold Howe II, Benjamin P. Payton, Mitchell Sviridoff, and Louis Winnick of the Ford Foundation; Regis Walther, George Washington University; and Phillis Wallace, Massachusetts Institute of Technology. Officials from the U.S. Civil Rights Commission and, in particular, the statisticians from the U.S. Bureau of the Census were helpful during the preparation of the volume. Mrs. Joyce K. Zickler and Karen C. Alderman helped in the research for Part II. And not least, the patient typing and proofreadings of the draft by Barbara Pease and Beverly Anderson and their final refusal to retype it again led to the completion of the volume.

This volume was prepared under a grant from the Ford Foundation to George Washington University's Center for Manpower Policy Studies. In accordance with the Foundation's practice, complete responsibility for the preparation of the volume has been left to the authors.

Sar A. Levitan
William B. Johnston
Robert Taggart

CONTENTS

xi

Part 3. Policy and Change

TABLES

FIGURES

Map

STILL A DREAM

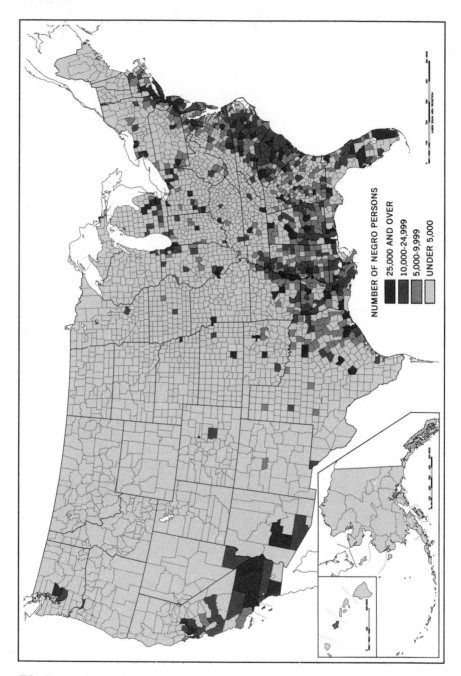

Black population by counties, 1970.

Source: U.S. Bureau of the Census, *1970 Census of Population, Supplementary Reports,* Series PC(S1)–1, "Distribution of the Negro Population, by County."

1

THE BLACK POPULATION

The social and economic status of blacks is a vital concern not only because blacks account for 11 percent of the population, but also because they include a disproportionate share of the disadvantaged, downtrodden, and disenfranchised. The domestic problems which beset our nation are closely intertwined with those of black citizens: continued poverty, urban blight, inequality, and alienation from government and other institutions. These problems are of our own making, and their existence is a shameful reminder of past and continuing exploitation and injustice.

Yet the present generation can take some pride in its efforts even though they have failed to end racial inequality. A variety of governmental initiatives were undertaken during the past decade to help the disadvantaged generally, and blacks specifically. It is important to determine the successes and shortcomings of these efforts in order to decide what can and will be done to sustain progress toward a more just and equal society.

Before either the social and economic status of blacks or the impact of governmental efforts can be understood, several aspects of the situation of the black minority must be recognized.

1. *Blacks are a minority of the population.* In 1972 there were 23.4 million blacks (defined in the census by self-identification rather than observation). They were the largest racial minority, outnumbering Mexican-Americans and Puerto Ricans by 3.5 to 1; they accounted

1

for nine-tenths of all nonwhites. Yet blacks constituted only 11.3 percent of the United States population, and even large percentages of
blacks with certain characteristics represent very small segments of the
total population.

	Millions	Percent
U.S. total	207.8	100.0
Blacks	23.4	11.3
Mexican-Americans	5.2	2.6
Puerto Ricans	1.5	0.7
Indians	0.8 (1970)	0.4

As an example, it is generally agreed that black teenage unemployment has reached crisis proportions, with a third counted unemployed
in 1972. A rate this size is frightening and may give the impression
that nothing can be done. Yet unemployed black teenagers averaged
only 6 percent of all unemployed persons and 0.2 percent of the
population age sixteen and above.[1] The creation of 165,000 jobs
would have reduced their unemployment rate to the white level. This
is not such an insurmountable task when it is considered that the
federally funded Neighborhood Youth Corps provided nearly
700,000 summer jobs in 1972. Similarly, it would have required only
$3.6 billion to raise all poor blacks to the poverty threshold in 1972,
less money than was paid to farmers in crop subsidies.[2]

The minority status of blacks, combined with their concentration
among those most in need, has other implications. Obviously, blacks
are limited in their potential influence over organizations and institutions. They tend to be disproportionately affected for better and for
worse by socioeconomic changes. For instance, if every firm decided
to increase the black percentage of its labor force by 1 percent, black
employment would grow by 10 percent. This leverage must always be
kept in mind when assessing the impact of change.

2. *A majority of the black population lives in the South and the
central cities of large urban areas.* Despite three decades of out-
migration, 52 percent of the black population still resides in the South
compared with only 29 percent of whites.[3] Most of the southern black
population is concentrated in Louisiana, Mississippi, Alabama, North

Carolina, and South Carolina. Fifty-five percent of all blacks reside in central cities compared with 28 percent of whites (table 1-1). In the South, only two of five blacks live inside central cities, but in the North, four-fifths, and in the West, two-thirds (map facing page 1).

Table 1-1. The black population in 1970 (thousands)

Residence	Total[a]	Northeast	North Central	South	West
Total	22,580	4,344	4,572	11,870	1,695
Metropolitan	17,103	4,230	4,305	6,941	1,626
Central city	13,330	3,404	3,717	5,074	1,135
Outside central city	3,772	826	587	1,867	491
Nonmetropolitan	5,478	113	266	5,029	68

Source: U.S. Bureau of the Census, Supplementary Report, *Population of Standard Metropolitan Statistical Areas Established Since the 1970 Census, for the United States: 1970 and 1960*, PC(S1)-17, May 1972, table 3.

[a] Total differs from other census counts because of sampling variability.

This bifurcated distribution, outside metropolitan areas in the South and within central cities in the North and West, may result in misleading averages for the entire black population. Blacks in rural areas of the deep South have the lowest living costs (as well as standards) in the nation. Those in large urban areas, especially those in ghettos where prices are inflated, pay more for everything. The dollar figures understate the real income of rural blacks and overstate the gains of those in urban areas. Shifts in the distribution of population may give a misleading picture of overall changes in income.

The employment problems of blacks in the nonmetropolitan South also differ radically from those in the urban North. Low-skill and low-paying jobs are more plentiful, though frequently unstable, in the North. Income support and "hustling" opportunities in the city provide alternatives to employment and encourage frequent entry and exit from the work force. In the nonmetropolitan South, however, where opportunities for the unskilled are much more limited, many potential workers may not appear in the unemployment statistics because they either give up their job search or are "underemployed" in agriculture or in other low-paying jobs. Low wages are relatively more of a problem for southern blacks, while unemployment is more frequent for those in the North, so that average employment and earnings data must be interpreted correspondingly.

There are also differences in patterns of socialization between rural southerners and urban northerners. As an example, there is apparently a more stable family tradition in rural areas; a third of all women age sixteen and over in urban areas are widowed, divorced, or separated compared with less than a fifth of those in rural farm areas.[4] Persons moving from rural to urban areas undoubtedly carry with them these differing values and attitudes.

3. *Migration has brought important changes for many blacks.* Blacks have been leaving the South at a steady rate of about 150,000 per year during the last twenty years, and they have been moving to the cities even faster. Almost all of the migrants from the South originated in nonmetropolitan areas. Between 1960 and 1970 net out-migration of blacks from southern farm areas totaled 1.3 million, representing a 23 percent decline in the rural black population. On the other hand, there was an increase of 124,000 blacks in southern cities due to net migration, and more than 2 million black migrants were added to urban populations in the North and West. Between 1960 and 1970 there was an increase of 14 million whites and 4 million blacks in the nation's cities. By 1970, 68 percent of whites and 74 percent of blacks lived in metropolitan areas (table 1-2).

This massive flow does not mean that blacks have been more mobile than whites. On the contrary, almost exactly four-fifths of both

Table 1-2. Population shares, 1960 and 1970 (percent)

	Black		White	
Area	1960	1970	1960	1970
South	60	53	27	28
North and West	40	47	73	72
Metropolitan areas	68	74	66	68
Nonmetropolitan areas	32	26	33	32

Source: U.S. Bureau of the Census, Department of Commerce, *The Social and Economic Status of the Black Population in the United States, 1971,* Series P-23, no. 42, July 1973, tables 4 and 8.

blacks and whites stay put each year and whites are more likely to move long distances. The transitional problems which accompany resettling are common to both groups. But the net redistribution for blacks is much greater than for whites. Whites are moving from the North and West to the South as well as in the reverse direction, so that the overall redistribution has not been marked, while for blacks there is more of a one-way flow. Also, migration for blacks may be of a different nature. The move from farm to city is much more dramatic than from an eastern to a southern suburb.

The predominant reason for the black migration is the quest for higher wages, more plentiful jobs, and more equal opportunities.[5] As the southern economy continues to shift away from farm employment, blacks are moving to urban areas where jobs are available and are being drawn to the states and cities where black-white earning differentials are lowest. In the South, blacks in 1970 received only 45 percent of average white earnings compared with 70 percent in the North and West.

The blacks who leave the rural South for northern cities are more skilled and better educated than those who stay behind and these rural areas may suffer from the depletion of black human resources. On the other hand, blacks migrating from the South have lower average education and skills than those raised and living in the North, thus the competition for low level jobs may be intensified in the cities and the pressure on the welfare system may sometimes be initially increased. But despite these temporary dislocations, migration in the end is an important avenue for economic improvement. Analyses of census data show that even with their educational disadvantages, southern born blacks who have been living in the North for longer than five years have higher median incomes, less chance of poverty or welfare status, and higher rates of labor force participation than northern born blacks.[6] Clearly, migration does not contribute significantly to the exacerbation of urban labor force and welfare problems, but rather may have the opposite effect by redistributing a more motivated segment of the black population to areas of greater economic opportunity.

4. *Increasingly, blacks live in areas which are predominantly black; stable, mixed neighborhoods are the exception rather than the rule.*

Though the concentration of blacks in rural counties in the Southeast is decreasing, their share of the population in the largest cities is steadily increasing because of both their own in-migration and the out-migration of whites. In the twelve cities with the greatest number of blacks, they averaged 21 percent of the population in 1950, 29 percent in 1960, and 39 percent in 1970 (table 1-3). Moreover, since

Table 1-3. Blacks as a percent of large city populations, 1950–1970

City	Number blacks 1970	Blacks as percent of total population		
		1970	1960	1950
New York	1,666,636	21.2	14.0	9.5
Chicago	1,102,620	32.7	22.9	13.6
Detroit	660,428	43.7	38.9	16.2
Philadelphia	653,791	33.6	26.4	18.2
Washington, D.C.	537,712	71.1	53.9	35.0
Los Angeles	503,606	17.9	13.5	8.7
Baltimore	420,210	46.4	34.7	23.7
Houston	316,551	25.7	22.9	20.9
Cleveland	287,841	38.3	28.6	16.2
New Orleans	267,308	45.0	37.2	31.9
Atlanta	255,051	51.3	38.3	36.6
St. Louis	254,191	40.9	28.6	18.0

Source: U.S. Bureau of the Census, *Negro Population in Selected Places and Selected Counties*, PC(S1)-2, June 1971, table 1.

1950 the proportion of these metropolitan blacks who live in the central city has increased from three-fourths to four-fifths. Whites have been moving in the opposite direction until by 1970 three-fifths of metropolitan whites lived in the suburbs. Between 1960 and 1970 the number of blacks in all central cities increased by a third while the number of whites remained constant, raising the black share from 16 to 22 percent.

The central city concentration of blacks is even more marked when regional variations are considered. Almost all blacks living in non-metropolitan areas reside in the South. In other areas nineteen of every twenty blacks live in metropolitan areas and up to 80 percent live in the central cities. The smaller the geographic unit, the more concentrated the black population. Census data for a sample of twenty large cities revealed that in 1970 half of blacks lived in tracts where blacks constituted 75 percent or more of the population, and only 17 percent lived in those where they were 25 percent or less of the population.

Concentration has major implications. First, since the incidence of social problems is higher among blacks, those who are trying to overcome these problems can be held back by others in their neighborhoods. Poverty, unemployment, crime, and drug addiction affect only a minority of blacks directly; but in central city ghettos, these problems have an indirect impact on many. Second, blacks and whites tend to have infrequent contact with each other, complicating efforts to achieve integration in education or housing. In neighborhoods and schools, the repeated pattern of the minority population increasing gradually up to a "tipping point" followed by accelerated white exodus leads whites to flee in fear of a "takeover" whenever blacks increase in numbers. Third, blacks may gain control of an increasing number of large cities as they become majorities or near majorities. In southern counties where they remain large proportions of the population, they may also achieve greater political power.

5. *Because of higher birth rates the black population is growing faster and is considerably younger than the white population.* From 1960 to 1972 the number of whites rose by 14.2 percent, while blacks increased by 23.4 percent. More important, the median age for black males in 1972 was 21.3 years compared with 27.8 years for whites. The median age of black females was 23.7 years compared with 30.6 years for whites. Viewed in another way, adult blacks had to provide

Blacks as a percent of U.S. population	
1940	9.8
1950	10.0
1960	10.5
1970	11.1
1971	11.2
1972	11.3

for more dependents than whites; even after adjustment for under-counting, there were 3.2 blacks age fourteen and under for each male age twenty-five to forty-four compared with 2.3 white children per adult white male in the same age category.[7] These demographic differences are crucial. For instance, the high incidence of poverty and dependency among blacks is, to some extent, related to the larger number of children and other dependents who must be supported by each breadwinner. Similarly, because discrimination and lack of skills have kept black youths at the back of the labor queue, the large number of blacks passing through their teen years over the last decade has intensified black youth unemployment.

The age mix is also a key to the future. The number of blacks now aged five through fourteen is 16 percent higher than the number aged fifteen to twenty-four, but for whites the differential is only 3 percent. As the younger group ages, the black teenage population will continue to grow rapidly. While white teenage labor market problems may be alleviated by a slowing population growth, this will not hold true for blacks. But the really significant demographic population pressure during the next decade will come among twenty-five to thirty-four-year olds, that is, the aging of those teenagers who experienced severe employment problems in the 1960s. The white population will grow by approximately 39 percent while the black group will increase by 66 percent so that there could be severe competition for limited oppor-tunities. This is the age when families are formed, homes purchased, employment patterns solidified, and the future generally determined. It is of critical importance that blacks get an equal chance at this juncture. Moreover, the prospective rise in the number of black females reaching the prime childbearing ages means that even if fertil-ity rates fall, the numbers of black children to be supported will continue to grow in the foreseeable future. Improvements in the earning power of black breadwinners must accelerate if the black population with this rising number of dependents is to move closer to economic equality with whites.

The black population differs in a number of other important but less quantifiable ways. A bitter history of slavery, injustice, discrimi-nation, and racial isolation has certainly had profound impacts on blacks individually and as a group. Black values, expectations, and attitudes—developed over the years in reaction to life in a white, racist society—may affect the present process of change in the black community. In studying the minutiae of recent data it is easy to lose sight of the longer term pattern and to try to explain too much with current variables.

There may be other important factors which are beyond the capabilities of researchers to evaluate. The interlocking system of discrimination in every facet of social and economic activity may produce effects which are greater than the sum of the parts. Discrimination in housing affects access to jobs and schools; unequal employment and education opportunity, in turn, might generate alienation which can be transmitted from one generation to the next. The combination of barriers may have impacts which are hidden from any single perspective. On the other hand, genetics may be a factor. Though there is little evidence on either side of this recently reexploding debate, it is not impossible that, compared to whites, blacks are inherently better at some things and worse at others.

To understand the causes and real meaning of change, and to understand the broader impacts of government programs and why they have succeeded or failed, it would be essential to consider in detail the historical, cultural, psychological, and genetic factors. Analysis would be needed of the overall patterns of discrimination and the applicability of existing concepts and measures. Yet a more limited presentation of the ever-expanding data dealing with the social and economic status of blacks can offer insight into their position in recent years and provide a vital first step toward more complete understanding.

PART 1

SOCIAL AND ECONOMIC CHANGE

2

THE COMMON DENOMINATOR: INCOME

A Matter of Perspective

Income is the common denominator underlying socioeconomic status. Money may not guarantee the good life, but given an adequate level of income, most of the necessary ingredients can be purchased and other goals are easier to attain. Many black problems can be traced to inadequate incomes.

Income can be quantified in dollars and cents, but the meaning of these figures is not always straightforward. For example, all of the following statements are true, yet each yields a different picture of black status.

1. In the Constitutional Convention of 1787, the founding fathers agreed that for purposes of representation three white men would count the same as five black slaves. After 185 years of "progress," though the census takers counted blacks equal to whites, the per capita income of blacks had still not reached three-fifths that of whites.

2. On the other hand, from 1947 to 1972 the black family median income rose by 135 percent in real terms. Within a single generation, blacks could afford more than twice as much of everything—more and better quality food, clothing, housing, entertainment, education, and other goods and services.

3. Yet the gap between black and white family incomes increased. In 1960 the white median was $3,566 higher (in 1972 dollars) than

that of nonwhites; by 1972 the gap had increased to $4,443. In more mundane terms, black families were becoming more able to buy automobiles and better housing, while whites were buying boats and second homes.

4. Although falling further behind in absolute income, nonwhites have made greater relative gains than whites. In 1950 the median family income of nonwhites was 54 percent of that of whites. By 1960 it had increased to 56 percent and by 1972 to 62 percent. Starting from a lower base, the purchasing power of nonwhite families has grown at a faster pace than that of whites.

Depending whether rates of change or current status are considered, and whether absolute or relative standards are used, there are grounds for either optimism or pessimism. There are no right or wrong interpretations; rather, some perspectives are more appropriate for specific purposes. The absolute real income measure is best used in considering the ability of blacks to purchase a diet with adequate nutrition, a home with central heating and indoor plumbing, medical care, and a multitude of other essential items. Poverty thresholds which estimate income required for vital goods and services are a good benchmark of inadequacy. But absolute measures are less useful in considering levels and gains above the minimum. As income rises, "necessities" require an ever-smaller part of the budget, and the adequacy of the goods and services becomes increasingly a matter of comparison with what others have.

One measure of relative status is the ratio of black/white incomes. This is appropriate to assess the rate of progress of blacks toward equality. But this ratio may rise and, indeed, has risen, while the gap between the incomes has increased. On the other hand, the widening absolute gaps may be less important when incomes are rising. The gap between $3,000 and $6,000 annual income is clearly more crucial than that between $20,000 and $26,000 even though the latter is twice as large. There is no proof whether blacks feel better off because of proportionate gains, or worse off because of widening dollar disparities; so both ratios and gaps must be considered in assessing relative progress.

Differentials and Trends

The real income of black families, and of both males and females, has increased dramatically since World War II and especially during the 1960s (table 2-1). The income gain of black males between 1960

Table 2-1. Median incomes of whites and nonwhites, 1948–1972 (1972 dollars)

Year	Median family		Median male		Median female	
	White	Nonwhite	White	Nonwhite	White	Nonwhite
1948	$ 5,762	$3,071	$4,365	$2,370	$1,970	$ 856
1952	6,492	3,687	5,134	2,814	2,112	815
1956	7,698	4,085	5,888	3,077	1,949	1,118
1960	8,152	4,562	6,069	3,189	1,905	1,181
1962	8,629	4,603	6,445	3,169	1,957	1,314
1964	9,252	5,177	6,661	3,775	2,042	1,439
1965	9,618	5,330	7,016	3,776	2,139	1,557
1966	10,047	6,016	7,206	3,991	2,210	1,682
1967	10,372	6,440	7,346	4,321	2,347	1,877
1968	10,747	6,723	7,532	4,600	2,499	2,029
1969	11,179	7,073	7,723	4,557	2,491	2,110
1970	11,026	7,031	7,556	4,563	2,442	2,246
1971	11,024	6,936	7,476	4,546	2,529	2,264
1972	11,549	7,106	7,814	4,811	2,616	2,502

Source: U.S. Bureau of the Census, *Social and Economic Status of the Black Population in the United States, 1972,* Series P-23, no. 46, July 1973, table 7; and Series P-60, annual issues.

and 1972 was 51 percent, and for black females 112 percent. The 1972 median income of black women remained only a little over half that of men, reflecting wage differentials based on sex. While the rate of increase of white median family incomes was relatively constant from 1948 to 1968, nonwhites were more affected by business cycles among other factors (figure 2-1). The long-term upward trend did not prevent periods of stagnation and decline for nonwhite income growth.

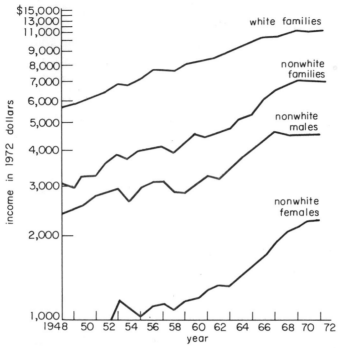

Figure 2-1. Nonwhite/white median real income, 1948–1972.
Source: Table 2-1.

The income of nonwhite families also increased relative to whites (table 2-2). Over the 1950s and the first half of the 1960s it averaged 54 percent of the white level, rising to an average of 63 percent for the subsequent six years. Black women made the most notable contributions to these relative gains, with their median income rising to 96 percent that of white women in 1972.

The gap between the median incomes of black and white families remained relatively constant during the 1960s, then grew in the recovery from the 1970–1971 recession as whites gained more quickly than blacks (figure 2-2). For males the gap widened during the decade, while for females it narrowed continuously.

Another way to compare black/white income differentials is in terms of the overlap of income distributions. As differentials decline and greater equality is achieved, the overlap should increase. This has

Table 2-2. Median nonwhite income as percent of white, 1948–1972

Year	Families	Male	Female
1948	53	54	43
1949	51	48	46
1950	54	54	45
1951	53	55	42
1952	57	55	49
1953	56	55	58
1954	56	50	54
1955	55	53	52
1956	53	52	57
1957	54	53	58
1958	51	50	59
1959	54	47	62
1960	55	53	62
1961	53	52	67
1962	53	49	67
1963	53	52	67
1964	56	57	70
1965	55	54	73
1966	60	55	76
1967	62	59	80
1968	63	61	81
1969	63	59	85
1970	64	60	92
1971	63	61	90
1972	62	62	96

Source: U.S. Bureau of the Census, *Social and Economic Status of the Black Population in the United States, 1972,* Series P-23, no. 46, July 1973, table 7; and Series P-60, annual issues.

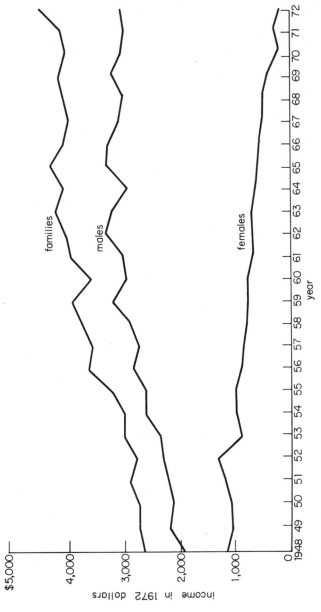

Figure 2-2. Nonwhite/white median income gap, 1948–1972.

Source: Table 2-1.

in fact occurred to a significant degree as family income distribution curves for 1961 and 1971 show (figure 2-3). An "index of integration" can be calculated by comparing the area under the curves with the 100 percent overlap which would exist if the black and white distributions were identical.[1] This index increased from 67 percent in 1961 to 75 percent in 1971. For unrelated individuals the index rose by less, from 84 percent in 1961 to 86 percent in 1971.[2]

The Underlying Factors

To better understand these relative and absolute income developments it is necessary to consider underlying factors such as changing family status, the impacts of migration and regional variations, the effects of improving black educational attainment, and the distribution of the gains among upper, middle, and lower income families.

1. Changing marital and family patterns among blacks are an

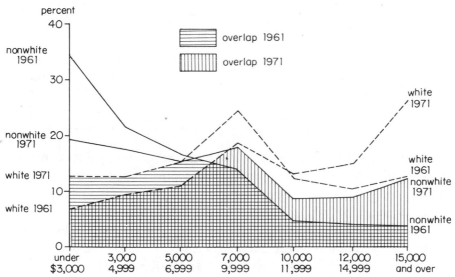

Figure 2-3. Overlap of income distributions of whites and nonwhites, 1960 and 1971.

Source: U.S. Bureau of the Census, *Money Income in 1971 of Families and Persons in the United States,* P-60, no. 85, December 1972, table 9.

important factor in income trends. The nonwhite/white median family income ratio rose only as fast as the ratio for males, even though the increase for females was much more rapid. The rise in female-headed families from 22 percent in 1960 to 33 percent in 1972 held down the relative income gains of black families.[3] The median income of nonwhite female-headed families has remained a relatively constant proportion of that for white female-headed families, but the median for nonwhite female-headed families is less than half as high as for families headed by a male (table 2-3).

Table 2-3. Median income of black families as a percent of whites, 1965–1972

| Year | All families | Male head | | | Female head |
		Total	Wife in paid labor force	Wife not in paid labor force	
1965	54	61	NA	NA	63
1967	60	67	72	60	62
1969	61	71	77	62	61
1971	60	72	78	65	62
1972	59	75	80	64	62

Source: U.S. Bureau of the Census, *Consumer Income*, Series P-60, annual issues.

2. Working wives played a big part in the income gains of black male-headed families. Black wives were more likely to work than whites (55 percent compared to 44 percent) and made almost as much money ($3,600 compared to $3,700). Thus, black families with both husband and wife working have gained most relative to whites. This trend is particularly noticeable among young couples. From 1959 to 1971, black husband-wife families increased their income from 57 to 74 percent of similar white families. If the head was younger than thirty-five, black husband-wife families took in 82 percent of the average for young whites. If the family was young and both

partners worked, blacks realized 90 percent of their white counter-part's income.[4]

3. Some of the black income gain is the result of continued migration from the South and into the cities where incomes (but also living costs) are higher. If the 1969 ratios of regional to national median incomes for whites and blacks are weighted by the percentage of the population in each region in 1960 and 1970, the weighted average rose 2.7 percent for blacks and 1.0 percent for whites (table 2-4). In other words, 1.7 percentage points of the relative income gain could be explained in a rough way by regional shifts. Rural to urban changes may have accounted for even more of the gain.

Though nonwhites are absolutely and relatively better off in the North and West, improvements have been greatest in the South (table 2-5). Median black family income in the South rose from 46 percent of white income in 1959 to 55 percent in 1972. On the other hand, even during the height of progress in the mid-1960s there was little relative improvement elsewhere. One reason was that the proportion of black families headed by females in the North and West rose from 25 percent in 1960 to 38 percent in 1972. The median income in husband-headed families in these regions increased from 76 to 86 percent of the level for similar white families, but the increased incidence of female-headed families checked the rise in the overall black family median.[5]

4. The relative status of better educated blacks improved more than that of the lesser educated. The increased educational attainment of blacks contributed very significantly to their income advance. From 1968 through 1971 black family heads with some college education had median incomes which averaged 1.4 times those of high school graduates and 1.7 times those for dropouts. The median incomes for dropouts, high school graduates, and blacks with some college were 68, 71, and 80 percent, respectively, of the white medians, suggesting a substantial payoff on education beyond the high school level. A comparison of nonwhite/white earnings ratios for males age twenty-five to sixty-four years in 1960 and 1970 shows that the better educated cohorts improved their relative status significantly over the decade.

Table 2-4. Regional population shifts and their impact on median family income, 1960 and 1970

	Population distribution		Median income 1969	Regional as percent of national median	Weighted income 1960	Weighted income 1970
	1960	1970				
Blacks	100%	100%	$ 5,999	—	99.2	101.9
South	60	53	4,987	83.1	49.9	44.0
Northeast	16	19	6,911	115.2	18.4	21.9
North Central	18	20	7,726	128.8	23.2	25.8
West	6	8	7,682	128.0	7.7	10.2
Whites	100%	100%	$ 9,794	—	99.3	100.3
South	27	28	8,764	89.5	24.2	25.1
Northeast	26	25	10,265	104.8	27.2	26.2
North	30	29	10,194	104.1	31.2	30.3
West	16	18	10,197	104.1	16.7	18.7

Source: U.S. Bureau of the Census, *The Social and Economic Status of the Black Population in the United States, 1972*, Series P-23, no. 46, July 1973, table 2.
Note: Details may not add to totals because of rounding.

Table 2-5. Regional black family income as a percent of white, 1959–1972

Region	1959	1966	1970	1972
United States	51	58	61	59
Northeast	69	67	71	64
North Central	74	74	73	70
West	67	72	77	71
South	46	51	57	55

Source: U.S. Bureau of the Census, *The Social and Economic Status of the Black Population in the United States, 1972,* Series P-23, no. 46, July 1973, table 8; and P-23, no. 42, July 1972, table 19.

Ratio of nonwhite to white mean earnings of men age 25 to 64 years, 1959 and 1969 (percent)

Years of education	1959	1969
8 years or less	62	70
9 to 11	63	70
12	64	72
13 to 15	58	69
16 and over	55	71

Source: Derived from U.S. Bureau of the Census, *Occupation by Earnings and Education,* Series PC(2)-7B, June 1963, table 1, and *Earnings by Occupation and Education,* Series PC(2)-8B, January 1973, table 1.

5. Both black and white income gains of the 1960s were broadly shared by all income groups. The proportion of nonwhite families with less than $3,000 annual income (in 1972 dollars) fell by 16 percentage points between 1960 and 1972, while the proportion with more than $10,000 increased by 21 percentage points (figure 2-4).

Real and Apparent Gains

Income levels and changes are not as clear-cut as the preceding data might suggest. Much income goes unreported, and a significant

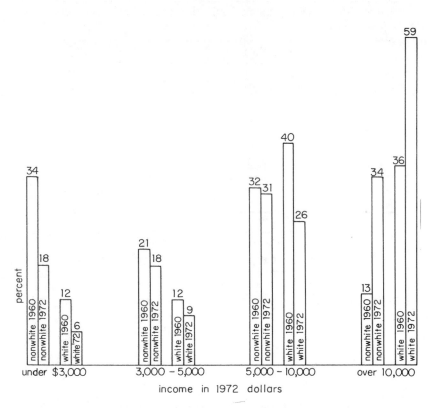

Figure 2-4. Income distribution, white and nonwhite families, 1960 and 1972.

Source: U.S. Bureau of the Census, *Money Income in 1972 of Families and Persons in the United States,* Series P-60, no. 87, June 1973, table 8.

number of individuals are missed by census enumerators. The census definition does not include some income sources which affect present or future well-being. Income must also be considered in light of cost-of-living changes which are not necessarily equal for all groups. While the absolute gains of blacks are so large that these considerations do not affect the overall picture, they do raise uncertainties about the extent of relative improvement. The following factors are probably responsible for an overstatement of relative black gains.

1. Time series census income data are adjusted by the Consumer Price Index (CPI), which is calculated to reflect typical consumption patterns unattained by many blacks, two-fifths of whom are poor or

near poor. The price of the "poverty market basket" rose more rapidly in the late 1960s and early 1970s than the CPI. Weighting the proportionate expenditures of poor and nonpoor families for different goods and services by the price changes for these goods and services, the rise for the poor was 32.9 percent between 1960 and 1970, while for the more affluent families it was 31.4 percent.[6] It may be estimated, therefore, that the CPI overstates the real income gains of lower income families by 1.0 to 1.5 percent. For blacks, other factors may also be involved. Discrimination in housing may have increased, or the flight of retail stores from the ghettos may have raised prices. The effects of these developments have not been measured; but it is clear that when inflation affects the cost of basic commodities such as food, lower income blacks are hurt more than upper class whites.

2. Migration to higher cost areas has raised living costs for blacks. Relative costs are highest for urban areas in the Northeast (106) and West (103), lowest for the South (92) and rural areas (87), and equal to the urban average in the North Central region. The nonwhite population grew rapidly in the first two highest-cost areas and only slowly in the low-cost areas.[7] Weighting the cost indices for each region by its share of white and nonwhite population in 1960 and 1970, the average cost of living rose by 1.6 percent for blacks, but only 0.3 percent for whites. If allowance could be made for the more dramatic cost increases involved in moving from farms to ghettos, it would not be surprising to find that black living costs rose even more compared to whites, significantly offsetting the relative black/white median income gains.

3. Income gains have been less for blacks than for all nonwhites. In 1972 the median income of black families was 3.4 percent less than for all nonwhites. The ratio of nonwhite to white family incomes, in constant dollars, rose from 0.54 in 1959 to 0.62 in 1972, while the black ratio rose from 0.52 to 0.59.[8] In other words, the relative gain was somewhat less for blacks than for other nonwhites.

4. Since the white population is growing more slowly than the black, and since the proportion of adults who are unrelated individuals has risen faster for blacks, relative per capita income has increased less than the family medians. Between 1959 and 1969 the nonwhite-to-white ratio of per capita incomes rose 8 percentage points while the family median ratio rose 11 percentage points.[9]

5. Capital gains, undistributed profits, and imputed income are not counted by the census income definition. Since whites are much more likely to be stockholders, businessmen, and homeowners, they receive a disproportionate share of the uncounted gains, which have been estimated to represent as much as a 50 percent supplement to cash income reported in the census survey. In 1968 consumer units with income over $25,000, of whom less than 2 percent were black, received 18 percent of uncounted income, while those with less than $4,000, 17 percent of whom were black, received only 4 percent of the uncounted income.[10] While it is not certain that capital gains, undistributed profits, and imputed income have increased or decreased relative to census-measured income during the past decade, or whether blacks have raised their share of unreported income, there is no doubt that the nonwhite/white census income figures present an inflated impression of the real income status of blacks.

6. Other forms of noncash compensation may have also augmented white real income faster than that of blacks. Vacation and holiday pay, insurance premiums, pensions, and educational stipends increased more rapidly over the 1960s than actual wages and salaries. In 1959, 85 percent of compensation in manufacturing was paid as wages and salaries. By 1970 this had fallen to 80 percent with the rest being absorbed in increased benefits.[11] There is evidence that blacks get a less than proportionate share of these "extras." For example, in 1968 they were only half as likely to be receiving private pensions, and these were only half as large as among white recipients.[12] During the 1960s "deferred wages" set aside to pay for future pensions amounted to $85 billion which, because of blacks' lower rate of coverage and earlier mortality, would be paid proportionately more to whites than blacks. Similarly, if blacks are less frequently covered by paid vacations and holidays (benefits which have a dollar value both to individuals and to companies) their real income gains are less than those of whites.

On the other hand, there is one very important positive development which does not show up in the income data. Over the last decade there was a dramatic growth of government in-kind programs such as Medicare, Medicaid, subsidized housing, food stamps, school lunches, and others which provide goods and services that would otherwise

have to be purchased. These programs provided much greater supplements to the incomes of blacks than whites because the proportion of
blacks in need was so much greater. It is estimated that blacks received about $3.4 billion more in in-kind aid in 1971 than in 1960,
which boosted their money incomes by about 7 percent. Though
whites received approximately $13 billion more from in-kind pro-
grams in 1971 than in 1960 this represented a supplement of only
about 2 percent to their total cash income. If they are valued at cost,
in-kind transfers increased black real incomes by about 5 percent
more than those of whites.

There is no way to quantify and balance all of these factors, but
certainly they raise doubts about the meaning of the measured improvements in the black/white real median family income ratio over
the last decade. It cannot be stated unequivocally that blacks improved their status relative to whites between 1960 and 1972, although in-kind government aid would appear to tip the balance in
their favor.

The Sources of Black Income

While the trends in black income are major concerns, income
sources are also important. In 1971, 86 percent of white income and
85 percent of black income was earned. Though these proportions
have fallen slightly for both races in recent years, earnings improvements still account for most black income gains (table 2-6). Over the
1960s nonwhite income increased $28 billion and 90 percent of this
resulted from increased earnings (table 2-7).

Within the earnings category, however, there are substantial differences between blacks and whites. Whites are much more likely to
write their own paychecks, with self-employment accounting for 7.3
percent of their income in 1972, compared to only 2.9 percent for
blacks. The self-employment income share has fallen for both groups,
from 14.9 percent of white and 6.4 percent of black income in 1959.
Self-employment income accounted for only 0.3 percent of black
earnings gains between 1968 and 1972 compared to 6.0 percent for
whites.

Table 2-6. Sources of income, 1968 and 1972

Income source	Blacks		Whites	
	1968	1972	1968	1972
	(billions)			
Total	$35.4	$53.3	$506.6	$715.3
Earnings	31.0	45.5	444.3	613.2
Wages and salaries	30.0	43.9	394.5	550.6
Nonfarm self-employment	0.9	1.5	42.3	52.0
Farm self-employment	0.1	0.1	7.6	10.5
Nonearnings	4.4	7.8	62.3	102.1
Social Security and railroad retirement	1.5	2.7	20.0	34.0
Dividends and interest	0.2	0.3	22.5	33.2
Public assistance	1.6	3.0	2.7	4.6
Public pensions and other	0.7	1.2	8.7	17.1
Private pensions	0.4	0.6	8.4	13.2
	(percent)			
Earnings	87.6	85.3	87.7	85.7
Wages and salaries	84.7	82.3	77.9	77.0
Nonfarm self-employment	2.6	2.9	8.3	7.3
Farm self-employment	0.3	0.1	1.5	1.5
Nonearnings	12.4	14.6	12.3	14.3
Social Security and railroad retirement	4.2	5.0	3.9	4.8
Dividends and interest	0.6	0.6	4.4	4.6
Public assistance	4.7	5.6	0.5	0.6
Public pensions and other	1.9	2.3	1.7	2.4
Private pensions	1.1	1.2	1.7	1.8

Source: U.S. Bureau of the Census, *Money Income of Families and Persons in the United States,* Series P-60, annual data.

Table 2-7. Income gains of families and unrelated individuals, 1959 and 1969

Race and income source	1959	1969	Percent increase 1959–1969
Nonwhite total (billions)	$19.2	$47.2	146
Earnings	17.0	42.2	148
Wages and salaries	15.8	40.3	155
Self-employment	1.2	2.0	60
Other income	2.2	4.9	128
White total (billions)	312.3	585.3	87
Earnings	277.8	514.5	85
Wages and salaries	231.1	459.4	99
Self-employment	46.7	55.1	18
Other income	34.5	68.6	99
Per capita income			
Nonwhite	936	1,852	98
White	1,966	3,293	67
Ratio			
White/nonwhite	.48	.56	—

Source: U.S. Bureau of the Census, *Sources and Structure of Family Income*, Series PC(2)-4C, June 1962, tables 6 and 7; and *Sources and Structure of Family Income*, Series PC(2)-8A, June 1973, tables 4 and 5.

Though nonearned income accounts for a small proportion of the total, it is a rising fraction for both blacks and whites, and detailed breakdowns show sharp racial differences. In 1972 both races received about the same proportion of their nonearned income from social security, and whites received slightly greater proportions from pensions and unemployment insurance. But dividends, interest, and rental income accounted for almost a third of nonearned white income, compared to less than 4 percent of blacks. On the other hand, two-fifths of black nonearned income came from welfare, compared to less than 5 percent of nonearned white income.

Reliance on welfare increased dramatically in recent years. Between 1968 and 1972 blacks added $1.4 billion in welfare money to their incomes, increasing the welfare share of total income by 1 percent. Though whites reaped nearly 2 billion new welfare dollars, this changed the proportion of welfare money in white incomes only a tenth of a percentage point. Between 1968 and 1972, 7 percent of black income gains came from welfare, compared to less than 1 percent for whites.

The racial differences in the sources of income show up most clearly in the black share of the different types of income. In 1972 blacks received 6.9 percent of money income, but the proportions ranged from 38.6 percent of welfare and 7.3 percent of wages and salaries to 0.9 percent of dividends and 0.6 percent of farm self-employment income (table 2-8).

Because of the imperfections in the collection of the data on income, these figures tend to underestimate the black/white disparities. Comparing reported income with national benchmark estimates of personal income, the Census Bureau estimated that in 1972 about 90 percent of all personal income appeared in its tallies. Underreporting was greatest for income from property and public assistance, and least for wages and salaries. Thus, the proportion of nonearned income for both blacks and whites is actually higher. If the income figures are adjusted for underreporting, blacks received about 7 (rather than 6) percent of their income from public assistance in 1972 and whites about 9 (rather than 5) percent from property.

Moreover, even adjusted payments to wealth holders may seriously underestimate the disproportionate white income gains. As has been noted, only money income is recorded, not capital gains, imputed rents, and undistributed profits. All of these income sources accrue almost exclusively to white wealth holders. If these are added, the income status of whites is even more enviable than the figures suggest.

Who earns or receives income can be as important as its source. Among blacks, women provide a larger share of total income than among whites. In 1972 women contributed 38 percent of total black income, while women accounted for 24 percent of total white income (table 2-9). The difference is especially significant in nonearned income; white women supply 40 percent of nonearned income, but black females provide 60 percent. Again, welfare payments are primarily responsible for this differential. In 1972, 55 percent of non-

Table 2-8. Money income sources, 1971

Income source	Total	Blacks	Black share
	(billions)		(percent)
Total	$777.5	$53.3	6.9
Earnings	666.5	45.5	6.8
Wages and salaries	601.7	43.9	7.3
Nonfarm self-employed	54.2	1.5	2.9
Farm self-employed	10.6	0.1	0.6
Nonearnings	111.0	7.8	7.0
Railroad retirement and Social Security	37.0	2.7	7.3
Dividends, interest, rents, royalties	33.8	0.3	0.9
Public assistance	7.7	3.0	38.6
Public pensions, unemployment and workmen's compensation	18.5	1.2	6.6
Pensions	14.0	0.6	4.4

Source: U.S. Bureau of the Census, *Money Income in 1972 of Families and Persons in the United States,* Series P-60, no. 90, December 1973, table 65.

Table 2-9. Female contributions to total income, 1972

Type of income	Black Total income	Black Percent female	White Total income	White Percent female
Total income (billions)	$53.3	38.2	$715.3	24.0
Earnings (billions)	45.5	34.6	613.2	21.3
Nonearnings (billions)	7.8	59.7	102.1	39.7
Welfare (billions)	3.0	85.1	4.6	72.1

Source: U.S. Bureau of the Census, *Money Income in 1972 of Families and Persons in the United States,* Series P-60, no. 90, December 1973, table 69.

earned black female income was welfare, compared to 8 percent for whites. One of every eight dollars of black female income is welfare, compared to one of every fifty dollars for white women.

Poverty—The Black (Wo)Man's Burden

Despite income gains which affected most blacks during the decade of the 1960s, a total of 7.7 million blacks still lived in what the census defined as poverty in 1972 (income less than $4,275 for a nonfarm family of four). Another 2 million were classified near-poor with incomes less than 25 percent above the poverty threshold (table 2-

Table 2-10. Number of persons in poverty, 1959–1972 (persons in thousands)

Year	All races	Black	Percent black
1959	39,490	9,927	25.1
1966	28,510	8,867	31.1
1967	27,769	8,486	30.5
1968	29,389	7,616	30.0
1969	24,147	7,095	29.4
1970	24,420	7,548	30.9
1971	25,559	7,396	28.9
1972	24,460	7,710	31.5

Number of persons who are poor or near poor (incomes below 125 percent of poverty)

1966	41,267	11,232	27.2
1967	39,206	10,701	27.3
1968	35,905	9,862	27.5
1969	34,665	9,507	27.4
1970	35,624	9,668	27.1
1971	36,501	9,739	26.7
1972	34,653	9,763	28.1

Source: U.S. Bureau of the Census, *Characteristics of the Low Income Population,* Series P-60, no. 86, December 1972, tables 1 and 3; and *Characteristics of the Low-Income Population: 1972,* Series P-60, no. 88, June 1973, tables 3 and 9.

10). Together, the poor and near-poor represented a staggering 42 percent of all blacks, and blacks were three times as likely to be poor as whites. Black poverty declined in the 1960s, but by less than whites, so that blacks increased from 25.1 percent of the poor in 1959 to 31.5 percent in 1972 (figure 2-5). Moreover, the decline in black

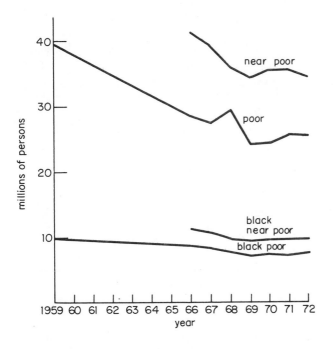

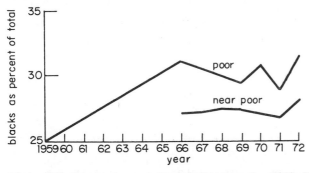

Figure 2-5. Persons in poverty and near poverty, 1959–1972.
    Source: Table 2-11.

poverty leveled off in the early 1970s. There were actually 100,000 more poor blacks in 1972 than in 1968.

The black poor are likely to live in the central cities of metropolitan areas or in the South (table 2-11). The number of poor blacks in the

Table 2-11. Poverty by region and residence, 1959 and 1972

Race and residence	1972		1959	
	Percent of poor	Incidence of poverty	Percent of poor	Incidence of poverty
Whites				
Total	100.0	9.0	100.0	17.9
Nonfarm	93.2	8.8	NA	NA
Farm	6.8	12.7	NA	NA
Metropolitan	55.1	7.4	41.7	
Central city	28.4	9.8	23.0	13.7
Outside central city	26.7	5.8	18.7	10.3
Nonmetropolitan	44.9	12.3	58.3	27.9
North and West	63.1	8.0	59.5	14.6
South	36.9	11.5	40.5	26.6
Blacks				
Total	100.0	33.3	100.0	54.0
Nonfarm	96.5	32.9	NA	NA
Farm	3.5	48.3	NA	NA
Metropolitan	68.1	29.4	50.4	42.0
Central city	56.5	31.2	38.4	40.3
Outside central city	11.5	23.0	11.9	48.8
Nonmetropolitan	31.9	46.3	49.6	71.0
North and West	37.7	26.2	24.4	33.4
South	62.3	39.8	75.6	67.4

Source: U.S. Bureau of the Census, *Characteristics of the Low Income Population, 1972,* Series P-60, no. 91, December 1973, tables 3, 7, and 8.

South declined by 2.7 million from 1959 to 1971, while in the North and West it rose by 200,000. Over the same period the proportion of poor blacks living outside metropolitan areas fell from 50 to 38 percent, while poor central city residents increased from 38 to 49 percent. Both migration to northern and metropolitan areas and the improving economic status of blacks in the South were responsible for these changes. It is important to note, however, that despite these improvements, two of every five blacks in the South remained poor in 1971 compared to only a fourth of those in the North and West. Almost half of those in nonmetropolitan areas and more than three-fifths of those on farms are also poor. The poverty conditions which have caused migration for decades still persist.

The characteristics of poor black families are predictable. They have little education, large families, and severe, persistent unemployment problems. In 1972 only one of every four poor black family heads had as much as a high school education (table 2-12). But, by itself, poor education accounts for less than a third of black poverty. The more severe problem is that at every education level blacks are more likely to be in poverty than whites. If the incidence of poverty were the same for blacks as whites at each educational level, the number of black poor in 1972 would have been reduced more than two-thirds. Only when blacks attain a college degree does the differential in poverty disappear, and during recession years in the early 1970s even among the college educated blacks were more likly than whites to have incomes below the poverty line.

Handicapped by the racial and sex discrimination, the growing numbers of female-headed families are a major cause of black poverty. In 1959 two of three poor nonwhite families was headed by a man; by 1972 the ratio was reversed, with 63 percent having female heads. By comparison, five of every six poor white families had male heads in 1959, and two of three in 1972. One consequence is that poor black children are likely to be doubly cursed by deprivation and broken homes. In 1972, 2.7 million black children—two-thirds of those in poverty—did not have a father present, an increase of 600,000 since 1966. Only two of every five poor white children were in female-headed homes.

Poor families are larger than those above the low income line, and

Table 2-12. Education of poor family heads age 25 years
and over, 1972

Years of schooling	Number poor	Percent of those in poverty	Incidence of poverty
	(thousands)		(percent)
Blacks	1,302	100.0	—
Less than 8	441	33.9	36.8
8	163	12.5	31.2
9–11	386	29.6	33.2
12	241	18.5	19.8
13–15	61	4.7	17.5
16 or more	10	4.7	3.8
Whites	2,989	100.0	—
Less than 8	912	30.5	18.5
8	478	16.0	9.2
9–11	603	20.1	8.7
12	690	23.1	4.5
13–15	165	5.5	3.0
16 or more	141	0.8	2.0

Source: U.S. Bureau of the Census, *Characteristics of the Low
Income Population, 1972*, Series P-60, no. 88, March 1973, table 4.

poor black families are larger than those of whites in poverty. Above
the low income level, there were an average of 2.6 children under
eighteen years old in black families with children and 2.1 in white
families in 1972; among the poor, the averages were 3.1 and 2.6,
respectively. Despite the prevailing stereotypes, female-headed families in poverty are smaller for both blacks and whites than those with
husbands present. Black female-headed families in poverty averaged
3.0 children in 1972 compared to black male-headed households
which had 3.4 children. For whites the figures were 2.3 and 2.8.[13]
But for those black women family heads who had large families the
chances of escaping poverty were slim. Doubly discriminated against

in the labor market, and often unable to work because of child care responsibilities, black women who were the heads of households with three or more children stood a 76 percent chance of being in poverty in 1972.

One encouraging note is that the number of children per family among the poor has been declining, especially for blacks. In 1967 poor black families averaged 3.6 children. If that rate still prevailed, there would have been more than 700,000 more children in poor black families in 1972.[14]

Separation, divorce, abandonment, and nonmarriage among black women explain much of the developing pattern of black female-headed poverty families. More than half of black women over twenty head their households, compared with less than a third of whites (table 2-13). Black women over age twenty were 58 percent more likely never to have been married, 55 percent more likely to be divorced, twice as likely to have their husband absent, and seven times as likely to be separated as white women. Black women with these marital problems are likely to have income problems as well. Of the 3.8 million black women over age twenty without husbands in 1972, 1.7 million, or 45 percent, were in poverty compared with only a fifth of white women in the same position.

Age is also a factor affecting poverty. Though the elderly are disproportionately represented in the poverty populations of both races, the old make up a larger proportion of white family heads, and relatively more black family heads are young. As younger female-headed families have risen as a proportion of the poor, and as poverty among the elderly has declined due to social security and other public and private pensions, the poor have become younger. Between 1967 and 1972 the median age of poor black family heads fell from forty-four to thirty-nine years and the percentage of family heads under age forty-four rose from 52 to 63 percent.

Some of the poor cannot work. Others can, but cannot find jobs, or when they do, cannot earn enough to support their families. In 1972, 51 percent of poor black family heads were not in the labor force at all during the previous year. More than half of these were "keeping house," another third did not work because of illness, and 6 percent could not find work (table 2-14). Among labor force participants,

Table 2-13. Marital and poverty status of women over 20, 1972 (numbers in thousands)

Marital status	White				Black			
	Total	Percent of total	In poverty	Percent in poverty	Total	Percent of total	In poverty	Percent in poverty
Total	61,016	100.0	6,248	10.2	6,992	100.0	2,217	31.7
Married	42,561	69.8	2,285	5.4	3,307	47.3	549	16.6
Married, husband present	42,107	69.0	2,124	5.0	3,181	45.4	506	15.9
Married, husband absent	454	0.7	161	35.5	126	1.8	43	34.1
Widowed	8,559	14.0	2,233	26.1	1,210	17.3	570	47.1
Divorced	2,744	4.5	625	22.8	486	7.0	205	42.2
Separated	1,188	1.9	437	36.8	904	12.9	497	55.0
Never married	5,964	9.8	669	11.2	1,086	15.5	397	36.6

Source: U.S. Bureau of the Census, *Characteristics of the Low Income Population, 1972*, Series P-60, no. 91, December 1973, table 16.

Table 2-14. Work experience of poor family heads, 1967 and 1972

Work experience	1967		1972	
	Black	White	Black	White
Total (thousands)	1,555	3,616	1,529	3,441
	(percent)			
Worked	63.3	54.2	49.1	55.8
50–52 weeks	33.9	29.6	20.5	24.8
Full-time	28.6	26.4	16.2	21.5
1–49 weeks	29.5	24.6	28.5	31.0
Reasons for working part-year:				
Unemployed	6.8	6.8	9.9	11.7
Other	22.7	17.8	18.5	19.4
Did not work	36.1	44.2	50.6	43.5
Reason for not working:				
Ill	12.5	12.6	15.5	14.3
Keeping house	17.2	12.8	27.0	14.9
Going to school	0.5	1.2	1.6	1.0
Unable to find work	0.8	0.4	3.3	1.8
Other	5.1	17.2	3.3	11.4
In armed forces	0.5	1.6	0.3	0.7

Source: U.S. Bureau of the Census, *Characteristics of the Low Income Population, 1972,* Series P-60, no. 91, December 1973, table 4.

only two-fifths worked full-year, and only a third worked full-time, full-year in 1972. A major reason for interrupted work was unemployment which affected 35 percent of those with less than full-year employment.

Even when working full-time, full-year, 247,000 black family heads remained in poverty in 1972. However, this number is declining. In 1967, 444,000 or 29 percent of the black poor were full-time, full-year workers. On the other hand, though low-wage problems were becoming less severe, other employment problems increased over this period because of the recession. In 1972, 18 percent of black poverty problems could be traced to unemployment, nonparticipation in the work force due to the inability to find jobs, and part-time work, compared to 13 percent in 1967.

However, income problems of the black poor are due less to shortcomings of the labor market than to other factors. Not working or not being able to work contributes much more to black poverty than unemployment, unavailability of jobs, or inadequate wages. As the burden of poverty has shifted to black women with children, home responsibilities have limited labor force participation. Between 1967 and 1972 there was an increase of 211,000 in the number of poor black household heads who remained out of the labor force, 145,000 of whom stayed home to keep house. Overall, the number of poor black families with no earners increased by 200,000, and the number with two or three earners declined by 265,000. Though recession-related employment problems added 67,000 family heads to the poverty totals between 1969 and 1972, those out of the labor force for other reasons increased by 151,000. These people will not escape poverty even when the labor market tightens.

Despite the continuing high incidence of black poverty and the slight rise in the 1970s, the long-run trend has been downward. And though the number of black poor did not decline between 1968 and 1972, those remaining in poverty made some gains. The total dollar gap for nonwhites—the number of dollars it would take to bring all families and persons up to the poverty level—declined between 1959 and 1972 from $5.5 billion to $3.6 billion. It would have taken $503 per poor person (in constant 1972 dollars) to bring all blacks up to the poverty threshold in 1959; by 1972 the figure had fallen to $439.[15]

This declining gap was the result of stable real incomes of the poor coupled with declining family size. Between 1969 and 1972 the average income of poor black families rose from $2,439 to $2,788. Adjusted for inflation, this equaled a negligible gain of $5 in 1972 dollars. But at the same time, the size of black families declined, lowering the average poverty threshold. Thus, relative to the poverty standard, blacks have gained slightly, even in recent years.

In light of the deteriorating employment situation and the declining labor force participation of the black poor, it is clear that these small improvements have come primarily from transfer payments. Although poverty figures themselves do not allow longitudinal analysis of the income sources, census data on those with the lowest incomes point up the trends. In 1959 nonwhites with incomes of less than $3,000 ($4,304 in 1972 dollars) earned 74 percent of their money and received 26 percent from other sources (table 2-15). By 1969 earnings accounted for only 58 percent of the income of nonwhites who made less than $4,000 ($4,565 in 1972 dollars), while other income, half of it public assistance, had jumped to 42 percent. Recently the nonearned and public assistance proportions of the income of the black poor may have risen even higher. In 1972, 55 percent of the income of black families below the census poverty line came from nonearnings, of which seven-tenths was public assistance. Although the white poor received a similar proportion of their income from transfer payments, most of these sources were pensions and social insurance, with public assistance accounting for only a fifth of their incomes in 1972. For both whites and blacks with low income, economic status is increasingly determined by government assistance.

The Balance Sheet

There can be no doubt that blacks have made substantial income gains since 1960. All major black income groups shared in the economic expansion of the 1960s, roughly doubling their total real income.

Other measures indicate that the gap between black and white incomes has also been reduced. Between 1960 and 1972 the ratio of black to white median incomes rose from 53 percent to 62 percent for men, from 62 percent to 96 percent for women, and from 56 to 62 percent for families. Moreover, these measures ignore the large increases in federal in-kind aid that may have added as much as 5 percentage points to the relative incomes of blacks. Yet the significance of these relative improvements is uncertain. Relative gains are overstated by a substantial margin because blacks have migrated to high wage, high cost areas, and because a large fraction of white property income is not included in the tallies. In addition, the closing

Table 2-15. Income sources of the poor, 1959–1969

	White						Nonwhite					
	1959[a]		1969[b]				1959[a]		1969[b]			
	Number	Percent	Number	Percent			Number	Percent	Number	Percent		
Families												
(thousands)	7,617	—	6,050	—			2,034	—	1,684	—		
Total	$1,615	100.0	$2,230	100.0			$1,471	100.0	$2,046	100.0		
Wages	730	45.2	911	40.9			987	67.1	1,143	55.9		
Self-employment	243	15.0	119	5.3			103	7.0	52	2.5		
Other	642	39.7	1,200	53.8			381	25.9	851	41.6		
Public assistance	NA	NA	(161)	(7.2)			NA	NA	(418)	(20.4)		

Source: U.S. Bureau of the Census, *Sources and Structure of Family Income, 1970*, Series PC(2)8A, 1973, table 5; and *Sources and Structure of Family Income, 1960*, Series PC(2)4C, 1963, table 7.
[a] Under $3,000 in 1959.
[b] Under $4,000 in 1969.

relative percentages are offset by widening absolute gaps. The absolute gains of men and families have not kept pace with comparable white advances, and the median family income differential widened by $853 between 1960 and 1972.

The very substantial absolute progress and the uncertain but probably more modest relative gains were due to expanding employment and earnings opportunities and government welfare programs. Since 1960 black wage and salary incomes nearly tripled, with the total growing by $25 billion during the 1960s. The long delayed entrance of black men into more skilled, better paying jobs and the rapid equalization of black and white women were responsible for this huge gain. But government aid also had a massive impact on those not sharing in the employment and earnings gains.

Despite the improvements, there are reasons for concern. Blacks have not been escaping poverty as fast as whites. The number of poor blacks actually rose in the early 1970s. More than half of the income of black poor in 1972 came from the government, compared with only a fourth in 1959. Moreover, very little black income originates from property or from self-employment. Blacks still control only a small fraction of the nation's income-producing assets, and they seldom own their own businesses. During the 1960s neither of these conditions improved. Whatever gains blacks have made, they have not won control over the sources of wealth which can be passed on from one generation to the next.

It is uncertain whether the slowing of progress for both poor and nonpoor blacks in the early 1970s was a temporary setback or a sign that a new plateau has been reached. It would be misleading to dwell on the progress of the 1960s as though much of the battle had been won. The gains resulted from the unique combination of social consensus, government commitment, and economic expansion. Even if the favorable conditions could be maintained and rates of gain sustained, it would take at least two generations before blacks would reach economic equality with whites. And no matter how one reads the conflicting evidence on relative gains, the fact remains that blacks still receive only about three-fifths as much income as whites and that millions of blacks remain locked in poverty. Though the 1960s saw the first steps toward income equality, there is a great distance still to be traveled.

3

EMPLOYMENT AND EARNINGS

Work is a prime determinant of a person's well-being, status, and prospects. In this critical area, blacks made major advances during the past decade. Black/white differentials remained significant and labor market problems persisted, but the trend was one of widespread progress toward equality.

The Job Gains

Blacks moved into better paying and higher status jobs. The proportion employed as managers and administrators, professional and technical workers, and craftsmen and kindred workers—the three highest paying occupations—almost doubled between 1958 and 1973, while the proportion employed in service work, nonfarm, and farm labor—the three lowest paying occupations—fell by one-third. Occupational patterns of whites did not change as much, so that nonwhites caught up somewhat (table 3-1).

The occupational gains of black women were more striking than those of black men. Most significant was the decline in the proportion of nonwhite women employed as private household workers. In 1960 one of every three was a household worker compared with 15 percent in 1972. During the same dozen years the proportion of nonwhite women in the clerical, sales, and professional categories rose from 19

Table 3-1. Relative occupational distribution of whites and nonwhites, 1958 and 1973

Occupation	Percent of nonwhites		Percent of whites		Percent nonwhites to percent whites in occupation	
	1958	1973	1958	1973	1958	1973
Total	100.0	100.0	100.0	100.0	1.00	1.00
Managers and administrators	2.4	4.1	11.7	11.0	0.21	0.37
Professional and technical	4.1	9.9	11.8	14.4	0.35	0.69
Craftsmen	5.9	8.9	14.3	13.9	0.41	0.64
Clerical	6.1	14.9	15.4	17.5	0.40	0.85
Operatives	20.1	22.2	17.9	16.3	1.12	1.36
Sales	1.2	2.3	6.9	6.9	0.17	0.33
Farmers and farm managers	3.7	0.7	5.0	2.1	0.74	0.33
Service	33.0	25.3	9.5	11.7	3.47	2.16
Nonfarm laborers	14.7	9.7	4.5	4.6	3.27	2.11
Farm laborers	8.8	2.1	3.0	1.6	2.93	1.31

Source: *Manpower Report of the President, 1974* (Washington: Government Printing Office, 1974), table A-12.

to 40 percent (table 3-2). Nonwhite men declined from 14 to 5 percent of those working as farmers or farm laborers, while those in professional, technical, and managerial occupations increased from 7 to 13 percent.

Younger blacks made the most notable gains. The proportion of nonwhite women under age twenty-five in private household work declined from 30 to 5 percent compared with a decline from 49 to 30 percent among nonwhite women age forty-five and over (table 3-3). The increase in professional, technical, and managerial jobs was more extensive among nonwhite men under age forty-five than among older workers.

Table 3-2. Occupational distribution of employed nonwhite workers, 1960–1972

Sex and occupation group	1960	1966	1972
Nonwhite male			
Total employed (thousands)	4,148	4,655	4,861
Percent	100	100	100
Professional, technical, and managerial	7	9	13
Clerical and sales	7	9	9
Craftsmen and foremen	10	12	15
Operatives	24	27	26
Service workers	15	16	16
Nonfarm laborers	23	20	17
Farmers and farm workers	14	8	5
Nonwhite female			
Total employed (thousands)	2,779	3,313	3,767
Percent	100	100	100
Professional, technical, and managerial	8	10	14
Clerical and sales	11	15	26
Craftsmen and foremen	1	—	1
Operatives	14	16	15
Service workers, except private households	22	26	27
Private household workers	35	28	15
Nonfarm laborers	1	—	1
Farmers and farm workers	9	4	1

Source: U.S. Bureau of Labor Statistics, unpublished tabulations.

The patterns of substantial gains in broad occupational categories is blurred when detailed occupations are considered. In most categories the greatest gains were made in the least prestigious and least paid occupations. Though blacks advanced dramatically as a proportion of most professions, they were still woefully underrepresented in the elite occupations (table 3-4). For example, in the professional and techni-cal category almost three-fifths of all blacks were either pre-college teachers, nurses, medical technicians, or social, personnel, or labor relations workers. Blacks were less than 3 percent each of accoun-

Table 3-3. Age and occupational distribution of employed nonwhites, 1960 and 1972

Occupational group	Under 25 years		25 to 44 years		45 years and over	
	1960	1972	1960	1972	1960	1972
	(percent)					
Nonwhite females	100	100	100	100	100	100
Professional, technical, and managerial	7	8	11	17	8	12
Clerical and sales	19	47	13	27	5	12
Craftsmen, operatives, and laborers	15	17	18	19	13	15
Private household workers	30	5	32	10	49	30
Other service workers	24	21	24	27	21	30
Farm workers	6	2	3	1	4	1
Nonwhite males	100	100	100	100	100	100
Professional, technical, and managerial	3	7	8	17	7	11
Clerical and sales	9	11	8	10	5	7
Craftsmen and foremen	7	10	13	17	11	15
Operatives	24	27	29	28	22	22
Service workers	18	19	13	12	19	20
Nonfarm laborers	22	22	21	13	21	19
Farm workers	18	5	9	3	16	6

Source: Derived from U.S. Bureau of the Census, *1960 Census of Population,* U.S. Summary, PC(1)-1D, table 204; data for 1972 are annual averages based on unpublished records of the Bureau of Labor Statistics.

tants, architects, physicians, dentists, editors, and reporters, and they were less than 2 percent of lawyers, designers, authors, or engineers. Though black rates of gain and proportional improvement were dramatic in each of these occupations, they remained seriously under-represented.

Similarly, though the number of blacks in managerial positions doubled during the 1960s, they still accounted for only 2.6 percent of

Table 3-4. Detailed occupations of employed black workers, 1960 and 1970 (numbers in thousands)

	1960		1970	
	Number	Blacks as percent of all	Number	Blacks as percent of all
Total	6087.5	9.4	7403.1	9.6
Professional and technical	319.0[a]	3.7	616.3	5.4
Accountants	3.6	0.8	16.2	2.3
Actors	0.3	3.5	0.6	6.7
Architects	0.1	0.4	1.3	2.3
Authors	0.3	1.0	0.4	1.6
Chemists	1.8	2.2	3.8	3.5
Clergymen	13.6	6.8	13.5	6.1
Dentists	2.3	2.7	2.4	2.6
Designers	0.7	1.1	1.9	1.8
Draftsmen	2.2	1.0	7.6	2.6
Editors and reporters	0.8	0.8	3.3	2.2
Engineers	4.2	0.5	14.3	1.2
Lawyers and judges	2.4	1.2	3.7	1.3
Librarians	3.8	4.5	7.9	6.5
Nurses, registered	32.8	5.6	65.2	7.8
Personnel and labor relations workers	1.5	1.5	14.9	5.1
Pharmacists	1.7	1.8	2.8	2.5
Photographers	1.1	2.3	1.9	3.0
Physicians	5.0	2.2	6.0	2.1
Public relations and publicity writers	0.3	1.0	2.3	3.2
Social and recreation workers	13.8	10.4	41.1	15.3
Social scientists	1.1	2.0	3.5	3.1
Teachers, elementary	90.3	9.0	134.6	9.4
Teachers, high school	33.6	6.5	65.5	6.6
Teachers, university	6.0	3.6	16.3	3.3
Managers, administrators, and proprietors	115.0[a]	1.6	166.2	2.6

Table 3-4. (continued)

| | 1960 | | 1970 | |
	Number	Blacks as percent of all	Number	Blacks as percent of all
Buyers, wholesale, retail trade	1.2	0.5	3.0	1.7
Funeral directors and embalmers	3.4[a]	9.0	3.4	8.5
Inspectors, public administration	1.7	2.2	5.2	5.2
Managers, superintendents, building	5.2	9.9	4.2	4.9
Officials, public administration	3.0	1.5	11.4	4.8
Officials, lodge, society, and union	0.8	2.4	2.8	5.8
Postmasters	—[b]	0.1	0.3	0.8
Railroad conductors	0.8	4.7	1.5	3.6
Managers, officials, salaried	27.7	1.1	48.7	1.9
Managers, officials, self-employed	46.4	2.4	23.0	2.5
Sales workers	96.8[a]	1.8	165.8	3.1
Advertising agents and salesmen	0.2	0.5	0.9	1.4
Hucksters and peddlers	2.5	4.8	2.5	2.0
Insurance agents and brokers	7.0	1.9	13.7	3.0
Newsboys	7.9	4.1	2.0	3.1
Real estate agents and brokers	3.6	1.8	4.6	1.8
Stock and bond salesmen	0.1	0.5	1.3	1.3
Salesmen and sales clerks, manufacturing	2.8	0.6	5.2	1.3
Salesmen and sales clerks, wholesale trade	3.1	0.6	9.4	1.5
Salesmen and sales clerks, retail trade	54.3	2.1	96.4	3.5

Table 3-4. (continued)

	1960		1970	
	Number	Blacks as percent of all	Number	Blacks as percent of all
Clerical and kindred workers	426.4[a]	4.0	1021.6	7.4
Bank tellers	0.6	0.5	10.5	4.2
Bookkeepers	8.0	0.9	44.6	2.9
Cashiers	14.1	3.0	52.4	6.4
File clerks	9.2	6.9	44.5	12.2
Mail carriers	19.8	10.1	29.6	11.7
Office machine operators	12.9	4.2	57.0	10.1
Payroll and timekeeping clerks	1.7	1.6	7.5	4.8
Postal clerks	35.5	16.7	64.9	22.1
Receptionists	3.6	2.6	16.1	5.2
Secretaries	21.4	1.5	91.1	3.4
Shipping clerks	29.6	10.7	54.8	13.3
Stenographers	5.6	2.1	5.8	4.5
Stock clerks and store keepers	33.4	10.1	50.7	11.2
Telephone operators	8.9	2.5	43.5	10.4
Typists	30.2	5.8	94.0	9.6
Craftsmen and kindred workers	418.6[a]	4.3	674.8	6.3
Bakers	8.7	8.2	13.1	12.0
Brickmasons and tile setters	22.7	12.2	29.2	14.9
Carpenters	36.6	4.4	46.9	5.5
Cement and concrete finishers	11.7	28.1	21.6	31.4
Cranemen, derrick operators	11.8	9.7	21.1	13.7
Electricians	4.8	1.4	15.0	3.1
Excavating machine operators	7.2	3.7	23.9	7.6
Foremen	18.4	1.6	58.8	3.7
Inspectors	4.5	3.8	9.0	6.7
Machinists	12.5	2.5	17.3	4.6

Table 3-4. (continued)

	1960		1970	
	Number	Blacks as percent of all	Number	Blacks as percent of all
Mechanics, automobile	44.9	6.5	76.4	9.4
Mechanics, airplane	3.1	2.7	7.1	4.9
Mechanics, television	4.3	4.2	7.6	5.4
Painters, construction, and maintenance	25.7	6.8	29.9	9.0
Plumbers and pipe fitters	10.2	3.3	18.4	4.8
Printing craftsmen	7.9	2.5	21.9	5.6
Roofers and slaters	4.7	9.8	6.9	11.9
Stationery engineers	4.6	1.7	8.0	4.6
Operatives	1309.8[a]	10.1	1749.2	12.7
Assemblers	36.5	6.0	113.9	12.1
Attendants, gas station and parking	44.7[a]	12.5	32.3	7.7
Checkers, examiners, and inspectors, manufacturing	17.5	3.6	55.0	7.9
Deliverymen and routemen	32.6	7.7	57.9	9.5
Drivers, bus	17.5	9.6	33.3	13.9
Drivers, taxi	30.5	18.7	33.3	21.6
Drivers, truck	217.6	14.0	186.2	13.4
Laundry and drycleaning operatives	136.2	35.4	113.7	32.4
Meat cutters, except manuf.	7.4	4.1	13.0	6.4
Miners	13.1	4.5	7.9	5.0
Packers and wrappers	49.0	11.0	71.7	14.0
Painters, construction, and maintenance	15.3	10.9	16.6	14.3
Sewers and stitchers	27.1	4.8	85.1	9.8
Welders	20.5	6.1	47.9	8.8
Laborers, except farm	816.1[a]	24.7	688.2	20.1

Table 3-4. (continued)

	1960		1970	
	Number	Blacks as percent of all	Number	Blacks as percent of all
Service workers, except				
private household	1128.6[a]	18.9	1484.0	17.1
Barbers	16.3	9.1	16.7	9.8
Bartenders	8.2	4.8	8.5	4.5
Cooks	124.2	22.0	159.6	19.2
Firemen	2.6	1.9	4.6	2.6
Guards and watchmen	13.0	5.3	33.4	10.4
Hairdressers and				
cosmetologists	34.4	11.3	35.4	7.3
Hospital attendants	96.0	24.5	183.4	25.3
Janitors and sextons	174.4[a]	23.2	273.7	22.5
Maids and cleaners	252.3[a]	44.5	239.9	37.6
Nurses, practical	33.0	15.9	51.1	21.7
Policemen and detectives	9.2	3.7	24.4	6.5
Waiters	66.0	8.0	63.6	6.2
Private household workers	947.5[a]	52.7	613.4	52.5
Farmers and farmworkers	509.6[a]	12.4	223.5	9.4
Owners, tenants, and				
managers	169.8	6.8	42.0	2.9
Foremen	0.8	3.2	2.5	7.7
Laborers, wage	288.8	25.5	150.7	20.1

Source: U.S. Bureau of the Census, *1970 Census of the Population Occupational Characteristics,* Series PC(2)-7A, table 39; *Population, 1960, Occupational Characteristics,* Series PC(2)-7A, table 3.

[a] Categories adjusted to match 1970 definitions.

[b] Total less than 50.

such workers. Significantly, black officials in unions and in public administration made the most progress during the decade, with the notable exception of postmasters who were still more than 99 percent white in 1970. Most of the opportunities for blacks (as for whites) were in salaried rather than self-employed jobs, with the number of self-employed black managers falling by 50 percent during the decade.

This pattern of underrepresentation in the best jobs is repeated in every occupational category. Blacks were less than 1.5 percent of advertising agents, manufacturing sales representatives, or stock and bond salesmen, but more than twice that proportion among retail sales clerks. They were overrepresented among telephone and office machine operators, postal clerks and carriers, and shipping and file clerks, but less than 6 percent of those with jobs which involved handling money or meeting the public such as secretaries, bank tellers, or receptionists. In the craft professions, black representation ranged from 3 percent of electricians and 4 percent of foremen to 32 percent of cement and concrete finishers. In operative jobs, blacks made the greatest gains in assembly line type occupations such as assemblers, packers and wrappers, checkers, and sewers and stitchers, jobs apparently being shunned by increasing numbers of whites. Though 288,000 fewer blacks serve in private households, they still make up more than half of such workers, the same percentage as in 1960. And lest the shift of blacks out of menial jobs be overestimated, it should be noted that the occupation in which the most new jobs opened for blacks during the decade was "janitors and sextons."

The evidence that blacks are still confined to low-rung jobs is confirmed by comparison of earnings levels and the black proportion in each occupation. In professional and craft jobs, for example, very strong rank order correlations are revealed: the better paid the occupation the less likely blacks are to be well represented (table 3-5).

Though these details reveal that black progress has been far from sweeping, they do not contradict the basic verdict that blacks improved their occupational status during the 1960s. When the present distribution of blacks on the occupational ladder is compared with that at the beginning of the 1960s, it is clear that blacks have advanced at least the first rungs upward.

Table 3-5. Professional and craft occupations in order of male earnings in 1969 and percent black in 1970

Professional and technical	Percent black	Craftsmen	Percent black
Physicians	2.1	Locomotive engineers	1.9
Dentists	2.6	Tool and die makers	1.7
Lawyers and judges	1.3	Foremen	3.7
Social scientists	3.1	Electricians	3.1
Engineers	1.2	Plumbers	4.8
Actuaries and statisticians	3.9	Aircraft repairmen	4.9
Accountants	2.3	Sheetmetal workers	3.3
Editors and reporters	2.2	Compositors and typesetters	5.4
Chemists	3.5	Job and die fitters	5.8
Designers	1.8	Machinists	4.6
Computer specialists	3.5	Brickmasons	14.9
Draftsmen	2.6	Plasterers	19.5
Secondary school teachers	6.6	Radio and TV repairmen	5.4
Social and recreation workers	15.3	Carpenters	5.5
Health technicians	9.0	Auto repairmen	9.4
Elementary school technicians	9.4	Cement and concrete finishers	31.4
Clergymen	6.1	Painters	9.0

Source: U.S. Bureau of the Census, *1970 Census of the Population,* Series PC(2)-7A, table 2; and *1960 Census of the Population,* Series PC(2)-8B, table 1.

Increased Earnings

Better jobs resulted in significant earnings gains for most blacks. In 1959 the average nonwhite male earned $2,900, or 53 percent of the average white. By 1971 earnings had increased to $5,300, or 66 percent of the white male mean. For nonwhite females the rise was even greater, doubling from $1,600 to $3,200 or from 62 to 90 percent of the mean for whites.[1]

The advances occurred throughout the labor queue. With the movement out of lower paid occupations, the percentage of nonwhite males earning less than $3,000 annually (in 1969 dollars) declined significantly from 40 percent in 1959 to 22 percent in 1969. For nonwhite females the proportion fell from 75 to 52 percent. The decline in low-paid whites was less than for blacks—from 16 to 14 percent for white males, and from 49 to 42 percent for white females. At the other end of the earnings spectrum, the proportion of nonwhite men earning over $10,000 (in 1969 dollars) rose from 3 to 9 percent, compared with an increase from 16 to 32 percent for white males. Among nonwhite females the rise was from less than 1 to 5 percent, compared with from 3 to 7 percent for white women.[2] These gains still left blacks far behind whites in the highest earnings categories, particularly among older workers whose long service and experience most often led to positions of seniority, authority, and top wages. In 1970 blacks were less than 4 percent of those with earnings above $10,000 and 1 percent of those with salaries above $15,000. Among those age fifty-five to sixty-four, there were 6,500 black men earning $15,000 or more compared to 800,000 white men.[3]

Black women advanced more than black men. Average earnings of nonwhite female workers in 1971 were 105 percent higher than in 1959, while the average for males was 86 percent higher. The number of female workers rose by half, compared to an increase of only 28 percent for nonwhite males. In the aggregate, then, the gains of females accounted for 38 percent of the growth in nonwhite wages and salaries over this period, as their share of nonwhite earnings rose from 29 to 34 percent. If the average earnings of nonwhite females had increased at the slower rate of nonwhite males, the women's aggregate gain would have been 13 percent less. If their numbers in the labor market had grown only as fast as nonwhite males, the increase in their aggregate earnings would have been 22 percent less. Clearly, the more rapid growth of the black female work force contributed even more than their rising earnings to boosting their share of total nonwhite earnings.

The rising wages and salaries of blacks resulted from a number of factors: broad occupational changes, upgrading into better jobs within these categories, and equalization of pay relative to whites in similar jobs. Share shift analysis of black male earnings gains reveals that if their occupational distribution had not changed since 1960

Table 3-6. Earnings gains within occupational categories of nonwhite males age 25 to 64 years, 1959 and 1969

Occupational category	Average earnings 1959	Nonwhite average as percent of average for all workers in category	Average earnings nonwhites 1969	Nonwhite average as percent of average for all workers in category	Estimated nonwhite earnings assuming 1959 shares in each category
Total	$3,260	56	$6,224	65	$5,509[a]
Professional and technical	5,519	63	10,160	77	8,361
Managers and administrators	4,823	51	9,379	68	7,004
Clerical and kindred	4,282	80	6,861	81	6,769
Sales	4,105	59	7,400	65	6,701
Craftsmen and foremen	3,757	67	6,576	75	5,862
Operatives	3,421	73	5,975	80	5,444
Service	2,922	74	5,215	78	4,922
Farmers and farm managers	1,551	45	3,579	52	3,074
Farm laborers	1,285	65	2,572	66	2,543
Laborers	2,802	65	4,952	81	3,957

Source: U.S. Bureau of the Census, *Earnings by Occupation and Education*, Series PC(2)-8B, July 1973, calculated from table 1; and PC(2)-7B, 1963, table 1.
[a] Calculated by weighting averages in each category by 1970 percent in each category.

their mean annual earnings would have been 8 percent lower. If within each category in 1969 nonwhite males earned the same percentage of the occupational average as in 1959, their mean annual earnings would have been an additional 11 percent less (table 3-6). Similar patterns hold for black females.

Toward Labor Market Equality

Broad-based occupational advancement improved the earnings of blacks, but they were still less likely than whites to get into the higher paying and status jobs. A crucial question is whether the persisting differentials are due to labor market inequities or to the underdevelopment of black human resources. One reason blacks have not gotten into better jobs is that they have not received adequate vocational and educational preparation. Employers are not discriminating when they choose more qualified whites over less qualified blacks. The issue is the extent of progress toward labor market equality given the differentials in education and training.

Vocational training is frequently informal and on-the-job, so that it is difficult to measure acquired work skills. However, data on completed formal training suggest that black males have less vocational preparation than white males though black women have completed formal training almost as frequently as white women. In 1970, 22 percent of black males age sixteen and over with less than four years of college had completed high school vocational courses, apprenticeship training, business, nursing, or trade courses in technical institutions, or vocational training in the armed forces; 28 percent of white males had completed similar training. For females the percentages were 20 for blacks and 22 for whites.[4]

The payoff on vocational training is very nearly equal for black and white females. Among black women with less than a high school education, those who had completed some training earned a third more than those who had not (table 3-7). The differential resulting from completion of training was 19 percent for black males with less than a high school education, compared to 31 percent for white males of the same education. Thus, training does not change the relative

Table 3-7. Completion of vocational training and average annual earnings, 1969

Level of training	Age 16 years and over		Age 25 to 34 years	
	Less than high school education	High school education	Less than high school education	High school education
Black male				
Completed	$4,974	$5,692	$5,228	$6,329
Did not complete	4,192	5,330	4,755	6,059
Differential	19%	7%	10%	4%
White male				
Completed	$7,544	$8,566	$7,698	$8,624
Did not complete	5,769	7,597	6,679	8,093
Differential	31%	13%	15%	7%
Black female				
Completed	$2,811	$3,569	$2,941	$3,837
Did not complete	2,100	3,124	2,379	3,362
Differential	34%	14%	24%	14%
White female				
Completed	$3,420	$3,945	$3,230	$3,772
Did not complete	2,608	3,360	2,612	3,319
Differential	31%	17%	24%	14%

Source: U.S. Bureau of the Census, *Vocational Training,* PC(2)-5C, May 1973, tables 11 and 12.

status of black women compared to whites, but it tends to expand rather than narrow the racial earnings differentials among males.

Educational attainment as well as vocational training data are needed to determine whether blacks with equal skills are getting equal jobs and pay. In 1969 black males age twenty-five to sixty-four earned three-fifths of white males' pay and black females four-fifths of white females. The differentials narrow substantially for whites and blacks with similar educational attainment and occupational distribution (table 3-8). The average earnings of nonwhite males age twenty-five

Table 3-8. Education and mean annual earnings of males and females age 25 to 64 years, 1969

Years of education	Male			Female		
	White	Black	Black/white ratio	White	Black	Black/white ratio
Total	$ 9,920	$5,936	60	$4,459	$3,550	80
8 or less	6,965	4,789	69	3,373	2,295	68
9 to 11	8,421	5,792	69	3,749	2,990	80
12	9,462	6,616	70	4,301	3,906	91
13 to 15	11,028	7,405	67	4,919	4,879	99
16	14,255	8,652	61	6,220	6,545	105
17 and over	16,145	11,755	73	8,061	8,412	104

Source: U.S. Bureau of the Census, Subject Reports, *Earnings By Occupation and Education*, PC(2)-8B, January 1973, tables 1, 2, 7, and 8.

to sixty-four was $6,224 or 63 percent of the $9,920 earned by whites in 1969. If nonwhite males had the same educational distribution as whites within each broad occupational category, their estimated income would have been 67 percent that of whites. Further adjusting their occupational pattern to that of whites would raise black average earnings to $7,472, or more than three-fourths those of whites. If the remaining differential, after "equalizing" education and occupation, is assumed to be a measure of discrimination and other impediments facing nonwhites, it amounted to a 25 percent handicap for adult males.[5]

While this difference is substantial, it represented some improvement since 1959. In that year, the nonwhite males earned an average of $3,260, or 53 percent as much as white males age twenty-five to sixty-four. If nonwhites had the same education in each occupation, their earnings would have been $3,437 or 56 percent of the white mean. Adjusting for occupation would have raised nonwhites to $4,100, leaving a 33 percent differential.[6] Occupational differences accounted for a larger share of the differential in 1959 than in 1969, and the shifts over the 1960s helped to equalize earnings.

The cohort age twenty-five to thirty-four is of special interest because they benefited most from recent educational improvements and expanding job opportunities. The annual earnings of the young black male workers in 1969 was $5,914 or 69 percent of whites. The differential was partly due to greater incidence of intermittent work among blacks. If the percentage of blacks in each occupation working full-year were the same as for whites, their earnings would have been $6,012, or 71 percent of the white level. If their educational distribution were also the same within each occupation, their earnings would have been $6,272. Making the final adjustment to the white occupational pattern would raise earnings to $7,009, or 82 percent of the white levels. Thus, adjusting for more frequently interrupted work, lower education, and a less favorable occupational distribution still leaves a substantial gap, but apparently less than for all nonwhite males age twenty-five to sixty-four.[7]

There is no such gap for females. Black women age twenty-five to thirty-four in 1969 earned $3,740 or 88 percent of whites. Adjusting for the percentage working full-year reduces estimated black earnings to 87 percent of whites, since black women are more frequently full-year workers. The educational adjustment within occupations raises income to 110 percent of the white level, while the occupational adjustment then lowers it to 108 percent.[8] This suggests that for a given level of education, black women tend to earn more than whites and to have a more favorable occupational distribution. Still, black women age twenty-five to thirty-four earn less than white women, and less than half as much as black male workers the same age. Additionally, black women are more likely than white women to be full-time as well as full-year workers. In 1972, 32 percent of employed female whites worked primarily at part-time jobs compared with only 25 percent of nonwhites. Consequently, the proportional hourly wage differential was larger than that for annual earnings.[9]

A critical uncertainty is whether the narrowed racial differentials of younger black workers will be maintained or whether they will increase later. Comparison of the experience of this group with that of older cohorts yields no clear-cut answers, since the differences can be assumed to be either the beginning of a favorable trend or part of a pattern of differentials which will increase with age. Black male college graduates age twenty-four to thirty-four working full-year earned 76 percent as much as whites in 1970, compared with 59 percent for those age thirty-five to fifty-four and 50 percent for older persons (table 3-9). It might be argued that better educated young blacks are getting slotted into higher level jobs where they will advance equally with whites. On the other hand, discrimination may still exist in the "internal labor markets" which determine the rate of advancement; educational quality differentials between whites and blacks may show up over time; or the value of the diploma may decline as the supply of college educated blacks continues to increase.

Social security earnings records provide some longitudinal perspective. Not all jobs are covered and there are no records of earnings above the maximum taxable rate. It is a reasonable assumption that a larger proportion of blacks work in noncovered jobs. On the other hand, only a tenth of black males, but more than half of whites age twenty-five to sixty-four had earnings over the social security maximum in 1969.[10] One would expect, therefore, that the gap between reported average earnings of blacks and whites would have declined

Table 3-9. Black/white annual mean earnings ratio for full-year workers, 1969

Years of education	Age 25 to 34	Age 35 to 54	Age 55 to 64
Males	.69	.60	.57
8 or less	.72	.70	.69
9 to 11	.72	.70	.70
12	.77	.71	.68
13 to 15	.79	.65	.60
16	.76	.59	.50
17 and over	.84	.70	.61
Females	.84	.77	.64
8 or less	.78	.68	.63
9 to 11	.81	.78	
12	.90	.88	.78
13 to 15	.95	.95	.93
16	.96	.94	.95
17 and over	.98	.97	.94

Source: U.S. Bureau of the Census, *Earnings by Occupation and Education,* Series PC(2)-8B, January 1973, tables 1, 2, 7, 8.

over time as more whites moved above the maximum and as coverage was extended so that more of the earnings of blacks were recorded. For a national cohort of black and white males over the 1960s there was, indeed, a declining gap up to 1965; but over the rest of the decade there was a slight dispersion (figure 3-1). For the cohort age twenty-five to twenty-nine in 1964 there was the same pattern of a widening gap in the late 1960s. It would appear, therefore, that the absolute differential between blacks and whites increases with age.

At any rate, the picture of progress which can be painted by concentrating on selected groups and on rates of gain needs to be tempered by consideration of the vast gaps remaining, of the slow manner in which improvements tend to shift the aggregates, and of the possibility that the improved relative status of younger blacks may not be a lifetime guarantee. Nevertheless, these considerations do not alter

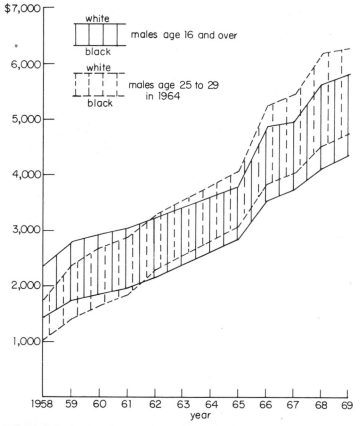

Figure 3-1. Average covered earnings of male cohorts, 1958–1969.

Source: Manpower Administration, U.S. Department of Labor, unpublished data from Continuous Work History Sample.

the picture of important occupational and earnings advances by black men and women.

The Persistent Problem of Unemployment

The labor market problems of many blacks were not alleviated by the decade's progress. Most crucially, blacks continued to have their earnings and employment interrupted by forced idleness, illness, and other factors. More than half of all adult nonwhite males worked full-year in 1972, compared with more than three-fifths of all whites (table 3-10). More than a fifth of nonwhite males had no work

Table 3-10. Work experience of whites and nonwhites age 16 years and over, 1972

Work experience	Males		Females	
	White	Nonwhite	White	Nonwhite
	(percent)			
Total	100.0	100.0	100.0	100.0
No work experience	15.7	23.1	48.3	45.9
Not in labor force	14.9	20.3	46.9	41.6
Could not find job	0.9	2.9	1.4	4.3
Part-year workers	23.5	26.3	24.6	23.8
Unemployment	8.2	10.8	3.9	5.6
Illness	2.9	4.0	1.9	3.2
School	7.3	6.7	5.2	4.1
Home	—	—	11.6	9.4
Retirement	1.6	1.0	0.4	0.3
Armed forces	0.5	0.5	—	—
Other	3.0	3.2	1.6	1.2
Full-year workers	60.8	50.6	27.1	30.2
Full-time	57.2	47.6	21.7	25.4
Part-time	3.6	3.0	5.4	4.8

Source: Anne M. Young, "Work Experience of the Population in 1972," U.S. Bureau of Labor Statistics, *Special Labor Force Report 162*, 1974, tables A-5, A-9, B-2, and D-2.

experience compared with 16 percent of whites; among men who were employed at some point, 34 percent of nonwhites, but only 28 percent of whites experienced work interruptions during the year. Nonwhite women were more likely than white women to have worked or looked for a job, and those with work experience were slightly more likely to have had full-year employment. However, unemployment or illness—involuntary factors—more frequently interrupted their work.

One consequence of these interruptions is that blacks tend to have less tenure on their jobs. In 1968 employed nonwhite males had been on their jobs an average of 3.3 years, compared with 5.0 years for whites; nonwhite female workers had 2.0 years of tenure compared with 2.4 years for whites (table 3-11). Differentials remain after

Table 3-11. Median years on current job, 1968

	Males		Females	
Age	White	Nonwhite	White	Nonwhite
16 years and over	5.0	3.3	2.4	2.0
16 to 24 years	0.8	0.7	0.8	0.6
25 to 34 years	2.8	2.4	1.6	1.5
35 to 39 years	6.0	4.1	2.4	3.2
40 to 44 years	8.7	5.8	3.2	3.4
45 to 54 years	11.6	9.2	5.2	4.9
55 to 64 years	15.1	11.8	8.8	7.8
65 years and over	13.7	11.6	9.8	11.1

Source: Edward J. O'Boyle, "Job Tenure of Workers, January 1968," U.S. Bureau of Labor Statistics, *Special Labor Force Report 112,* September 1969, table B.

adjusting for age. Since tenure on a job is a major determinant of wage levels, privileges, and eligibility for benefits from pension and other welfare plans, work interruptions have serious long-run consequences beyond the immediate problems they cause.

Unemployment and its immediate consequences, however, are more critical concerns than these long-range effects. Unemployment is much more frequent and much more volatile among blacks. Nonwhites are more often "the last to be hired and the first to be fired," and their unemployment rates fluctuate more than for whites over the business cycle (figure 3-2). Nonwhites of all ages, especially males, benefited more than proportionately from the tight labor markets in the middle 1960s. Even black teenagers were helped during this period, though this only briefly offset the disturbing long-run trend of rising unemployment.

In relative terms, using the unemployment rates for white males age twenty and over as the base, nonwhite males the same age have made

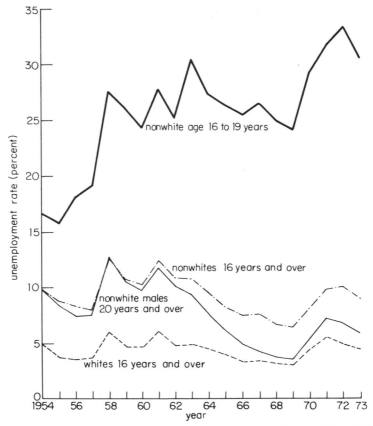

Figure 3-2. Annual average unemployment rates of nonwhites, 1954–1973.

Source: *Manpower Report of the President, 1973* (Washington: Government Printing Office, 1973), table A-6.

some gains. There have been some setbacks for nonwhite females which are shared by white females. Nonwhite teenagers have lost ground relative to everyone, including white youths (figure 3-3).

Unemployment rates at any point in time tell only part of the story. Equally important is the incidence and duration of unemployment over the course of the year. Twenty-two percent of the nonwhite males in the work force experienced some period of unemployment in 1972, as did 23 percent of nonwhite females; this compared with 14 and 15 percent, respectively, of whites (table 3-12). Nonwhites who experienced some unemployment were more likely to have two or

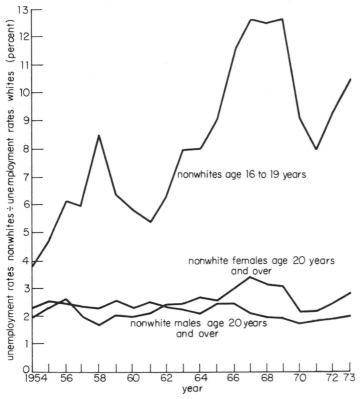

Figure 3-3. Unemployment rates for nonwhites relative to those for white males age 20 years and above, 1954–1973.

Source: *Manpower Report of the President, 1973* (Washington: Government Printing Office, 1973), table A-5.

more spells, and thus 43 percent of nonwhite males compared with 34 percent of whites were out a total of fifteen or more weeks. Much of the black/white differential is thus associated with individuals who are "unemployment prone," having recurrent problems.

The causes of black unemployment are varied. One factor is their concentration in occupations where unemployment tends to be high, such as among nonfarm laborers, operatives, and service workers. If the unemployment rate for experienced workers in each occupation in 1972 is weighted by the percentage distribution of whites in these occupations, the weighted unemployment rate is 4.8 percent. If the

Table 3-12. The incidence and duration of unemployment, 1972

	Males		Females	
	White	Nonwhite	White	Nonwhite
	(percent)			
Total working or looking for work	100.0	100.0	100.0	100.0
Persons with unem- ployment as per- cent of total	14.4	22.1	14.7	22.6
Weeks of unem- ployment	100.0	100.0	100.0	100.0
1 to 4	32.3	29.6	39.2	34.0
5 to 10	21.2	18.0	18.3	16.1
11 to 14	12.7	9.7	10.0	10.1
15 to 26	21.0	23.3	18.7	20.5
27 or more	12.8	19.3	13.7	19.3
Spells of unem- ployment	100.0	100.0	100.0	100.0
1 spell	65.6	62.1	71.6	68.4
2 spells	16.6	15.3	15.0	14.8
3 spells or more	17.8	22.6	13.4	16.8

Source: Anne M. Young, "Work Experience of the Population in 1972," U.S. Bureau of Labor Statistics, *Special Labor Force Report 162,* 1974, table C-1.

occupational distribution of nonwhites is used, the weighted rate is 5.8 percent.[11]

Education is correlated with unemployment for blacks as well as whites, and some of the racial differential is related to educational differentials. Yet, blacks of all ages and all educational levels were more frequently unemployed than whites. Nonwhites with some college education had the same unemployment rate in March 1972 as whites who had completed high school (figure 3-4).

Another explanation of the higher unemployment rates of blacks is that a large minority are trapped in a "secondary labor market" where

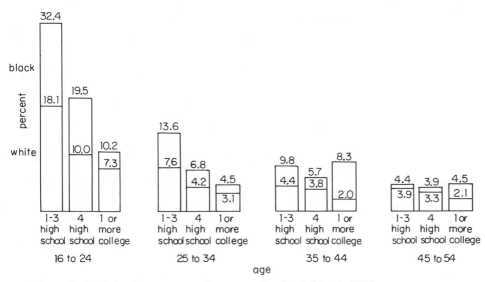

Figure 3-4. Unemployment rates by years of school, March 1972.

Source: William V. Deutermann, "Educational Attainment, March 1972," U.S. Bureau of Labor Statistics, *Special Labor Force Report 148,* November 1972, table L.

there is no reward for tenure, and where wages and working conditions are barely preferable to street life and welfare. Whether or not there is such a definable secondary labor market, high quit rates, frequent layoffs, and periods of nonparticipation tend to prevail more frequently for blacks than whites. On the average in 1973, nonwhite labor force participants were 1.8 times more likely to have lost and quit their jobs, and 2.3 times more likely to be experiencing reentry or first entry problems (table 3-13). While the increasing number of job losers accounted for more than half of the rise in nonwhite unemployment during the recession between 1968 and 1971, the nonwhite rates of quitting, job loss, reentry, and first entry problems were all at least twice as high in the tight labor markets of 1968.

Declining Labor Force Participation

In 1950, 86 percent of all nonwhite males age sixteen and over were labor force participants, the same proportion as for whites. By 1960 both rates declined to 83 percent. The participation rate for

Table 3-13. Distribution of unemployment by cause, 1968 and 1973

Unemployment rate by cause	1968		1973	
	White	Nonwhite	White	Nonwhite
	(percent)			
Total	3.2	6.7	4.3	8.9
Lost last job	1.2	2.5	1.7	3.1
Left last job	0.5	1.0	0.7	1.2
Re-entered labor force	1.0	2.2	1.3	3.0
Never worked before	0.4	1.1	0.6	1.6
Percent of unemployed				
Total	100.0	100.0	100.0	100.0
Lost last job	38.1	37.4	39.8	34.5
Left last job	15.5	14.5	16.2	13.7
Re-entered labor force	32.3	33.2	30.0	33.4
Never worked before	14.1	15.9	14.0	18.4

Source: *Manpower Report of the President, 1974* (Washington: Government Printing Office, 1974), table A-21.

whites continued downward to 80 percent in 1973, but for blacks it fell precipitously to 74 percent. Among nonwhite females, there was a slight increase in participation from 47 percent in 1950 to 49 percent in 1973; but over the same period the white female rate rose substantially from 33 to 44 percent.[12]

Participation patterns of both the white and nonwhite populations changed between 1960 and 1973 (figure 3-5). Nonwhite male teenagers and young men in their early twenties were less likely to be in the work force, while white male teenagers' participation increased. Rates were lower for both white and black males age fifty-five and over, as they retired at an earlier age. Perhaps the most alarming change was the reduced participation of nonwhite males age twenty-five to fifty-four, considered prime working years.

The 1973 participation rate of nonwhite women age twenty to thirty-four was substantially higher than thirteen years earlier, but the comparable rate for middle-aged women declined. White women's participation increased at all ages, but retained its "bimodal pattern"

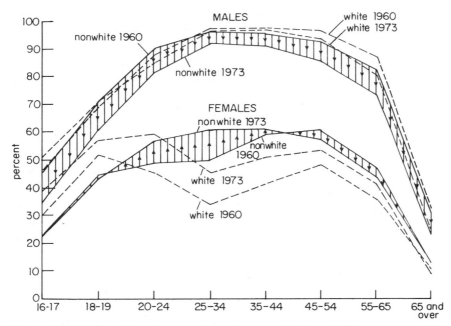

Figure 3-5. Civilian labor force participation rates, 1960 and 1973.

Source: *Manpower Report of the President, 1973* (Washington: Government Printing Office, 1973), table A-4.

with participation peaking in the late teens and early twenties before the birth of children and then again in the forties after the children are grown. Black women do not share this pattern, having their highest participation rates in the middle years.

The critical issue is the declining participation of black males. If each of the nonwhite age cohorts had the same participation rates in 1973 as they did in 1960, there would have been half a million more black male job seekers and workers in the latter year. Alternatively, if the participation rate of each cohort had declined at the same rate as among white males, 300,000 nonwhites would have joined the labor force.[13] Various hypotheses are offered to explain the exodus of black males from the workplace: the "work ethic" has been eroded; an increasing shortage of well-paying jobs has discouraged job seeking; favorable developments, such as increased school attendance and earlier retirement, have contributed.

1. Looking first at the positive factors, much of the decline in labor force participation among younger blacks is associated with rising school enrollment. Between 1967 and 1972 the annual average proportion of nonwhite males age sixteen to twenty-four outside the labor force rose from 32.5 to 36.8 percent. Over the same period, the proportions not participating because of school attendance rose from 25.7 to 28.3 percent. Rising school attendance "explained" about three-fifths of the declining participation among young nonwhite males.

The falling participation rate for blacks age sixty and over is due largely to earlier retirement, though detailed data do not go back far enough to prove this point. Between the fourth quarter of 1968 and 1972, the participation rate of older nonwhite males fell from 41 to 38 percent; the proportion of those outside the labor force giving retirement as their primary reason increased from 54 to 64 percent.

One explanation for the declining participation of prime-age nonwhites is ill health and disability. Between 1967 and 1972 the proportion of nonwhite males age twenty-five to fifty-four out of the labor force due to ill health or disability rose from 2.5 to 3.9 percent, while the participation rate fell from 93.5 to 90.3 percent.[14] It is likely that this rise reflects the increasing availability of disability coverage, rather than deteriorating black health.

2. While ill health, school attendance, and retirement are "acceptable" reasons for nonparticipation, they are not fully explanative. More white than black students work, fewer white males have disabilities, and "retirement" may disguise a forced retreat from the labor market. Many blacks not counted in the labor force are "discouraged" workers who want jobs but believe that work is not available and give up the search, sometimes claiming that they are disabled, retired, or in school. By definition, discouraged workers are restricted to those who are not seeking work because they think they cannot find a job. In 1972, 2.9 percent of nonwhites not in the labor force said they were discouraged from seeking work, compared with only 1.1 percent among whites. The 188,000 discouraged nonwhites accounted for a fourth of all discouraged workers, which might be expected from the fact that they had much more to be discouraged about.[15] Among black males not in school and under age sixty-five, the number of discouraged workers rose from 0.76 to 1.85 percent of labor force

participants between 1968 and 1972, explaining some of the participation rate decline in these years.[16]

3. The falling labor force participation rates for males may also be
due in part to changing attitudes toward work which, in turn, are
related to expanding income options. It is sometimes alleged that
though jobs are plentiful, blacks will no longer take them because of
unrealistic wage expectations. Rising crime and welfare rates are
offered as evidence that more blacks are supporting themselves by
illegal activities or are living off the increasing number of welfare
mothers.

The existence of alienated black males supported by the "hustle"
and of those who refuse dead-end jobs cannot be denied, but the
frequency of such behavior is too often overstated and ascribed to all
low-income "disadvantaged" blacks. One study based on intensive
interviews with three groups of disadvantaged black males—those
participating in a training program, those with intermittent work
experience, and others who had never worked—revealed substantial
differences despite similar age and education patterns. Program participants had a strong "work ethic" while those who had never worked
filled the stereotype of the "street dude" (table 3-14). Intermittent
workers—the "swing" group moving in and out of work both volun-
tarily and involuntarily—in all probability account for the bulk of
younger low-income males. When they are out of money, when hustling
is not productive, or when the "heat" is on, they may be willing to take
a low-wage job they would spurn on Monday after payday. Their attitudes toward work, labor force participation, and street corner activities depend largely on their financial status. But their attitudes also
depend on the availability and attractiveness of employment opportunities. If these improve, more will choose work over socially less
desirable activities.

The existence of some unknown number of black males who do not
want to work does not wipe away the hundreds of thousands who are
looking for but cannot find jobs. If more jobs are available, blacks will
take them. Between 1961 and 1969, when the aggregate unemployment rate dropped from 6.7 to 3.5 percent, the number of employed
white adult males rose by 9 percent, compared with a growth of 16
percent for black adult males. Whatever the measured participation
rates, opening more jobs for blacks will draw in more black workers.

Table 3-14. Attitudes of three groups of disadvantaged black males

Characteristic	Percent with characteristic		
	Program participant	Sometime worked	Never worked
Married with spouse present	38	20	6
Feeling that jobs involve too much red tape	19	18	55
Feeling of being bossed around on job	33	30	52
Unnecessary language requirement on job	5	7	32
Prefer working with blacks	54	75	72
Perceive discrimination	37	32	42
Perceive opportunities for hustling	53	80	76
Prefer regular job to hustling	91	59	23
Feel regular work is one of most satisfying parts of life	55	20	15

Source: Philip B. Springer, *Work Attitudes of Disadvantaged Black Men*, U.S. Bureau of Labor Statistics, Report 401, 1972, pp. 5–14.

Inadequate Employment and Earnings

Black employment problems are disproportionate and diverse. They earn less than whites, are forced to work irregularly, have trouble finding jobs, and are more frequently discouraged from even looking. Low earnings, intermittent employment, discouragement, unemployment, and falling labor participation all interact. While there is no exact way to determine the interrelationships and net impact of these problems, a useful conceptualization is provided by the employment and earnings inadequacy (EEI) index, which measures the number of workers with employment problems who are unable to earn an adequate income to support their households.[17] The index counts all persons age sixteen through sixty-four (excluding students age sixteen to twenty-one) who are unemployed, discouraged, involun-

tarily employed part-time for economic reasons, household heads working full-time at poverty level wages, and heads working intermittently
and earning too little to raise their families above the poverty thresholds. Members of households which have above average income are excluded even if the individuals have an employment or earnings problem, since they are presumably not in need.

According to this definition 2.2 million blacks, compared with 7.6
million whites, had inadequate employment and earnings in March
1972; these represented 25 and 10 percent, respectively, of the black
and white labor forces. More than half of blacks with inadequate
employment and earnings lived in poverty with a mean annual household income of only $4,500, and the unemployed accounted for only
28 percent of the total (table 3-15). Nearly a third of black labor

Table 3-15. Characteristics of blacks with inadequate employment and
earnings, March 1972

Characteristic	Number blacks (thousands)	Percent of blacks	Blacks as percent of total
Total	2,185	100.0	22
Unemployed	613	28	22
Discouraged	185	8	34
Low-paid, fully-employed heads	484	31	20
Employed part-time involuntarily	224	10	20
Other low-earning heads	679	31	20
Family heads	1,226	56	21
Wives	206	9	16
Other relatives	426	19	36
Unrelated individuals	372	17	22
Metropolitan residents	1,510	69	24
Central city residents	1,201	55	34
Nonmetropolitan residents	675	31	19

Source: Sar A. Levitan and Robert Taggart, *Employment and Earnings Inadequacy:
A New Social Indicator* (Baltimore: The Johns Hopkins University Press, 1974).

force participants outside metropolitan areas had inadequate employment and earnings compared with 24 percent of those in central cities
and 20 percent in the suburbs.

The inadequacy index (calculated by dividing the number with
inadequate employment and earnings by the number in the labor
force, including discouraged workers) provides some evidence that
despite the recession, conditions improved for blacks, both absolutely
and relatively, between March 1968 and 1972. Their inadequacy
index fell from 27 percent to 25 percent, while over the same period it
rose for whites from 8 percent to 10 percent; the black/white ratio
thus declined from 3.2 in March 1968 to 2.5 in March 1972 (figure 3-
6). These gains resulted for the most part from a decrease in the
percentage of black males in the low earnings categories. Where 19.5
percent of black male labor force participants in 1968 earned less
than poverty wages in the preceding year, only 14.5 percent had this
problem in 1972.

The Work and Wage Record

The labor market progress of blacks in the 1960s was extensive,
with the following major developments.

1. The black occupational distribution moved closer to that of
whites as blacks progressed at a much faster rate out of the lowest
paying categories and penetrated into higher paying occupations.
Though much of the upward movement was into the lower rungs of
the higher occupational categories, the advances were still notable.

2. The mean annual earnings of black males increased from 53 to
66 percent of those for whites between 1959 and 1971, and average
black female earnings moved very close to equality with the earnings
of white females.

3. The job gains were widespread and affected broad categories of
black workers. The percent of black males earning less than $3,000
annually (in 1969 dollars) dropped from 40 to 22 percent between
1959 and 1969, while for females the decline was from 75 to 52
percent. The proportion earning over $10,000 (in 1969 dollars) rose

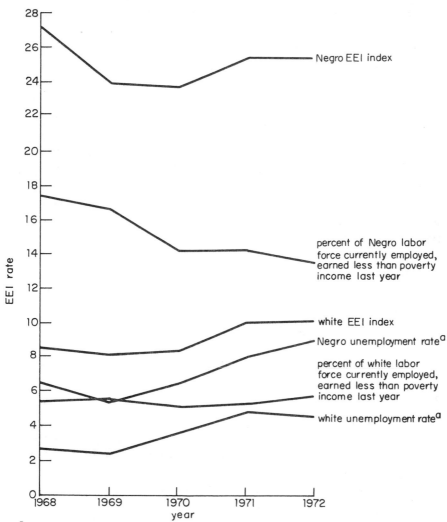

Unemployment rate excludes 16 to 21-year-old students and persons
65 and over.

Figure 3-6. Black and white employment and earnings inadequacy, 1968–1972.

Source: Sar A. Levitan and Robert Taggart, *Employment and Earnings Inadequacy:
A New Social Indicator* (Baltimore: Johns Hopkins University Press, 1974).

from 3 to 9 percent for black males and from 1 to 5 percent for black females.

4. Blacks received 6.4 percent of all wages and salaries at the beginning of the 1960s, but 8.1 percent at the end. Over the period, increased earnings accounted for 90 percent of the growth in real income.

The severe employment problems of blacks persisted, but improvement can be noted. Black teenage unemployment rates rose throughout the decade, absolutely and relatively, but the critically important unemployment rate—that of adult black males—declined. Labor force participation rates fell among black males of all ages, but the pull of alternatives to work such as school, retirement, and more readily available disability benefits were apparently the major contributing factors. Measured by a specially designed index of employment and earnings inadequacy, absolute and relative improvement apparently continued through the 1969–1971 recession. The problems remain severe, but the progress made suggests that they are not intractable.

4

EDUCATION: QUANTITY AND QUALITY

The growing importance of education has challenged American ideals of equality. Education increasingly separates the economically successful from the disadvantaged and the powerful from the helpless. Despite a massive national investment in educational institutions, inequalities of educational opportunity persist. Those with better education make more money and gain more power, and the children of the successful and powerful get better education. Conversely, blacks with poor schooling have lower incomes, and children of low-income blacks tend to get poor schooling.

To break this cycle it is not enough to equalize years of school. If all are to compete on an equal footing in American society, education must produce individuals whose innate competence is as equally developed as possible. In order to obtain truly equal opportunity, education must seek to minimize environmental advantages or disadvantages and to compensate for social and economic inequalities. The vital questions concern not only gains in school attainment, but whether the education of blacks is really equivalent to that of whites, and whether it is sufficient to insure blacks equal mobility in society.

Educational Attainment

Measured by years in school, blacks are increasing their educational attainment both absolutely and relative to whites. Between

79

1960 and 1972 median years of black education rose from 8.2 to 10.3. Though whites were also staying in school longer, their lead narrowed from an average of 2.7 years in 1960 to 2.0 years in 1972. Proportionately, the white/nonwhite differential declined from 33 percent in 1960 to 19 percent in 1972.

	Nonwhites[a]			Whites[a]		
	1950	1960	1972	1950	1960	1972
Median years of school	6.9	8.2	10.3	9.7	10.9	12.3
Male	NA	7.9	10.0	NA	10.7	12.3
Female	NA	8.5	10.5	NA	11.2	12.3

[a] Age 25 and over.

Most of the improvement in educational attainment has come from reduced high school dropout rates. Although black college graduates are increasing rapidly, they still do not contribute substantially to the average educational attainment. From 1950 to 1972 the proportion of nonwhites with fewer than five years of education fell from 33 to 13 percent; those with high school diplomas increased from 14 to 37 percent. In both categories, the nonwhite rate of gain was faster than the white. Nonwhite college graduates increased from 2.3 to 6.9 percent while white graduates increased from 6.6 to 12.6 percent (table 4-1).

These educational gains result mostly from the increased school attainment of the younger black population. Among blacks between the ages of twenty-five and twenty-nine, the proportion of high school graduates leaped from two-fifths in 1960 to two-thirds in 1972, while college graduates more than doubled from 5.4 to 11.6 percent. Whites also gained but at slower rates (table 4-2).

Not all blacks gained equally and there are still differences in attainment between various regions and residences. In 1972 blacks in the South and those in nonmetropolitan areas lagged far behind both whites and blacks elsewhere. In suburban areas and in the West, on the other hand, blacks are much nearer equality in educational attainment (table 4-3).

Table 4-1. Comparative levels of education of the population 25 and over, 1950–1972

Years of education	Nonwhite			White		
	1950	1960	1972	1950	1960	1972
Percent						
Less than 5 years	32.6	23.4	12.8[a]	8.9	6.7	3.7
Less than 1 year high school	72.5	59.6	38.2[a]	45.8	39.8	23.3
4 years high school or more	13.9	21.7	39.1[a]	36.4	41.4	60.4
4 years college or more	2.3	3.5	6.9[a]	6.6	8.1	12.6
Numbers (in thousands)						
High school graduates	1,074	2,049	4,531	28,151	38,575	60,121
Some college	414	757	1,575	11,132	15,537	23,906
College graduates	176	335	797	5,108	7,253	12,567

Source: U.S. Bureau of the Census, Census of the Population, 1960, *General Social and Economic Characteristics of the Population, U.S. Summary,* PC(1)C, table 76; and *Educational Attainment: March 1972,* Series P-20, no. 243, November 1973, table 2.
[a] 1972 includes blacks only.

Table 4-2. Black 25- to 29-year-old high school and college graduates, 1940-1972 (percent of age group)

Year	Black and other races		White	
	4 years of high school or more	4 years of college or more	4 years of high school or more	4 years of college or more
1972	66.6	11.6	81.5	19.9
1970	58.4	10.0	77.8	17.3
1964	48.0	7.0	72.1	13.6
1960	38.6	5.4	63.7	11.8
1950	23.4	2.8	55.2	8.1
1940	12.1	1.6	41.2	6.4

Source: U.S. Bureau of the Census, *Characteristics of American Youth: 1972,* Series P-23, no. 44, March 1973, table 18.

Table 4-3. Median years of school, 1972

Residence	Black	White
Total	10.3	12.3
Metropolitan	10.9	12.4
Central city	10.9	12.3
Outside central cities	11.0	12.4
Nonmetropolitan	8.3	12.1
Northwest	11.3	12.2
North central	11.3	12.3
South	9.1	12.2
West	12.2	12.5

Source: U.S. Bureau of the Census, *Population Characteristics,* "Educational Attainment, March 1972," Series P-20, no. 243, November 1972, tables 2 and 3.

School Enrollment

The increasing educational attainment of blacks relative to whites reflects more equal enrollment ratios. At every age level (except, significantly, college years) blacks are nearly as likely—and among preschoolers, more likely—to be enrolled in school as whites (table 4-4). Between the ages of six and sixteen when education is mandatory, almost all blacks and whites are enrolled and enrollment rates of youths through age seventeen to nineteen are nearly equal. Although blacks are still less likely to complete high school, the dropout rate is declining. In 1967, 22.8 percent of blacks between age fourteen and twenty-four had dropped out of high school without finishing, compared to 12.4 percent of whites. By 1972 the proportions were 17.5 percent for blacks and 11.3 for whites.[1]

Though blacks are less likely than whites to be attending college, they are narrowing this gap also. Between 1960 and 1973 the number of blacks enrolled in college increased by approximately 540,000, a gain of 370 percent which raised the ratio of blacks to whites from 1 in 20 to 1 in 12. In 1973, 16 percent of blacks and 25 percent of

Table 4-4. School enrollment by race, 1973 (numbers in thousands)

Age	Black				White			
	Enrolled in school	Percent	Enrolled in college	Percent	Enrolled in school	Percent	Enrolled in college	Percent
3–4 years	292	28.9	—	—	1,364	23.2	—	—
5–6 years	835	89.9	—	—	5,270	93.0	—	—
7–9 years	1,587	99.2	—	—	9,291	99.1	—	—
10–13 years	2,210	99.0	—	—	13,812	99.3	—	—
14–15 years	1,070	96.7	—	—	6,926	97.6	6	0.1
16–17 years	967	87.7	37	3.4	6,183	88.3	247	3.5
18–19 years	377	37.8	194	19.5	2,849	43.4	2,281	34.8
20–21 years	176	20.5	164	19.2	1,924	31.3	1,865	30.3
22–24 years	156	12.4	140	11.0	1,322	14.6	1,292	14.3
25–29 years	97	6.1	89	5.6	1,174	8.7	1,152	8.5
30–34 years	67	5.0	60	4.5	502	4.5	481	4.3
18–24 years in college	—	—	498	16.0	—	—	5,384	24.7

Source: U.S. Bureau of the Census, *School Enrollment in the United States: October 1973* (Advance Report), Series P-20, no. 261, March 1974, table 2.

whites in the eighteen to twenty-four age group were enrolled in college. This represented a substantial improvement over 1960, when 8 percent of blacks and 20 percent of whites were in college.

	College enrollment (thousands)			
	1960	1965	1970	1973
Black	146	274	522	684
White	2,743	5,317	6,759	7,324

Source: Derived from U.S. Bureau of the Census, *The Social and Economic Status of Negroes in the United States, 1970,* Series P-23, no. 3, table 69; *School Enrollment in the United States: October 1973* (Advance Report), Series P-20, no. 261, table 2; and *Census of the Population, 1960, U.S. Summary,* Series PC(1)-1C, table 75.

The universality (if not the uniformity) of the American educational system is evident from the fact that enrollment figures do not vary significantly among regions or residence areas. The variations in educational attainment between the South and North, and between central city children and suburban ones, cannot be explained by discrepancies in enrollment. Southern blacks are slightly less likely to be in school in most age groups, but the differences are very small. Among college age youth (eighteen to twenty-four years) southern blacks are more likely to be in school.[2] The differences in school enrollment between central city and suburban and metropolitan and nonmetropolitan blacks are also insignificant. Whatever the problems of central city schools, black residents are as likely to be in school as those from other areas. In fact, between ages seven and fifteen, 98 percent or more of blacks from all types of residence areas attend school.[3]

Educational Achievement and the Quality of Black Education

Black enrollment and attainment gains at the precollege level are paradoxical, for elementary and secondary education has become the area in which black progress is most bitterly debated. The reason for this concern is that black educational achievement on various tests and standards has not improved relative to whites. Though the extra years of education have had positive impacts, the achievement gains and the ultimate payoffs for education have been less for blacks than for whites at each level of attainment.

A number of indicators document the achievement differentials. Black children are much more likely to be enrolled at grade levels below their age groups, and this differential increases in higher grades (figure 4-1). Whereas some white children also fall behind, this group does not seem to increase as schooling progresses. But more and more blacks fall further and further behind. By age seventeen, more than half of black males are behind their "modal" class, and 30 percent are back two grades or more. Females are less likely to fall behind, but the

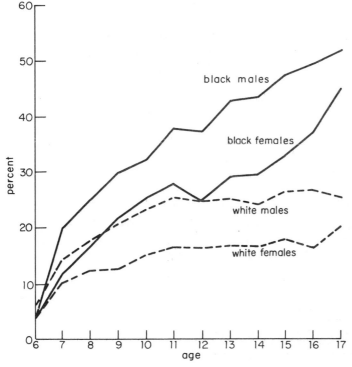

Figure 4-1. Children enrolled below modal grade, 1969–1971.

Source: U.S. Bureau of the Census, *School Enrollment: October 1970,* Series P-20, no. 222, June 28, 1971, table 7; and *Social and Economic Characteristics of Students: October 1971,* Series P-20, no. 241, October 1972, table 16.

black-white differential is still present. Moreover, despite compensatory efforts to improve the elementary and secondary education these figures are not improving. In 1972 a slightly greater proportion of black children were behind in school than in 1968.[4]

Tests also demonstrate lagging black achievement. The Equal Educational Opportunity survey sponsored by the Department of Health, Education, and Welfare in 1965, showed that black reading achievement was 1.5 years less than whites in the sixth grade, 2.25 years in grade nine, and 3.25 years in the senior year of high school.[5] These data are now nine years old, and no comparably broad study has been made more recently; but surveys of educational needs in Title I schools and reports from heavily black central city school districts do not indicate that there has been any general improvement since 1965.[6]

The inability of the school system to upgrade black educational achievement is also indicated by results of mental tests of draftees (table 4-5). Between 1950 and 1971 blacks were more than four

Table 4-5. Mental disqualification of draftees, 1950–1971

Year	Black	White
	(percent)	
1971	33.9	4.7
1970	33.0	5.3
1969	38.2	8.1
1968	39.0	8.0
1967–1950	53.6	13.1
Average 1950–1971	49.8	11.5

Source: Department of the Army, Office of the Surgeon General, *Results of the Examination of Youths for Military Service, September 22* (Washington: Government Printing Office, 1972), table 10.

times as likely to be rejected for military induction on the basis of mental tests as whites. Both black and white rejection rates have declined in recent years as a result of more universal education and larger draft calls which tapped better educated individuals. But the gap between blacks and whites has narrowed little.

Taken together, these figures cast a shadow on the recorded gains in black educational attainment. Not only are blacks likely to be in lower grade levels than whites, but when they are tested against the standards of those grade levels, they do more poorly. Though the census records all who have completed twelve years of school as high school graduates, it is clear that some blacks with such attainment may not have educations equivalent to those of whites.

Failures of Institutions or Individuals?

These findings, of course, touch the rawest nerves of racial friction and raise fundamental questions about the American educational system. Three explanations and policy prescriptions have been offered for dealing with the evidence. At one extreme, some argue that a large and ineradicable part of the achievement differentials lies in genetic differences. A second and much larger group feels that the responsibilities for failure rest primarily with the schools, whose rigid and often racist teaching policies and unequally distributed resources have insured the failure of blacks. In-between are those who downplay genetic differences but who replace them with social and environmental factors, thus leaving little room for the schools to effect change. There are libraries of rhetoric and evidence on every side of these issues—so much that "resolving" them is almost a matter of personal predisposition. There is only room to summarize the conflicting arguments.

Intelligence and Genetic Differences

Of the few academics who have publicly argued that genetic differences may be responsible for interracial differences in measured intelligence (I.Q.) and achievement, the most noted spokesman has been Arthur R. Jensen, a professor of educational psychology at Berkeley.

In a highly controversial article in the *Harvard Educational Review* in 1969, Jensen suggested that within population samples as much as 80 percent of the variance in intelligence was related to genetic factors. He cited evidence that the intelligences of monozygotic twins reared apart showed a median correlation coefficient of .75, while those of unrelated children reared together correlated at .24. Groups with various genetic and environmental similarities (for example, siblings and adopted children) had intelligences which correlated according to the pattern of presumed genetic dominance. Moreover, Jensen found that environment acts as a "threshold variable." Extreme deprivation could prevent children from achieving their potential, but enriched environment could not push children beyond natural limitations.

Jensen hypothesized that some of the observed differences in average intelligence between blacks and whites (which, he reported, averaged approximately one standard deviation, or 15 I.Q. points) could be due to genetic differences. He cited a study which estimated that after controlling for socioeconomic status, an average difference of 11 I.Q. points remained between the races. He noted that no study had ever found the I.Q.s of blacks and whites to be equal no matter how many environmental or educational factors were controlled. With similar reasoning, he presented the Coleman findings on American Indian children who scored a half a standard deviation higher than blacks, despite the fact that Indians had a higher index of social and economic disadvantages.

Jensen's evidence and his interpretation have been sharply criticized. It has been argued that his estimates of heritability are too high, and that they cannot be applied to interracial population differences. It has been pointed out that most of the data on the genetic origins of intelligence were derived for white and north European populations and thus cannot legitimately be applied to blacks. Others have criticized his statistical methods and use of sources. Analyses have been cited in which all interracial differences in I.Q. are explained by environmental variables. Others have argued that many of the environmental disadvantages which blacks suffer are not measurable, or have cumulative effects which are ignored. Another widely supported view is that I.Q. tests measure only a small part of intelligence and are culturally biased against blacks. It is noted that black children tested by blacks score several points higher on the average than when tested by whites. These criticisms suggest that Jensen's hypothesis remains unproven, and that the relation between genetics and intelligence is still far from clear.

Whatever the resolution of the debate, its policy implications may be limited. If genetic hypotheses were to be confirmed, they would not relieve the schools of their responsibility to equalize educational opportunity and to compensate for environmental disadvantages. Genetics could prove an ultimate boundary of educational improvement, but much remains to be done before other barriers to inequality are removed.

Home Environments and Individual Attitudes— The Coleman Report

The ability of schools to effect change has not been questioned only by geneticists. Many psychologists and educators have argued that family backgrounds and individual and peer group attitudes are more important determinants of performance than the characteristics of schools. In 1966 the Department of Health, Education, and Welfare's *Report on Equal Educational Opportunity* (the Coleman Report) buttressed these beliefs with a mountain of evidence. After surveying and testing 675,000 students and nearly 20,000 teachers, the researchers reported that family background and student attitudes explained far more of the variance in student test scores than differences in schools, and that the most important differences within schools were the attitudes and backgrounds of the student body—that is, variables also related to the socioeconomic environment.

Designed and executed under great time pressures, the data and the conclusions of the Coleman Report have also been questioned. Critics have argued that the survey used resource allocation data which were averaged over school systems (and thus failed to reflect true differences in resources) and that the report's technique of controlling for student background first in the regressions understated the amount of variance explained by school resources.[7] Though these critiques have cast doubt on some of the Coleman Report conclusions, a reanalysis of the data published in 1972 confirmed the basic findings that students and their backgrounds are far more important than schools in determining achievement.[8]

Statistical proof is hardly needed to show that, compared to poor children, students from upper income, college educated families will not only have the prerequisites to learning—adequate food, shelter, and medical care—but will also be far more likely to be exposed to books, vocabulary, travel, and even toys which will develop their cognitive abilities.

Blacks, of course, are not only less likely to have such advantages, but they are far more likely to be disadvantaged. Sixty-nine percent of black children in 1970 were in homes in which the head had less than a high school education, a third were receiving welfare or had inadequate diets, and a quarter were living in substandard housing (table 4-6).

The Coleman Report found that differences in students' backgrounds—size and type of family, education, reading and other mate-

Table 4-6. Disadvantaged black children, 1970

Characteristic	White	Black
Total children under 18 (thousands)	59,125	9,463
	(percent)	
With one parent	10	33
With neither parent	3	9
Family head not a high school graduate	38	69
Family head with 8 years or less of education	19	39
Family income less than $3,000	9	34
Family receiving welfare	6	33
Living in substandard housing	6	26
Inadequate diet	19	34

Source: Derived from U.S. Bureau of the Census, *U.S. Census of Population, 1970,* PC(2)4B, tables 3-6; *Characteristics of the Low-Income Population, 1971,* Series P-60, no. 86, tables 1 and 4; *Statistical Abstracts of the U.S., 1972,* table 491; U.S. Congress, Senate, Select Committee on Equal Educational Opportunity, *Toward Equal Educational Opportunity,* 92nd Cong., 2d Sess., December 1972, p. 73; White House Conference on Children, *1970 Profiles of Children* (Washington: Government Printing Office, 1971), table 57.

rial at home, and parents' interest in and educational aspirations for their children—accounted for between 15 and 25 percent of all the variance in individual and verbal test scores.[9] Further analysis of the data revealed that student achievement was directly related to the socioeconomic status of the parents. Black students in the sixth grade achieved at an average grade level of 4.4, but those who had backgrounds of "high" socioeconomic status averaged 5.3 grades. Among seniors in high school, the black average was 8.8 grades, but for upper status black children it was 10.7.

Additional evidence of the preeminent importance of the home has been suggested by a study which compared the estimated dollar value of parents' educational services with those of the schools. The researchers concluded that college educated parents had three times more educational impact on their offspring than all the school inputs combined. In dollar terms, by the time a child entered school the value of the educational services provided by the average white mother (11.2 years of school) was $9,310. In comparison, the services of the average nonwhite mother (8.5 years of education) were worth $5,242. By the twelfth grade there was a differential of $15,000 per child between the imputed parental investment of college trained parents and that of grade school educated parents.[10]

When the Coleman researchers turned to school variables, they found that environmental factors—characteristics and backgrounds of other students—were nearly ten times more important than the impacts of school facilities, curriculum, or teacher characteristics. A predominantly middle class student body had a positive effect on the achievement of all students, especially the disadvantaged. If a high proportion of students planned to go to college, spent long hours studying, had more educated parents, or lived in homes with encyclopedias and other books, all students tended to do better. Moreover, these effects were greater for black than white students.

Evidently, racial isolation has a double-barreled impact on blacks. Not only do more blacks come from disadvantaged homes, they are far more likely to be in schools with students from similar deprived backgrounds. As the Coleman researchers pointed out, the impact of segregation had less to do with racial isolation per se than with the characteristics which were associated with white students.

Of all the variables found to affect student achievement, individual attitudes, such as self-concepts, interest in learning, and sense of control over environment, correlated most with performance. Correlation, of course, does not determine which is cause and which is effect. Students may have achieved more poorly because they had negative attitudes, or they may have developed negative attitudes because they were unsuccessful in school. Nevertheless, attitudes should not be ignored since they were found to account for between 15 and 30 percent of achievement variations in the Coleman study.

The researchers found that both black and white students expressed high self-concepts, interest in school, and desire to achieve. Blacks were more likely than whites to want to stay in school and to finish college. They more frequently wanted to be best in school and studied longer hours. But more blacks also felt unable to influence their environments, that luck or other factors controlled their lives. Apparently, many blacks did not translate their school interest into achievement because they did not feel that their efforts would be successful. White children from advantaged backgrounds, on the other hand, reacted more to their self-concept—if they thought themselves bright or capable, they performed accordingly.

These findings suggested that integration might have conflicting effects on disadvantaged students. Going to school with advantaged white students might make blacks less likely to consider themselves top students. On the other hand, middle class beliefs in personal control over the environment might "rub off" on disadvantaged students, encouraging them to perform up to the limits of their capabilities.

School Policies and Resources

The Coleman Report, psychologists of child development, and geneticists have seemingly painted the schools into a rather small corner. What some have explained in terms of genes, others have interpreted as the effects of family background and peer attitudes. But clearly, there are differences in the effectiveness of schools. And since the schools are the variable in the equation of learning most susceptible to public policy, attention has focused on them. Three policy alternatives have received the most attention: desegregation, equalization of school resources, and reform of instructional methods.

1. *Integration.* Integration has proceeded rapidly since 1965, though de facto segregation in urban areas remains a problem. Despite prevailing assumptions that socioeconomic and racial integration would improve the achievement of disadvantaged students, the results have been mixed. Almost all reports indicate that black students in integrated schools do better than apparently similar black students in segregated schools. The Coleman Report concluded that blacks who went to school with middle class whites scored better than those who did not. Another large survey of black adults found that those who had attended desegregated schools scored two to three points higher on a verbal test than those who had been to school in segregated surroundings.[11] But these and other surveys with similar findings may have been biased by unknown differences in the integrated and segregated populations.

Follow-up studies of students in newly-segregated schools have not provided more conclusive evidence. Longitudinal studies of black inner city children bused to white suburban schools in New Haven and Hartford, Connecticut showed significant gains accruing over time. But the complete integration of the Berkeley, California school district had little effect on the test scores for most grade levels.[12] In Riverside, California and Ann Arbor, Michigan desegregated black students improved their I.Q. levels but lost ground to whites who improved faster.[13] In Boston, a year of busing revealed no significant improvements compared to a control group of brothers and sisters.[14]

Integration's effects on student attitudes, as well as on academic performance, have been examined. It has been claimed that the self-image and academic aspirations of black students suffer when they are transferred to predominantly white schools, and that racial friction increases.[15] Others have argued that more realistic aspirations promote greater achievement, and that the raised awareness of racial identity is a positive development which has little to do with school integration.[16]

While the many studies are subject to different interpretations, the weight of the evidence seems to suggest that integration in the schools can make small improvements in black I.Q. and achievement, if it is accompanied by no dilution of school services, and if it includes socio-economic as well as racial desegregation.[17]

2. *Equalizing school resources.* A second strategy for improving black education is to equalize school facilities, staff, and curriculums. A growing body of evidence indicates that there are large differences in expenditures between rich and poor school districts, and between schools within districts. In 1972–1973 state expenditures per pupil ranged from $680 per pupil in Alabama to $1961 in Alaska.[18] Within the states, the range of expenditures between districts was even greater. In Illinois, one district spent $2,295 per pupil, while another spent only $391, a ratio of 5.9 to 1. Ratios ranged from 1.4 in West Virginia to 23.6 in Wyoming.[19]

But it is within school districts that the disparities have the greatest racial impacts. There is evidence that schools with high concentrations of low-achieving black students tend to get fewer resources than those with high-achieving whites. Testimony before the Senate Select Committee on Equal Educational Opportunity revealed that in the District of Columbia, black ghetto elementary schools spent an average of $216 per child, while affluent white schools averaged $627. In 1970 the richest elementary schools received as much as $1,719 more per student than the poorest schools.[20]

These differences in expenditures translate into different qualities and quantities of school resources. Spending more per student means lower teacher-pupil ratios, higher teacher salaries (and correspondingly better trained teachers), more library books, and a host of other resources and facilities. The Coleman team found that blacks were slightly more crowded in schools and less likely to have physics labs; they had fewer library books per student, more frequent textbook shortages, and teachers who scored lower on verbal tests.

But in every case the averages were quite close and on many criteria—such as availability of cafeterias and teachers' experience—blacks fared better (table 4-7). The Coleman Report also debunked the idea that teacher attitudes were markedly different between the schools that white and black students attended. Though the researchers found teachers of blacks rated their students lower on effort and ability and were less willing to continue teaching at their present

Table 4-7. School resources, secondary schools, 1966

Resource	White	Black
Pupils per classroom	31	34
Pupils per teacher	22	24
Cafeteria	65%	72%
Auditorium	46%	49%
Shop with power tools	96%	89%
Gymnasium	74%	64%
Physics lab	94%	80%
Language lab	56%	49%
Sports field	98%	89%
Volumes per student in library	5.8	4.6
Sufficient number of textbooks	95%	85%
Percent of texts less than 4 years old	62%	61%
Days in school year	180	181
Average hours in academic day	6.3	6.4
Average hours of homework expected	1.8	1.9
College preparatory curriculum offered	96%	88%

Source: James S. Coleman and others, *Equality of Educational Opportunity* (Washington: Government Printing Office, 1966), tables 2.21.3, 2.21.7, 2.21.12, 2.23.13, 2.23.15.

school, they were somewhat more likely to be career teachers and to believe that compensatory education could succeed (table 4-8). But, again, most of the differences were small. The inescapable conclusion was that despite wide differences in expenditures, actual school resources were not severely inequitably distributed along racial lines. At least in terms of hardware and staff characteristics, the discrimination against black students was not as great as had been expected.

Since the publication of the Coleman Report's conclusion that school resources are relatively equally distributed, and that the small variations make little difference in academic achievement anyway, a great deal of effort has gone into proving the opposite case. One review of the literature (used to support the contention of unequal treatment in a Michigan court case) compiled a long list of studies which had found unequally distributed resources. The researchers reported significant relationships between attributes of staff (verbal

Table 4-8. Characteristics of school staffs, secondary schools

Characteristic	White	Black
Verbal facilities of teachers	23.2	21.2
Years of experience of teachers	10	11
Teachers' years at this school	6	7
Salary (thousand dollars)	6.6	6.4
Hours preparing for class	3.2	3.4
Number of days absent last year	2.8	3.2
Requested assignment to present school	26%	45%
Would reenter teaching	43%	42%
Teach until retirement	33%	38%
Would continue teaching at present school	51%	46%
Average teacher turnover per year	11.5%	7.3%
Teacher exam for employment	10%	29%
Prefer white students	28%	6%
Prefer students of high academic ability	39%	28%
Believe in busing for desegregation	26%	39%
Believe in compensatory education	59%	66%
Believe in racial mixing of students and faculty	42%	57%
Rating of student effort[a]	2.3	1.8
Rating of student ability[a]	2.4	2.0
Perception of school's reputation[a]	2.8	2.6

Source: James S. Coleman and others, *Equality of Educational Opportunity* (Washington: Government Printing Office, 1966), pp. 151–175, tables 2.33.3, 2.34.3, 2.34.7, 2.34.13, 2.35.3.
[a] Scale of 1 to 5.

abilities, academic preparation), access of students to staff (pupil-teacher ratios, the number of counselors), physical facilities (age of building, presence of language and science labs), and student performance.[21] The conclusion was that schools do indeed make a difference and that some schools make bigger differences. The Coleman Report itself found that teachers' characteristics had some impact on students. They also found that some of the school facility variables had small but measurable relationships to achievement.

But though the correlations reached statistical significance, they were unimportant compared to other factors. The clear message of the

Coleman analysis was not contradicted by the Michigan study: school resources as they are currently distributed are not substantially responsible for the inequality of achievement reported among individuals and races. Apparently, there is little prospect that redistribution of school resources can do a great deal to remedy inequalities in education.

3. *Revamping education.* Because the measured impacts of schooling are small, it has been almost impossible to establish innovative school policies based on firm evidence of what works and what does not. The assumption has been that the quality of teaching, including hard-to-measure variables such as attitudes and enthusiasm, has most to do with student achievement. But there is little consensus as to which facilities, types of teachers, or methods of schooling can maximize the capabilities of students from diverse backgrounds.

Despite, or perhaps because of, this lack of consensus, the strategies for dealing with black underachievement have proliferated. Some have argued that traditional educational methods, such as ability grouping and achievement testing, need to be reformed. Because blacks reach school with educational disadvantages, and because they fall behind in achievement during school, "tracking" on the basis of I.Q. and achievement tests has the effect of racially isolating black children. Coleman found that 75 percent of high school districts practiced tracking. In secondary schools, 19 percent of white students but 31 percent of blacks were in the lowest track; in the highest groups, 21 percent of whites but 17 percent of blacks were represented.[22]

The rationale of tracking is that children do better if they compete against others more nearly their equals in ability rather than with those who are far above or below them. Moreover, tracking may encourage peer reinforcement of academic goals among bright, motivated students, enabling their teachers to devote more time to education rather than control. Though these arguments sound logical, the evidence is inconclusive. One review of the research on ability groups revealed that tracking was as often harmful as helpful to students from both talented and slow groups. Some researchers found that fast tracks raised the bright student's test by 1 or 2 points, but other studies have shown that tracking has little effect on fast learners.[23]

Traditional intelligence and achievement tests may be even more detrimental to blacks because they tend to measure the kinds of information and abilities which white middle class children are more likely to acquire. Blacks may be unfairly labeled as slow learners on the basis of biased tests which are not reflective of their abilities.

Jensen himself noted that many teachers distrusted I.Q. tests because they conflicted with the teachers' own observations of the native quickness and intelligence of disadvantaged children.[24] Jensen hypothesized different types of learning ability from this evidence, but many educators have argued from such results that I.Q. tests, and indeed testing and schooling procedures in general, are educational instruments which simply do not fit the culture or backgrounds of black children. The harm which such tests may do was illustrated by one experiment in which teachers were told that tests had shown certain students to be exceptionally able or slow. Though the students were actually chosen at random, their later achievement reflected the self-fulfilling expectations of their teachers.[25]

Other researchers have not been able to replicate these findings, and have cast doubt on the hypothesis that students learn according to their teachers' expectations. But the evidence of racial and socioeconomic segregation caused by tracking, and the unfairness of the tests used to establish the tracks, was convincing enough to lead a federal district judge to outlaw ability grouping in Washington, D.C., schools in 1967.[26] In many other school systems, the practices have either been abandoned or modified to give blacks a more equal chance.

Other critics of traditional school practices have argued that the greatest problems concern the attitudes of teachers and administrators who, they claim, often underestimate, ignore, or give up on black children and seldom try to understand or motivate them. Yet, administrative safeguards frequently protect these unsympathetic or ineffective teachers from removal despite repeated parental protests. The best solution to the problems, critics contend, is to turn control of the schools, including budgets and personnel policies, over to the communities which the schools serve. After often bitter disputes, partial community control has been won in some urban areas, notably New York and Detroit. On a smaller scale, the United States Office of Education has supported pilot projects to test the effectiveness of neighborhood school control. The impact has varied, with small projects supported by enthusiastic parents and innovative administrators often reporting significant improvements. Attempts at large-scale reform over longer time periods, however, have often met with community apathy and administrative intransigence.

Other strategies aimed at improving the quality of schooling for disadvantaged students include the use of paraprofessional teachers' assistants and the training of teachers in ghetto schools to be more responsive to the needs of minority students. These methods have achieved some success, especially when they have been concentrated on small numbers of students. Among the other proposed methods for improving compensatory education are open classrooms; special language programs, including Spanish and "Black English"; use of new technologies, such as teaching machines and television; and greater use of community resources, including not only the traditional museums and public buildings, but parents' homes and work places. Again, the success of these programs seems to hinge primarily on the enthusiasm and effort generated by interested parents and educators. Their applicability to national educational policy remains to be determined.

Higher Education

Most of the debate over the quality of black education has focused on elementary and secondary schooling, while the small but growing numbers of blacks who go on to college are generally assumed to have succeeded. There is no doubt that the college sheepskin is becoming more important to occupational advancement, economic success, and social status, and that black gains in the future will depend crucially on college education. Yet it is not just the number who receive degrees, but the institutions from which they graduate and the fields in which they specialize which will determine the later payoffs on college training. In college, as in high school, both quality and quantity must be assessed.

1. In 1966 blacks were less than half as likely as whites to attend schools charging more than $1,000 a year tuition. Two of three black students, compared to three-fifths of whites, attended colleges charg-

ing an annual tuition of less than $500.[27] This is not surprising since 72 percent of black college students in 1971 came from families with annual incomes of less than $10,000, while 71 percent of white college students were from families that made more than $10,000.

Still income inequality explains only part of the differential between black and white college enrollment. In families with incomes between $3,000 and $10,000, blacks are almost as likely as whites to attend college. But as the income level rises, the proportion of whites going to college increases more than the proportion of blacks (table 4-9). If

Table 4-9. Likelihood of attending college full-time, families with members age 18 to 24, 1971

Income	Number (in thousands)		Percent with members in college	
	Black	White	Black	White
Total	1,260	8,272	23	40
Under $3,000	298	429	11	16
$3,000–$4,999	299	623	20	22
$5,000–$7,499	250	1,036	26	30
$7,500–$9,999	141	1,288	30	33
$10,000–$14,999	124	2,236	34	43
$15,000 and over	69	2,043	39	59

Source: U.S. Bureau of the Census, *The Social and Economic Status of the Black Population in the United States, 1971*, Series P-23, no. 42, July 1972, p. 86.

blacks had the income distribution of whites but the same enrollment rate in each income category, their weighted enrollment rate would be 31 percent, rather than the actual 23 percent.

2. Almost half of black students are in schools with fewer than 2,500 students compared to a quarter of white students in such schools. The ratios are reversed at schools greater than 10,000. These figures are explained almost entirely by the fact that black colleges, where two of every five blacks are enrolled, are comparatively small. Howard University with 6,500 undergraduates (1970) is the largest predominantly black college in the country and only three other black colleges have as many as 4,000 students.

3. Blacks are slightly more likely to attend public and junior (two-year) colleges and to go to school part-time. In 1972 four of every five black students were enrolled in public colleges compared to 76 percent of whites; 28 percent of blacks attended junior colleges compared to 22 percent of whites; among whites, 76 percent attend school full-time, while 72 percent of blacks did so.[28]

4. Blacks are underrepresented in the nation's highest rated and most prestigious undergraduate institutions. In 1966 they were twice as likely to be in schools rated low according to freshman aptitude scores and a third less likely to be in high-rated schools as whites. Nearly one of every four white students was enrolled in a high-rated college, but only one of every twelve black students.[29] In 1970 the Office of Civil Rights found that blacks constituted 7 percent of a very large sample of college students, but only 5 percent of those in Ivy League schools and 4 percent of those in sixty-three highly prestigious schools (table 4-10). Blacks were least represented on the main

Table 4-10. Blacks as a proportion of undergraduate enrollment, 1970 (numbers in thousands)

School	Number of blacks	Number of students of all races	Percentage of blacks in institutions	Percentage of black students	Percentage of all students
Total all schools	344.8	4,965.8	6.9	100.0	100.0
Ivy League	2.1	40.4	5.1	.6	.8
Main campuses of state universities[a]	15.3	567.7	2.7	4.4	11.4
Prestigious colleges[b]	6.5	165.2	3.9	1.9	3.3
Military academies	.5	12.9	3.9	.2	.2
Black colleges	147.1	156.8	93.8	42.7	3.2

Source: U.S. Department of Health, Education, and Welfare, *Racial and Ethnic Enrollment Data from Institutions of Higher Education, Fall 1970* (Washington: Government Printing Office, 1970).

[a] Includes only those states in which blacks make up at least 2 percent of the population.

[b] Colleges ranked "most selective" or "highly selective" in *The Comparative College Guide* by James Cass and Max Birnbaum.

campuses of state universities. Even when states with few black residents were excluded from the totals, blacks accounted for only 3 percent of enrollment on main state university campuses. Though these institutions served 11 percent of all white college students, they were educating only 4 percent of blacks.[30] In the military academies the picture is similar. In 1973 there were 505 black cadets and midshipmen, approximately 4 percent of total enrollment. Even this percentage represented a spectacular improvement since 1963, when there were only 10 blacks in an entering class of 2,712 at the military academies.

5. Blacks are much less likely to go to graduate school than whites. Five percent of whites but 2 percent of blacks have five or more years of college. Only 1.1 percent of blacks between the ages of twenty-one and thirty-four were attending graduate school in 1971, compared to 3.3 percent of whites.[31]

6. A large proportion of blacks still attend black colleges. Though the proportion of blacks in predominantly black schools fell from 51 percent in 1966 to 43 percent in 1970, seventeen states still operate essentially segregated systems of higher education.[32] Blacks who go on to graduate school are also frequently enrolled in black institutions. Howard University and Meharry Medical College accounted for 72 percent of all black dental students in 1970, and the same two institutions were educating 40 percent of upcoming black doctors. Predominantly black colleges accounted for one of every five law students (though Harvard and Yale had the third and fifth largest number of black law students). In other types of graduate schools, 21 percent of blacks attended black schools in 1970.[33]

The large numbers of blacks in predominantly black undergraduate and graduate schools is important because the quality of these schools has been questioned. An evaluation of black colleges in 1966 found black medical and law schools to be very inadequate.[34] Although this report was denounced because it was written by whites, some black educators have accepted its conclusions. One noted black economist, citing specific evidence on the quality of students, libraries, and faculty members, concluded that not one black college "ranks with a decent state university."[35] This damning conclusion may overstate the case, but it does suggest that the equalization of college enrollment ratios may overstate black educational gains.

7. Once enrolled in college, the dropout rate of blacks and whites does not differ substantially. An estimated 69 percent of whites and 68 percent of blacks who enrolled in 1967–1969 were still in school during 1969–1971.[36]

8. On the other hand, blacks tend to choose study areas with less certain economic payoffs. Only 8 percent of blacks major in engineering, science, or math compared to 12 percent of whites; nearly a fifth of blacks had not decided on a field of study, compared to 10 percent of whites.[37]

Overall, the record of black involvement in college is encouraging, despite the questions of quality. Blacks more frequently attend smaller, lower cost, less prestigious, and all-black institutions, and they more often attend school part-time or study "softer" disciplines. But the most important fact is still that there were 684,000 blacks in college in 1973, almost five times the number in 1960. With the ever-growing importance of the college credential, this represents progress.

Final Examination

Given society's growing needs for educated individuals, and the controversial but real importance of credentials in determining social and economic success, the equalization of school enrollment ratios and the narrowing gap between black and white educational attainment are healthy trends. By 1973 blacks at all ages through seventeen years, and in almost all areas and residential environments, were as likely to be in school as whites. These strides in enrollment have been translated into attainment. Sixty-seven percent of blacks age twenty to twenty-four had completed high school in 1972, and the median educational attainment for blacks over twenty-one stood at 10.8 years. Black education at the college level has also improved, though blacks are still much less likely to be enrolled in college or to have attained a college degree than whites. From 1960, when blacks were 5 percent of college students, the proportion increased to nearly 9 percent in 1972, when 18 percent of blacks age eighteen to twenty-four were enrolled.

The record of black progress in education is clouded by evidence that the advancement represented by these years in school may not be

equivalent to that of whites. Blacks from more impoverished backgrounds begin school at a disadvantage; they are often culturally
isolated or attend schools with fewer resources than those attended by
children from affluent homes. On the average, blacks are more likely
to fall behind one or more grade levels and to score lower on
achievement tests. Of those who do succeed in high school and go on
to college, a large proportion attend black schools or integrated institutions with limited facilities and resources. One consequence is that
the payoff on black educational credentials is less than for whites.
Black male high school graduates may expect to earn about 24 percent more than nongraduates, while whites average 29 percent more
with a diploma. A sheepskin is worth about 33 percent more to a
black but it raises white earnings by 53 percent.

It would be unfair and misleading, however, to direct attention
primarily toward the quality of black education as though this were
evidence of overall stagnation of black educational progress. While
comparisons of test scores are reminders that equality of educational
opportunity is a difficult and distant goal, they do not outweigh significant black enrollment and attainment gains. The schools, whatever
their shortcomings, prepare individuals for productive roles in society.
Whether they still fail many blacks, few observers have suggested that
those who have no schooling are better off than those who graduate.
The educational advantages which blacks have gained since 1960 may
be far less than optimum, and far less than what is necessary to establish true equality of opportunity, but they are crucially important steps
toward that goal.

5

THE BLACK FAMILY

Black marital and family patterns are a crucial dimension of socio-economic status. The family is the basic earning and consuming unit whose needs are determined by its size and age composition. Work patterns are affected by the presence or absence of children or a second breadwinner. Education begins in the home and vitally influences later success in school and the whole life thereafter. The health of children depends on the diet and medical care provided by the parents. The size and age distribution of the family determines its housing needs. Finally, values and attitudes are engendered in the home.

Some standard is necessary to measure progress or deterioration in family status. In the United States that norm is the nuclear husband-wife family, supporting and raising children. There are, of course, other arrangements which might be as feasible for childrearing, for example a communal group with several parents dividing the labors of childrearing and economic support. Moreover, analysis of black culture from the vantage point of husband-wife units ignores the close blood and friendship ties which often unite grandparents, brothers, sisters, aunts, uncles, or neighbors into extended black families. These arrangements may take the place of or fulfill some of the functions of the nuclear family. But the husband-wife unit is not an arbitrary standard or a peculiarly white, middle-class institution. It is, in fact, the most common, most accepted arrangement among all races and social classes. It is sanctioned by law and prevailing morality. It is a natural structure for providing love, support, and role models for developing children. In a society in which men have great financial advantage it has become the most desirable economic position for women with children. Though the status of the black nuclear family may be an incomplete picture of black social structure, it is clearly an important element.

The Salient Features

It is heroic to generalize about black marital and family characteristics, but the following facts are relatively clear-cut and have widespread implications.

1. *Nonwhite birth rates are declining but still exceed those of whites.* In 1970 there were 25.2 births per thousand nonwhites, a substantial decline from 32.1 per thousand in 1960 (figure 5-1). Over the same

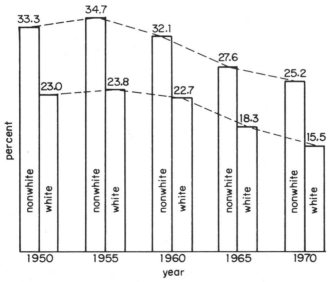

Figure 5-1. Birth rate per 1,000 population, 1950–1970.

Source: U.S. Bureau of the Census, *Statistical Abstract of the United States, 1972* (Washington: Government Printing Office, 1972), p. 50.

period, however, this birth rate rose from 141 to 163 percent that of whites. Proportionately more black women are in the childbearing years, but this accounts for only part of the difference. The fertility rate, which is the number of births per thousand women age fifteen to forty-four, was 114.3 for nonwhites in 1970 compared with 83.9 for whites. Though the nonwhite rate had declined from 158.8 in 1960, the ratio of nonwhite/white fertility had dropped only slightly from 1.40 to 1.36.[1]

Another measure is the "intrinsic rate of natural increase," which is the population growth rate that would prevail if current birth and death rates remained constant. Because blacks have a more youthful population profile, they have a larger proportion of women in childbearing years as well as lower mortality rates. The intrinsic rate of natural increase for nonwhites was, therefore, 1.6 percent in 1968, or four times the rate for whites. While the nonwhite rate had declined from an average of 2.8 between 1960 and 1964, it had risen in relative terms from being only two-thirds higher than for whites.[2]

Between 1960 and 1971 the falling black birth rate occurred mostly among younger women, with rates for women under twenty-nine falling while those of women over thirty rose (table 5-1). Whether birth rates will continue to decline depends on the behavior of the younger cohorts as they age. Surveys of birth expectations

Table 5-1. Children ever born per black woman, 1960–1973

Age	1960	1965	1969	1973
All women 15 to 44 years	2.0	2.1	2.0	1.6
15 to 19 years	0.2	0.2	0.1	0.1
20 to 24 years	1.3	1.2	1.0	0.7
25 to 29 years	2.4	2.6	2.3	1.7
30 to 34 years	2.9	3.4	3.1	2.6
35 to 39 years	2.9	3.5	3.7	3.5
40 to 44 years	2.8	3.1	3.5	3.4

Source: U.S. Bureau of the Census, *The Social and Economic Status of the Black Population in the United States, 1971*, Series P-23, no. 42, July 1971, p. 109; and U.S. Bureau of the Census, *Birth Expectations of American Wives: June: 1973*, Series P-20, no. 254, October 1973, p. 8.

suggest that younger black wives, like younger whites, expect to have fewer children; but the birth expectations of whites have fallen faster, and the average expected number of births for blacks remains higher among most age groups (table 5-2). It is significant to note that the

Table 5-2. Average birth expectancies of wives age 18 to 39 years, 1967 and 1973

Age	Black		White	
	1967	1973	1967	1973
18–39 years	3.7	3.0	3.1	2.6
18–24 years	2.8	2.3	2.9	2.3
25–29 years	3.4	2.8	3.0	2.3
30–34 years	4.3	3.3	3.2	2.8
35–39 years	4.2	3.9	3.2	3.2

Source: U.S. Bureau of the Census, *Birth Expectations of American Wives, June 1973*, Series P-20, no. 254, October 1973, p. 5.

number of births is related to income, education, labor force participation, and residence in urban areas. Among black women thirty-five to forty-four years in 1970, the average number of children born was 3.5. But there were only 1.9 children ever born to mothers who graduated from college, 3.1 to mothers in the labor force, and 3.2 to those from urban areas.[3] Continued migration, improved education, and increasing rates of labor force participation should thus contribute to a continuing decline in the black fertility rate.

In contradiction to Malthusian notions, fertility data suggest a more rapidly declining birth rate among the poor than among the more affluent. Between the first and last halves of the 1960s, the average annual births of nonwhite women in poverty declined 26 percent, compared with only 3 percent for more affluent families (table 5-3). The increasing proportion of females without husbands among low-income families was probably responsible for this decline in births.

2. *There are more mouths to feed in black families.* As a result of higher birth rates, black husband-wife households had, on the average, two-fifths more children in 1971 than similar white households; fe-

Table 5-3. Average annual births per 1,000 women age 15 to 44 years, 1960–1970

Income	1960–1965		1966–1970	
	White	Nonwhite	White	Nonwhite
Poverty	134.4	186.0	113.5	136.9
100% to 125% poverty	152.6	160.6	113.4	132.9
More than 125% poverty	97.2	108.5	78.3	104.9

Source: Frederick S. Jaffe, "Low-Income Families: Fertility Changes in the Sixties," *Family Planning Perspectives* (January 1972), p. 45.

male-headed black families had 90 percent more children on the average. Nearly a fifth of all black families had four or more children, while only 8 percent of white family heads had such a heavy burden to support.

Consideration of family size drastically changes the relative income status of blacks. The mean family income of husband-wife black families in 1971 was 73 percent that of whites. On a per capita basis it was only 62 percent as high (table 5-4). If total family income is divided by the aggregate number of children, the black income per child is only 53 percent that of whites. For female-headed families, the income per child is less than two-fifths as high in black as in white units. Female black family heads raise their children with roughly one-fifth the income to support and invest in their children as white husband-wife units.

3. *More nonwhite than white children are born out of wedlock.* Though recorded illegitimacy rates may be biased, the racial disparities are too great to be completely discounted. In 1968, the latest year for which national data were available, there were an estimated 184,000 births out of wedlock among nonwhites compared with only 155,000 reported for whites; the illegitimacy rates were 86.6 and 13.2, respectively, per 1,000 unmarried women age fifteen to forty-four years in 1968 (table 5-5). There was some improvement relative to whites during the 1960s. The illegitimacy rate for nonwhites fell from 98.3 per thousand unmarried women in 1960, while it rose from 9.2 for whites. The nonwhite cohort aged twenty to twenty-four ex-

Table 5-4. Family income and family size, 1971

Type of family	Mean income		Black/ white income	Per capita income		Black/white per capita income	Per child income		Black/white per child income
	Black	White		Black	White		Black	White	
All families	$7,695	$11,997	64%	$1,899	$3,460	55%	$4,215	$ 9,834	43%
Husband-wife families	9,229	12,570	73	2,214	3,558	62	5,383	10,170	53
Female-headed families	4,632	7,030	66	1,180	2,338	51	2,173	5,745	38

Source: U.S. Bureau of the Census, Department of Commerce, Consumer Income: Money Income in 1971 of Families and Persons in the United States, P-60, no. 85, December 1972, table 19.

Table 5-5. Estimated illegitimacy rates by age of mother, 1940–1968 (rates per 1,000 unmarried women)

Age and race of mother	1940	1950	1960	1968
Black and other races				
Total, 15 to 44 years	35.6	71.2	98.3	86.6
15 to 19 years	42.5	68.5	76.5	82.8
20 to 24 years	46.1	105.4	166.5	118.3
25 to 29 years	32.5	94.2	171.8	104.4
30 to 34 years	23.4	63.5	104.0	80.6
35 to 39 years	13.2	31.3 ⎫	35.6[a]	25.2[a]
40 to 44 years	5.0	8.7 ⎭		
White				
Total, 15 to 44 years	3.6	6.1	9.2	13.2
15 to 19 years	3.3	5.1	6.6	9.8
20 to 24 years	5.7	10.0	18.2	23.1
25 to 29 years	4.0	8.7	18.2	22.1
30 to 34 years	2.5	5.9	10.8	15.1
35 to 39 years	1.7	3.2 ⎫	3.9[a]	4.7[a]
40 to 44 years	0.7	0.9 ⎭		

Source: U.S. Bureau of the Census, *The Social and Economic Status of Negroes in the United States, 1968,* Series P-23, no. 29, 1970, p. 78.
[a] 35 to 44 years.

perienced a significant decline, as a growing proportion of women this age postponed both marriage and childbearing. Yet, for black teenagers, there was a continuing rise over the decade.

Despite these falling illegitimacy rates, the proportion of all live births born out of wedlock increased steadily from 17 percent in 1940 and 18 percent in 1950 to 22 percent in 1960 and 33 percent in 1968.[4] The reason for this rise was that the birth rate among wives fell even faster than among unmarried women, and a larger percentage of black women postponed marriage.

The proportion of black women who bear a child out of wedlock is even higher than the proportion of all births which are illegitimate. The 1964–1966 National Natality Survey indicated that 57 percent of the first births among nonwhite fifteen- to nineteen-year-olds, and 46 percent among fifteen- to forty-four-year-olds, were born out of wedlock, compared with 15 and 9 percent, respectively, among whites. On the other hand, 34 percent of the children born to white females age fifteen to nineteen years came less than eight months after marriage, compared with 26 percent among nonwhites, suggesting that the "shotgun marriage" reduces white illegitimacy.[5]

It is important to note the very substantial differences in the handling of illegitimacy among blacks. One estimate suggested that in 1968 and 1969 two-thirds of white children born out of wedlock were adopted, institutionalized, or placed under foster care compared with only 7 percent of blacks.[6] In some cases, adoption or institutionalization might be better for both the child and the mother, but it is also reasonable to interpret these differential rates as a "hidden strength of black families" mitigating the consequences of higher black illegitimacy.

4. *Blacks tend to marry later and to have less stable marriages than whites.* In 1970, 17 percent of black females age twenty-five to thirty-four were single compared with only 9 percent of white females (figure 5-2). Older black women are as likely as whites to have been married because of more frequent marriage at later ages and because the marital rates are lowest in the younger cohorts. Among black females born between 1935 and 1939, 75 percent were married at age twenty-four or younger, a proportion nine-tenths that of whites in this cohort. For black women born between 1945 and 1949, however, only 62 percent were married by age twenty-five, a proportion 82 percent that of whites.[7]

Black marriages have historically been less stable than whites, and they were affected by the developments in the 1960s which tended to weaken family stability generally. Despite the widespread belief that divorce is a white, upper-class phenomenon, the incidence of divorce is nearly half again higher among nonwhites than whites. Moreover, divorce rates are rising faster among nonwhite than white males, though this is not true for nonwhite females (table 5-6). Once divorced or widowed, black women are less likely to remarry than

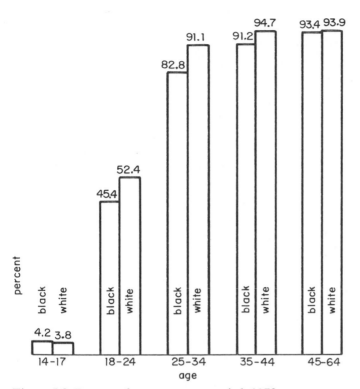

Figure 5-2. Percent of women ever married, 1970.

Source: U.S. Bureau of the Census, *Persons by Family Characteristics,* Series PC(2)4B, January 1973, table 2.

whites. In 1970, 49 percent of black women age twenty-five to thirty-four who had been widowed or divorced had remarried compared with 69 percent of whites.[8]

Separation without divorce is also much more common among blacks than whites. In 1970, 17 percent of black married women were currently separated, compared with only 2 percent of white married women.[9]

Delayed marriage and more frequent divorce and separation mean that at any point in time, more black women and their children are living without the presence and support of a husband and father. The key statistic is that in 1970 two-fifths of all black women fourteen and over were married with a husband present, compared with three-fifths of whites. Only 56 percent of black women compared with 82 percent

Table 5-6. Divorced as a percent of all persons age 15 years and over, 1960–1971

Sex and race	1960	1965	1970	1971
Male				
White	2.0	2.4	2.4	2.8
Nonwhite	2.2	3.4	3.4	3.4
Female				
White	2.7	3.1	3.8	3.8
Nonwhite	4.8	4.5	4.8	5.6

Source: U.S. Bureau of the Census, *Statistical Abstract of the United States, 1972* (Washington: Government Printing Office, 1972), table 86.

of whites in the primary childbearing years, age twenty-five to thirty-four, had a husband present (table 5-7).

5. *A large and increasing percentage of black families are headed by women.* In 1972 a third of all nonwhite families were female-headed—more than three times the proportion among white families and a substantial increase over the 22 percent of all nonwhite families with female heads in 1960. Nearly two-fifths of black youths under age eighteen were not living with both parents in 1972, or close to

Table 5-7. Marital status of black and white women, 1970

| Marital status | Black | | White | |
	14 years and over	25–34 years	14 years and over	25–34 years
	(percent)			
Single	28.7	17.2	21.8	8.9
Married	53.2	73.7	62.2	85.6
Spouse present	41.5	56.3	59.0	81.7
Separated	8.9	13.8	1.5	2.0
Other, spouse absent	2.8	3.6	1.7	1.9
Widowed	13.2	2.6	12.3	1.1
Divorced	5.0	6.4	3.7	4.4

Source: U.S. Bureau of the Census, *Persons by Family Characteristics,* Series PC(2)4B, January 1973, table 2.

four times the rate for whites. There has also been some decline in subfamily living patterns, which in the past provided support for deserted wives and their offspring and women with illegitimate children. In 1970 only 2.3 percent of all nonwhites fourteen years and over were members of subfamilies compared with 3.1 percent in 1960. Yet, 6.7 percent of all black women age eighteen to twenty-four were heads of subfamilies in 1970 compared with only 1.5 percent among white females this age.[10]

The problems of female family heads are complicated by more children. In 1971 husband-wife black families had an average of 1.7 children under eighteen compared with 2.1 in female-headed units. Most of the difference is due to the larger number of husband-wife families with no children, since the average number of children under eighteen in households with children is roughly the same.[11] But the problem of supporting and raising these dependents is certainly greater when the responsibility falls on the woman's shoulders alone.

6. *Black wives play a more important economic role than whites.* In March 1971, 53 percent of black married women with their husband present were in the labor force compared with 40 percent of whites. This greater participation occurred at all income levels despite the fact that black wives had more small children requiring care (table 5-8). Forty-one percent of nonwhite wives with children under six and a husband's income of less than $3,000 were in the labor force in March 1971 compared with 35 percent of whites; for those with a husband's income over $10,000, the rates for blacks and whites were 47 and 21 percent, respectively. Not only do black wives work more frequently, but they also contribute a larger share of family earnings. In 1970, 35 percent of the earnings of black husband-wife families in which the wife worked came from the wife's earnings, compared with 29 percent among white families with working spouses. Overall, white wives accounted for less than a fifth of all earnings in husband-wife families, while nonwhite wives accounted for three-tenths.[12]

The Reasons for Greater Fertility

While the black marital and family characteristics are fairly well documented, the causal factors are difficult to disentangle. This is

Table 5-8. Labor force participation rates of women by number of children, March 1971

Presence and age of children and color	Total	Income of husband				
		Under $3,000	$3,000 to 4,999	$5,000 to 6,999	$7,000 to 9,999	$10,000 and over
		(percent)				
Black and other races						
All wives	52.5	39.4	51.9	57.4	59.8	56.1
No children under 18 years	51.7	35.5	52.7	62.4	60.0	69.7
Children 6 to 17 years only	60.5	51.0	58.9	64.5	69.8	55.5
Children under 6 years	46.9	40.5	46.2	47.8	51.1	46.7
White						
All wives	39.7	34.1	38.2	44.9	44.9	36.3
No children under 18 years	41.3	31.1	35.6	46.9	50.2	42.5
Children 6 to 17 years only	48.4	52.2	55.4	56.9	53.8	42.2
Children under 6 years	27.6	34.7	31.4	34.1	30.7	20.5

Source: U.S. Bureau of Labor Statistics, "Marital and Family Characteristics of the Labor Force, March 1971," *Special Labor Force Report 144,* January 1972, table J.

especially true when it comes to explaining fertility and illegitimacy. Several general conclusions seem warranted, however.

1. *Black women have more children because they want more.* As indicated previously, black wives age eighteen to thirty-nine expected to have 3.0 children compared with 2.6 for whites in 1973. The major reason for this continuing disparity is that a small proportion of black women expect to have very large families. Even though 17.7 percent of black women age eighteen to thirty-nine expected one or no

children compared with only 12.6 percent of whites, 18.7 percent expected five or more compared with 8.0 percent of whites.[13]

2. *Black married women have more unwanted and unplanned births.* Data from the 1970 National Fertility Survey for currently married women under forty-five years of age suggest that if blacks could eliminate unwanted births, their theoretical fertility rate would be reduced by over a fifth (table 5-9). If they had the same proportion of unwanted births as whites, their fertility rate would be only 10 percent rather than 28 percent higher.

3. *Black women are less aware of contraceptive techniques and employ them less frequently.* A fourth of a national sample of married black women under forty-five in 1970 reported never having used contraceptives, compared with 15 percent of whites. This proportion had actually increased since 1965 because of the rise in wives under age thirty not using contraception. Two-fifths of the black wives were not currently using any birth controls compared with 34 percent of whites.[14]

The lack of knowledge is a major and especially critical reason among younger blacks. A 1970 national sample of young women age fifteen to nineteen years found that only 18 percent of blacks correctly identified the time of highest fertility within the menstrual cycle compared with 42 percent of whites, and the differences were not explained by income or education of the parents.[15]

4. *Blacks may find birth control less acceptable.* A national opinion survey in 1971 found that 18 percent of black men and women but only 8 percent of whites opposed the government's dissemination of information on contraception. Only a third of blacks as compared to half of whites felt that abortion should be left to the discretion of the couple and the doctor. Fourteen percent of blacks but only 5 percent of whites felt abortions should never be performed. Finally, 22 percent of blacks but only 12 percent of whites felt that sterilization should be illegal.[16] These attitudes may reflect black suspicions of white government interference, or fears that white institutions are subtly encouraging genocide.

Table 5-9. Unwanted fertility in the United States, 1970

Race and education	Most likely number of births per woman	Percent of births 1966–70 unwanted	Percent of births 1966–70 unplanned	Theoretical births per woman without unwanted births
All women	3.0	15	44	2.7
College 4+	2.5	7	32	2.4
College 1–3	2.8	11	39	2.6
High school 4	2.8	14	44	2.6
High school 1–3	3.4	20	48	2.9
Less	3.9	31	56	3.0
White women	2.9	13	42	2.6
College 4+	2.5	7	32	2.4
College 1–3	2.8	10	39	2.6
High school 4	2.8	13	42	2.6
High school 1–3	3.2	18	44	2.8
Less	3.5	25	53	2.9
Black women	3.7	27	61	2.9
College 4+	2.3	3	21	2.2
College 1–3	2.6	21	46	2.3
High school 4	3.3	19	62	2.8
High school 1–3	4.2	31	66	3.2
Less	5.2	55	68	3.1

Source: Report of the Commission on Population Growth and the American Future, *Population and the American Future* (Washington: Government Printing Office, 1972), p. 97.

5. *Black women tend to have earlier sexual contact.* According to one extensive national survey in 1971, four-fifths of young black women reported having intercourse by age nineteen compared with only two-fifths of whites (table 5-10). Some of the difference between whites and blacks is related to the education level of parents, their income, and the area of residence, but racial patterns predominate over all these factors. And this activity may have become more

Table 5-10. Percent of women age 15 to 19 years who have ever had sexual experience, 1971

Age	White	Black
15–19 years	23.4	53.6
15 years	10.8	32.2
16 years	17.5	46.4
17 years	21.7	57.0
18 years	33.5	60.4
19 years	40.4	80.0

Source: John F. Kantner and Melvin Zelnik, "Sexual Experience of Young Unmarried Women in the United States," *Family Planning Perspectives* (October 1972), p. 9.

common in recent years. Only 8 percent of black females age nineteen reported having had intercourse by age fifteen; black girls currently age fifteen reported a 22 percent incidence.[17]

The differing fertility patterns between blacks and whites are thus related to a number of factors: attitudes toward sex, marriage, and childbirth, ignorance of contraceptive techniques, the desire for more children, and, possibly, earlier sexual experience. Increased use of the pill alone will not equalize black/white birth rates unless contraception is supported by changes in personal beliefs and prevailing mores.

The Causes of Marital Instability

A number of possible explanations have been offered for the increasing instability of black marriages.

1. *Welfare may have encouraged family breakup.* The number of black mothers on welfare rose from 317,000 in 1961 to 1,007,000 in 1971.[18] Among the 690,000 net additions to the Aid to Families with Dependent Children (AFDC) rolls, 30 percent had been separated from or deserted by their husbands, 9 percent divorced or legally separated, and 46 percent had never been married. Obviously, the growth of welfare came mainly from those with marital and family problems. This does not mean, however, that welfare *caused* the

breakup or nonformation of most of the black families newly added to welfare rolls. The proportion of eligible broken families who received assistance also increased rapidly. From 1967 to 1971 the ratio of black female AFDC recipients to black female family heads rose from 43 to 47 percent. Much of the caseload increase must, therefore, be attributed to a greater reliance on welfare by women from otherwise split homes or with fatherless children, rather than being the result, much less the cause, of an increase in split homes or illegitimate births.

With these reservations, there is still no doubt that welfare has had a massive impact. Between 1960 and 1970 the number of female-headed families increased by half a million, so that even if only 100,000 to 200,000 female-headed family formations were related to welfare, it was a very significant factor.[19]

However, the availability of welfare is not the only factor involved, even when a husband deserts his wife and children and his family goes on relief. In some cases, there may be a rational decision that this is the best course of action in order to "maximize" total income, but the availability of welfare may simply tip the balance where the marriage lacks cohesion for other reasons.

2. *There may be a shortage of marriageable black males.* In 1970 the census counted only eighty-six males age twenty to twenty-four for each one hundred females, and eighty-four males for each one hundred women age twenty-five to thirty-five. Additionally, 4.5 percent of the males compared with only 0.5 percent of black women these ages were in institutions (mostly prisons or jails).[20] There is an admittedly large undercount of black males, but one estimate based on birth and death rate projections suggests that there are still only ninety-three males age twenty to twenty-four and ninety-six age twenty-five to thirty-four for every one hundred females, *before* subtracting the 4 percent who are "out of circulation."[21] Also, black men more often than black women marry members of a different race. In 1970, 1.5 percent of all married black males with a wife present had a spouse of another race compared with only 0.8 percent of black females. Among blacks age twenty to thirty-four, the comparable interracial marriages were 2.1 and 1.0 percent, respectively, removing another 1 percent of males from the "eligible" category.[22]

The sexual imbalance of the black population would be greater if drug addicts and other severe problem cases not considered "eligible" suitors for most black women were subtracted. This shortfall probably has some influence on marital and family attitudes as well as courtship patterns.

3. *Less education and lower income explain part of the disparity between black and white marital and family patterns.* Marriage is more frequent among males age twenty-five to thirty-four with a high school or college education, and divorce and absenteeism are less frequent (table 5-11). In each age-education group, however, marital instability is substantially greater among blacks than whites.

Black males who are financially capable of supporting a family are more likely to do so. Among black males age twenty-five to thirty-four with $3,000 to $3,999 income in 1969, 64 percent were married with

Table 5-11. Education and marital status of males age 25 to 34 years, 1970

Educational attainment	Total	Single	Married spouse present	Other
		(percent)		
Elementary school or less				
Black	100.0	27.2	57.1	15.7
White	100.0	20.1	70.9	9.0
1 to 3 years high school				
Black	100.0	20.3	62.8	16.9
White	100.0	10.9	80.1	9.0
4 years high school				
Black	100.0	18.3	67.5	14.2
White	100.0	11.8	81.6	6.6
1 or more years college				
Black	100.0	21.2	66.5	12.3
White	100.0	17.7	77.2	5.1

Source: U.S. Bureau of the Census, *Marital Status,* PC(2)-4C, December 1972, table 4.

Table 5-12. Income and the marital patterns of males, 1970

Age and income	Blacks Whites	Single	Married spouse present	Married spouse absent	Widowed or divorced
			(percent)		
All age 14 years and over	Blacks	35.5	48.3	8.6	7.6
	Whites	27.7	64.1	2.7	5.4
Without income	Blacks	84.2	6.8	5.5	3.5
	Whites	88.2	6.6	2.3	3.0
$1–$999	Blacks	58.1	23.7	8.3	9.8
	Whites	73.3	17.9	2.6	6.3
$1,000–$2,999	Blacks	31.5	44.3	10.8	13.4
	Whites	41.5	43.3	4.0	11.2
$3,000–$4,999	Blacks	20.6	61.7	10.6	7.1
	Whites	24.2	64.7	4.0	7.2
$5,000–$6,999	Blacks	13.6	71.3	9.0	6.0
	Whites	14.2	77.3	3.3	5.2
$7,000–$9,999	Blacks	9.0	77.6	7.3	6.1
	Whites	7.9	85.7	2.4	4.0
$10,000–$14,999	Blacks	6.6	82.1	6.0	5.3
	Whites	4.7	90.1	1.8	3.3
$15,000 or more	Blacks	7.6	81.0	5.6	5.7
	Whites	3.3	92.0	1.7	3.0
Age 24 to 34 years	Blacks	21.1	63.9	11.1	3.9
	Whites	14.7	78.7	3.3	3.5
Without income	Blacks	54.0	15.3	24.3	6.4
	Whites	59.8	20.8	11.3	8.1
$1–$999	Blacks	45.1	31.9	17.2	5.8
	Whites	45.6	39.8	7.7	6.9
$1,000–$2,999	Blacks	31.5	48.4	15.1	4.9
	Whites	35.3	52.5	6.3	5.8

Table 5-12. (continued)

Age and income	Blacks Whites	Single	Married spouse present	Married spouse absent	Widowed or divorced
			(percent)		
$3,000–$4,999	Blacks	20.7	64.2	11.6	3.5
	Whites	23.2	66.7	5.3	4.8
$5,000–$6,999	Blacks	15.1	72.7	9.0	3.2
	Whites	15.5	77.0	3.8	3.7
$7,000–$9,999	Blacks	11.7	77.5	7.1	3.7
	Whites	10.4	84.3	2.4	2.8
$10,000–$14,999	Blacks	10.4	80.0	6.3	3.2
	Whites	7.3	88.5	1.8	2.5
$15,000 and more	Blacks	10.1	77.2	7.6	2.2
	Whites	6.8	89.1	1.9	2.3

Source: U.S. Bureau of the Census, *Marital Status,* Series PC(2)4C, December 1972, table 7.

spouse present, and 15 percent were widowed, divorced, or separated, compared with 80 and 10 percent, respectively, in the $10,000 to $15,000 income class (table 5-12). But income alone is not the only factor. If black males age twenty-five to thirty-four had the income distribution of whites, 65.4 percent would have been stably married rather than 63.9, compared with 73.5 percent among whites. In other words, the limited income capacity of the black male, that is, his inability to support a family, explains only a part of the differences relative to whites. Moreover, the fact that the black marriages became less stable between 1960 and 1970 while average income and education were rising demonstrates the incompleteness of these factors in explaining marital patterns.

Other explanations have been proposed for the differing and changing marital and family patterns of blacks. The migration of blacks from rural areas to central cities may have contributed to family instability. There is no firm proof that the city discourages stable marriages, but it is a fact that black women age twenty-five to thirty-four from the rural-nonfarm South are over a fifth more likely to be married with a husband present than those who live in urban areas in the Northeast (table 5-13). A number of analysts have pointed to the

Table 5-13. Marital patterns of women age 25 to 34 years, 1970

Marital status	South	Rural nonfarm South	Northeast
		(percent)	
Single	16.7	17.3	19.6
Married, husband present	59.1	64.1	52.3
Separated	12.3	8.5	18.2
Married, husband absent	3.3	4.1	3.1
Widowed	3.2	3.3	2.3
Divorced	5.3	2.6	4.6

Source: U.S. Bureau of the Census, *Negro Population,* PC(2)-1B, May 1973, table 5.

slave heritage which emphasized the female's role as a mother rather than a spouse as well as the subservience of the male. The more rapid gains of black females in the labor market and the increasing availability of welfare have improved black women's relative economic status. An alternative explanation is that instability may breed instability. When marriage is undertaken with neither party expecting much and leaving all options open, it is bound to be less stable; if as the statistics suggest, failed marriages are more often the norm, the higher incidence may encourage easier acceptance of broken families.

The Implications

Because of their impact on the next generation, marital and family patterns are of critical importance, but the intergenerational effects are poorly documented and highly controversial. In the middle 1960s a report by Daniel P. Moynihan, *The Negro Family: The Case for*

National Action, generated a furor with its theme that "at the heart of the deterioration of the fabric of the Negro society is the deterioration of the Negro family." The report was criticized because the evidence of family deterioration was equivocal, its proof of intergenerational impacts insubstantial, and its interpretation dependent on value judgments about optimal family patterns. Whatever the merits of the Moynihan assertions, the divorce, separation, illegitimacy, and welfare rates cited in the study have become worse since the mid-1960s. It is therefore vital to determine the socioeconomic implications of marital and family changes.

There are two polar scenarios: according to one explanation, the developments of the 1960s could be followed by a generation of alienated, discontented, and dependent young blacks with severe handicaps that forestall their realization of greater opportunity. Upbringing in female-headed homes will guarantee a low income with all its concomitants. Youths brought up in homes where both the mother and father work or the female head supports them alone are likely to lack supervision and to become prey to negative peer group influences. Crime, illegitimacy, and dependency could become an even more frequent pattern of life.

Others suggest that poor blacks might continue to find that it pays to have fewer children, with a declining birth rate permitting a greater investment per child. Rising education and income would lead to more stable marital patterns. Meanwhile, the negative consequences of illegitimacy and broken homes are minimized by social patterns in the black community, such as informal mechanisms for child care and "temporary fathers" who contribute to family income and provide some male influence.

There are no facts which can resolve these differing interpretations. Clearly, split homes usually result in or are related to low income, but it is difficult to separate the effects of inadequate parental guidance from the influence of poor housing, diet, and medical care. A more adequate guaranteed income or welfare payment could alleviate economic deprivation, and it is entirely possible that this would eliminate most of the negative consequences of growing up in a female-headed home.

The limited evidence of negative intergenerational effects is also unconvincing because of the difficulty of separating cause from effect. The Moynihan Report, for instance, cited evidence that black children with their fathers present had significantly higher average intelligence scores than those with their fathers absent, that those living with both parents were more likely to be enrolled in school, and that the percentage falling behind in school was higher for youths from split homes.[23] Yet, female-headed families are more likely to have low income, pressuring the youth to drop out of school to work. Since stable families are more likely to have educated heads, the advantages are likely to be transmitted to their offspring.

On the other hand, the arguments that black marital and family changes are of little importance are even more unconvincing. There is a broad body of literature which supports the fact that the husband-wife unit is the most effective mechanism for childrearing.[24] Claims to the contrary have no comparable documentation. Moreover, an assertion of underlying strengths in the black family upbringing must necessarily minimize the importance of family factors in the higher incidence of crime, illegitimacy, and dependency. When other socio-economic variables are controlled, only a part of black/white differentials in these problems are explained, laying the burden of responsibility on cultural factors such as family structure.

Whatever the exact implications, it is clear that the changes in black marital and family status are not positive developments. Because of their cultural, historical, and economic heritage, blacks entered the 1960s with a much less firmly established pattern of family and marital stability. They were affected more by economic and social changes, and as a result their marital and family patterns were dramatically altered. The process of migration from rural settings and concentration in the central cities was a disrupting influence. New job openings increased opportunities for women to gain economic independence. Welfare encouraged or facilitated family breakup and nonformation. Rising divorce was a general societal problem which affected blacks more than proportionately because of the less sturdy nature of the black marital and family tradition. The long-run positive impacts of rising education and income did not balance the negative factors, and in the short-run may have contributed to apparent family problems: young blacks delayed marriage in pursuit of longer education and more married women reduced childbirth expectations, resulting in a rise in the proportion of children born out of wedlock.

Though it has been buffeted by social and economic change, the stable husband-wife family still remains the rule rather than the exception. Even if it is assumed that the stable family is an essential ingredient of a healthy society, it is an overstatement to view the changes in marital and family status over the last decade as signs of a decaying fabric of black society. But the potentially debilitating consequences of the developments during the past decade should not be ignored. Efforts are needed to alleviate disrupting factors in the welfare system as currently administered, to expand programs which will help eliminate unwanted births, and to reach the children in female-headed homes to assure that adequate resources are invested in their development.

6

HEALTH AND ITS IMPACTS

Chronic or frequent illnesses can limit participation and enjoyment at home, on the job, and in school. They can be costly in terms of medical care and earnings losses. And they can shorten the years of activity as well as of life. Health is related to a number of variables. Certain afflictions are income-related, caused by the inability to afford adequate diet, preventative care, or a proper living environment. Other health problems are related to social problems such as drinking, drugs, and violence. Some are culturally or racially related, for instance, nervous disorders among more competitive groups, or genetically-carried diseases such as sickle cell anemia.

Because of lower income, a different culture, a greater incidence of social problems, and perhaps genetic differences, the health patterns of blacks differ from those of whites. In some ways their health is better; but on balance it is worse. To some extent, these differences explain variances in other areas such as earnings, sources of income, and general well-being.

Mortality

Life expectancy and mortality rates are crude but basic indices of comparative health. By definition, the least healthy are those who do not survive. Blacks have improved relative to whites in recent years, and they now have slightly lower mortality rates than whites (table 6-

Table 6-1. Life expectancy, 1920–1971

Age and sex	1949–1951		1959–1961		1969	
	Nonwhite	White	Nonwhite	White	Nonwhite	White
Remaining years of life expectancy						
At birth						
Male	58.9	66.3	61.5	67.6	60.5	67.8
Female	62.7	72.0	66.5	74.2	68.4	75.1
Age 20						
Male	43.7	49.5	45.8	50.3	43.9	50.1
Female	46.8	54.6	50.1	56.3	51.2	56.9
Age 50						
Male	20.3	22.8	21.3	23.2	20.8	23.3
Female	22.7	26.8	24.3	28.1	25.4	28.8
Age 65						
Male	12.8	12.8	12.8	13.0	12.6	13.0
Female	14.5	15.0	15.1	15.9	15.7	16.6

Mortality rates
(per thousand)

	1920	1930	1940	1950	1960	1965	1970	1971
White	12.6	10.8	10.4	9.5	9.5	9.4	9.4	9.3
Nonwhite	17.7	16.3	13.8	11.2	10.1	9.6	9.5	9.1

Source: U.S. Bureau of the Census, *Statistical Abstract of the United States, 1972* (Washington: Government Printing Office, 1972), tables 75, 77.

1). But blacks of both sexes can expect fewer years of life at every age, ranging from the 7.3 year difference between white and black males at birth, to the half year gap between the life expectancies of sixty-five-year-old males. Since 1967 black and white death rates have been almost identical: about 9.5 deaths annually per thousand population. But the black population is significantly younger than the white, so black mortality rates must fall well below white rates before the two races have equal longevity expectations.

The differences in health between the races begin at birth and perhaps even before. Infant deaths among nonwhites are almost twice as common as among whites. These rates are falling for both races, but black infant mortality is decreasing more rapidly. Between 1960 and 1972 infant mortality declined 33 percent among nonwhites compared with 29 percent for whites (table 6-2).

Table 6-2. Maternal and infant deaths, 1950–1972

	1950		1960		1972	
Death rates	Nonwhite	White	Nonwhite	White	Nonwhite	White
Maternal deaths per 100,000 births	221.6	61.1	97.9	26.0	66.6[a]	18.1[a]
Infant deaths per 1,000 births	44.5	26.8	43.2	22.9	29.0	16.3
during the first 28 days	27.5	19.4	26.9	17.2	20.6	12.3

Sources: National Center for Health Statistics, U.S. Department of Health, Education, and Welfare, *Vital Statistics Report, Annual Survey for the United States, 1972* (Provisional Statistics) (Washington: Government Printing Office, 1973), p. 5; *Statistical Abstract of the United States, 1972* (Washington: Government Printing Office, 1972), table 78, p. 57.
    a 1968.

The risks of childbearing are also greater for black mothers. In 1968 they were almost four times as likely as whites to die as a result of complications during and after delivery. Maternal death rates are declining rapidly, but in this case blacks do not seem to be closing the gap between their rates and those of whites.

It is difficult to explain the disproportionately high risk of childbearing for nonwhites. In the past, unequal and inadequate health care explained much of the difference between black and white natal deaths, but this is a much less important factor today. The percentages of births taking place in hospitals and of births attended by physicians have become nearly equal for the two races. By 1968 nineteen of twenty mothers of both races had professional medical care during child birth.[1]

One factor affecting maternal deaths is abortion. The most recent statistics on childbearing deaths were collected in 1968 when most abortions were illegal and crudely performed. Blacks were estimated to be more than twice as likely to undergo illegal abortions in 1967, and one-fifth of all maternal deaths among nonwhites were the result of complications from abortion.[2] It is uncertain whether black women are now taking advantage of legal and safer methods of abortion.

Another contributing cause may be higher birth rates during the early higher risk years of the mother's life. In 1968, 13 percent of nonwhite babies were born to mothers under eighteen, compared to 4 percent of whites.[3]

The high incidence of infant death presents an even cloudier question. One suggestive statistic is the average weight of nonwhite babies: 6 pounds, 14 ounces compared to 7 pounds, 5 ounces for white babies.[4] This probably indicates some nutritional deficiencies which could be partly responsible for infant mortality, since baby weight and infant mortality correlate very closely.[5] A second factor which may be involved is premature births which increase infant mortality rates and which may often be caused by poor diets, insufficient exercise, or other inadequacies of the mother's personal health care. In 1968, 18.2 percent of black births were premature, compared to 8.2 percent among whites.[6] Also, a greater percentage of the white babies that die do so during the first twenty-eight days after birth, while more nonwhite children die between the second and twelfth months.[7] This may indicate poor postnatal care in black families rather than inadequate hospital treatment.

The chances of mortality, which are higher at birth, remain higher. Adjusting for age, blacks are more likely to suffer almost all kinds of fatal illnesses and accidents. Though the overall incidence of heart disease and cancer are lower among blacks, standardization by age reveals that blacks are 25 to 35 percent more likely than whites to die from these two most serious diseases.[8] These ratios have changed little during recent decades. Though deaths from heart disease have declined slightly among both blacks and whites since 1950, cancer-related deaths have been increasing rapidly (table 6-3). Since 1940 cancer has surpassed accidents, pneumonia, tuberculosis, and homicide to become the second leading killer of nonwhites.

Sharp differentials are evident for other diseases. Pneumonia, dia-

Table 6-3. Major causes of death, 1939–1968 (annual rates per 100,000)

Cause	Nonwhite			White
	1939–41	1949–51	1968	1968
All causes	1,343	1,097	988	963
Heart and circulatory diseases	479	586	432	523
Cancers	77	104	135	163
Accidents	75	70	71	56
Motor vehicle	—	—	30	27
Pneumonia and influenza	124	57	46	32
Homicide	30	28	32	4
Diabetes	17	14	24	18
Cirrhosis of the liver	5	6	18	14
Tuberculosis	125	62	8	2
Suicide	4	4	5	12

Source: *Metropolitan Life Bulletin* (April 1970), p. 7, and U.S. Department of Health, Education, and Welfare, *Vital Statistics of the United States, 1968* (Washington: Government Printing Office, 1972), tables 1–8.

betes, and cirrhosis of the liver are twice as common among blacks as whites. Moreover, though deaths from pneumonia have been decreasing, fatalities from diabetes and cirrhosis of the liver have been on the upswing. On the other hand, tuberculosis, once the third leading killer of nonwhites, has been brought under control during the last two decades. Although blacks are still far more likely than whites to suffer death from this disease, they have only one-sixteenth the chance of dying from it as their parents had.

It is worth noting that sickle cell anemia, a disease which is currently the topic of a great deal of publicity and debate, is rarely fatal even among blacks. Although it may cause many problems during their lifetimes, only three black persons per 100,000 die from all types of anemias—fewer, for example, than the number who die of hernias.[9]

The only major disease for which the white mortality rate is higher than blacks is emphysema (13.0 compared to 5.2). Whether this reflects rural housing environments of more blacks, variations in smoking habits, or some other factor is unknown.

Deaths from causes other than disease are also more common among blacks. Accidents are the third most common cause of death, and blacks are 30 percent more likely to meet accidental death than whites. Black men are more than twice as vulnerable to fatal accidents as white men.[10] A smaller proportion of nonwhite accident deaths, however, result from automobile accidents, probably because many fewer black households have access to an automobile.

By far the largest differential between black and white death rates is homicide, which is eight times more common among blacks. One of twenty black men dies by murder and among black men aged twenty to twenty-four, one of every three deaths is a homicide, compared with only one of thirty among white males the same age.[11] Suicide, on the other hand, is far more common among whites than nonwhites, though the rate for blacks has risen recently.

Health Problems

It is misleading to describe health problems as though they consist only of fatal diseases. Clearly, poor health is more of a problem to those who must keep living than to those who die.

Most chronic health problems are more prevalent among blacks than among whites (table 6-4).

1. Blacks are 43 percent more likely to be in mental institutions than whites and twice as likely to suffer fatal consequences from psychoses or neuroses.

2. Blacks are more than eight times as likely to become institutionalized for drug addiction as whites. Death from alcoholism is three times more common among blacks, and studies of problem drinking find it is considerably more common among blacks than whites.[12] Though there are no national totals on alcoholism, one survey in Rochester, New York indicated that nonwhites were ten times as likely to be alcoholics as whites.[13]

3. Venereal disease is thirteen times more common among blacks than whites.

4. Tuberculosis is more prevalent among blacks than whites. In

Table 6-4. Comparative health statistics

Illness	Black	White
Inmates of mental institutions[1] (per 1,000 over 14)	4.6	2.7
Residents of homes for the aged[2] (per 1,000 over 65)	30.3	48.5
Tuberculosis (new cases per 1,000 over 14)	1.0	0.2
Drug addiction[3] (per 1,000 over 14)	2.8	0.3
Venereal disease[4] (per 1,000 over 14)	28.7[a]	2.2
Gonorrhea	25.6[a]	1.9
Syphilis	3.1[a]	0.3
Injured annually[5] (per 1,000)	191.1[a]	261.6

Sources: 1. National Institute of Mental Health, 1970, unpublished data (OMB Study). 2. U.S. Bureau of the Census, *General Social and Economic Characteristics,* Series PC(1)C1, table 89. 3. Bureau of Narcotics and Dangerous Drugs, unpublished data, and U.S. Census of the Population, *Persons by Family Characteristics,* Series PC(2)4B, table 2. 4. Department of Health, Education, and Welfare, Center for Disease Control, Morbidity & Mortality, *Summary 1971,* table 9, p. 15. 5. National Center for Health Statistics, unpublished data.
[a] Nonwhites rather than blacks.

1970 new tuberculosis cases were six times more likely to strike blacks than whites.

5. Elderly blacks are less likely to be in homes for the aged; but rather than better health in old age, this reflects higher incomes for whites (since most nursing homes are private and costly) and the extended family structures among blacks, who are more likely to care for grandparents in the home.

The health picture for blacks is not totally pessimistic. There are some indications that in the teens and twenties, blacks may actually be healthier than whites. For example, whites are consistently more often disqualified from military service for medical reasons than nonwhites.

	1971	1970	1969	1968	1950– 1967
Percent black	28.7	24.5	23.7	19.8	13.9
Percent white	41.3	35.9	33.3	30.3	22.5

Source: Office of the Surgeon General, Department of the Army, *Supplement to Health of the Army, Results of the Examination of Youths for Service, 1971*, September 1972, table 10.

In investigating this phenomenon, the Defense Department found that some of the variation could be explained by educational differences, that is, educated whites were more likely to develop well-documented histories of medical problems. But even when this variable was considered, blacks were less likely to have medical problems warranting disqualification.[14]

Ill Health and Restricted Activity

While health problems are discomforting, often costly, and sometimes deadly, one of their most unfortunate impacts is the limiting of full participation in life's activities. Due to health-related problems, blacks spend more days in bed and more days out of work than whites (table 6-5). Young nonwhites actually have less frequent disabilities, and as a result miss fewer days of school, but as the years go by the differential shifts sharply in favor of whites. Nonwhites age forty-five to sixty-five spent an average of twelve days in bed in 1971 and lost nine days of work, compared with seven and six respectively for whites.

Chronic health problems are also more likely to restrict the activities of blacks. In 1971 a national sample found that though the same proportion of whites and nonwhites had activity limitations, white health limitations were more likely to be minor, while nonwhites were

Table 6-5. Days of disability per person per year, 1971

Age	Total	Bed-disability days	Work-loss days[a]	School-loss days[b]
Black and other races				
Total	18.0	7.6	7.5	4.9
Under 17 years	8.7	3.8	—	4.9
17 to 44 years	15.5	6.9	6.6	—
45 to 64 years	31.9	12.1	9.1	—
65 years and over	57.9	26.0	10.3	—
White				
Total	15.4	5.9	4.8	5.6
Under 17 years	11.3	4.9	—	5.6
17 to 44 years	11.8	4.5	4.3	—
45 to 64 years	19.9	6.9	5.8	—
65 years and over	31.8	12.1	5.0	—

Source: U.S. Bureau of the Census, *The Social and Economic Status of the Black Population in the United States, 1972,* P-23, no. 46, July 1973, table 73.

Note: A day of restricted activity is defined as a day on which a person reduced his normal activities for the entire day as a result of illness or injury.

[a] Per currently employed persons.

[b] Includes children age 6 to 16 years only.

nearly a third more likely to have serious problems. In general, nonwhites tended to have about the same incidence of limitations when they were young, but relatively more severe problems with age. While 16 percent of whites sixty-five and over reported being unable to carry on their major activity because of ill health, 26 percent of nonwhites claimed such limitations.[15]

The differences between whites and nonwhites in activity restrictions are explained almost entirely by the lower income of blacks. In families with less than $5,000 income, 25 percent of whites but only 17 percent of nonwhites reported any limitations in their activities; in those with over $5,000 income, overall limitations were about the same. On the other hand, for persons age sixty-five and over in both income categories, nonwhites were more than half again as likely as whites to have a complete restriction of their activities.[16]

Some of the difference between whites and nonwhites may be related to situational factors. The greater frequency with which whites report minor health limitations may result from greater expectations or health consciousness. The poor black may accept an allergy or vision problem as a fact of life while the more affluent white might see it as a restriction. Conversely, the nonwhite with a laborer's job might be restricted from work by a number of ailments which would only be a hindrance to a white college professor.

Perhaps the most crucial limitation is the inability to continue working and earning an income. In 1970, 6.4 percent of black males aged eighteen to sixty-four were completely work disabled compared with only 3.4 percent of whites (table 6-6). The percentages among

Table 6-6. Incidence of partial and complete work disabilities, 1970

| | Percent with partial disability | | | | Percent with complete disability | | | |
| | Male | | Female | | Male | | Female | |
Age	White	Black	White	Black	White	Black	White	Black
Total	8.7	7.8	4.6	6.5	3.4	6.4	4.7	8.2
18 to 24 years	6.2	5.6	2.5	3.4	1.3	2.2	1.3	2.4
25 to 34 years	5.0	5.3	2.9	4.5	1.2	3.0	1.8	3.8
35 to 44 years	6.6	7.3	4.2	6.8	2.0	5.0	3.1	6.8
45 to 49 years	9.6	9.3	5.7	8.5	3.3	7.6	5.0	11.4
50 to 54 years	11.3	11.1	6.8	9.8	4.7	9.9	7.0	13.8
55 to 59 years	12.8	12.6	7.6	10.6	7.5	14.4	10.5	18.7
60 to 64 years	14.3	13.7	8.1	11.4	13.2	20.8	14.9	25.1

Source: U.S. Bureau of the Census, *Persons with Work Disabilities*, PC(2)-6C, January 1973, table 1.

males forty-five and over were 14.5 and 8.1 percent, respectively. Black females were also much more likely to be completely disabled, with even higher rates for them than for black males.

Work disabilities by definition affect labor force activities, and disabilities among blacks more frequently limit earnings than among whites. Among black males age eighteen to sixty-four with partial disability, 14 percent did not work in 1969, compared with 7 percent of whites. Only a fourth of black males with complete disabilities worked, compared to 31 percent of whites. Blacks with disabilities who did work averaged 65 percent of the earnings of similar whites.[17] If the incidence of disability among blacks were the same as whites, the black male labor force participation rate would have been 2 percentage points higher, and total black earnings would have been 1 percent higher. If there were no disabilities, aggregate black earnings would have been 8 percent higher in 1969.

Income and Ill Health

The low income of blacks and other minorities is clearly a major factor in their health problems. Obviously, when the poor cannot afford or are not provided adequate care, their problems intensify. Less obviously, but equally important, low income means limited funds for an adequate diet, for proper hygiene, and for a healthy living environment.

Health expenditure data indicate that nonwhites spend 30 percent less per capita than whites on health expenses, medical care, and insurance premiums. In families with more than $5,000 annual income, the spending patterns are roughly comparable, but for lower income families the differences are marked. Nonwhites with less than $5,000 annual income spend less than half as much on health as whites in the same income class, even when differing age distributions are considered. Comparable per capita health expenditures in 1969–1970 were:

	White	Nonwhite
All	$190	$133
Income less than $5,000	188	87
Income $5,000 to $9,999	163	162
Income $10,000 and over	213	196

Source: National Center for Health Statistics, Department of Health, Education and Welfare, unpublished data.

Particularly critical is the fact that blacks are less likely to purchase hospital insurance coverage or to have it purchased for them. In 1970 only three-fifths of nonwhites under sixty-five were covered, compared with four-fifths of whites, and there were differences at every income level (table 6-7). Blacks are clearly less protected against the risks of illness and this may be one reason why they receive less care.

Poor blacks, probably even more than poor whites, depend on government health services. But even though these expanded significantly over the 1960s, blacks still received less care. In 1971 nearly 66 percent of nonwhites compared with 73 percent of whites had one or more visits with a physician. Thirty percent of nonwhites received dental attention compared with 50 percent of whites (table 6-8).

Inadequate diet is also a detriment to the health of nonwhite youths, more than a third of whom live in poverty. Proportionately more black than white children in 1970 were found to have unacceptable levels of essential nutrients.

One major reason was low income. Among preschool children those in the lowest income quintile were much more likely to lack essential vitamins and minerals than those in the upper quintile. Evidence indicates that the poor do not eat the balanced diet which the Agriculture

Table 6-7. Hospital insurance coverage for persons under 65 years of age, 1970 (percent)

Age	Total		Under $5,000		$5,000–9,999		$10,000 and over	
	Non-white	White	Non-white	White	Non-white	White	Non-white	White
Total	60	80	38	50	71	82	87	90
Under 17 years	54	78	31	37	66	80	87	90
17 to 24 years	60	75	50	60	67	77	78	84
25 to 44 years	68	84	43	48	75	84	89	92
45 to 64 years	65	83	44	57	81	87	92	93

Source: U.S. Bureau of the Census, *The Social and Economic Status of the Black Population in the United States, 1972,* Series P-23, no. 46, July 1973, table 74.

	Hemoglobin	Vitamin A	Vitamin C	Riboflavin	Thiamin
Percent black	34	23	12	21	13
Percent white	15	15	9	7	5

Source: 1970 White House Conference on Children, *Profiles of Children* (Washington: Government Printing Office, 1970), table 57.

Table 6-8. Visits to physicians and dentists, 1971

		Annual family income		
Subject	Total	Under $5,000	$5,000 to 9,999	$10,000 and over
Black and other races				
Percent with one or more visits to:				
Physician	66	66	64	71
Dentist	30	24	31	42
Average number of physician visits per person:				
Total	4.4	5.1	3.8	4.2
Under 65 years	4.2	4.8	3.7	4.2
65 years and over	7.1	6.9	8.7	4.4
White				
Percent with one or more visits to:				
Physician	73	72	72	75
Dentist	50	32	44	61
Average number of physician visits per person:				
Total	5.0	5.8	4.8	4.9
Under 65 years	4.8	5.4	4.7	4.8
65 years and over	6.7	6.7	6.2	7.6

Source: U.S. Bureau of the Census, *The Social and Economic Status of the Black Population in the United States,* Series P-23, no. 46, July 1973, table 72.

Department envisions when it calculates the poverty threshold. In 1965–1966, it was estimated that 70 percent of persons in households with under $1,000 income had deficient diets, as did 62 percent of those in homes with incomes between $1,000 and $2,000, and 60 percent of those in the $2,000–$2,999 income class.[18]

Final Diagnosis

It is possible that blacks may be innately more healthy than whites. Before age seventeen blacks lose fewer days of school due to ill health; young black men are less frequently rejected for military service for medical reasons; blacks are less likely than whites to suffer activity limitations when income is controlled. But neglect catches up, resulting in significantly poorer black health in adulthood. Social patterns which give low priority to health care, inadequate health education, and possibly residential isolation from health care facilities apparently reinforce the effects of low income. Moreover, cultural factors which result in a high incidence of violence and accidents raise death and disability rates particularly for young black males. Consequently, blacks have shorter life expectancy and a higher mortality from most diseases and traumas. On the average, they suffer more frequent chronic health problems, disabilities, activity restrictions, and work limitations.

Better medical care, longer education, and higher incomes have improved the life expectancy and health of blacks during the past few decades. Particularly important gains were made in maternal and infant mortality, tuberculosis, pneumonia, and other problems which are susceptible to medical treatment. As black life expectancies have increased, however, the causes of black mortality have shifted more to those of whites—heart disease and cancer. Though the absolute black death rates for these diseases remain below white rates, blacks are much younger as a group. Thus, most of the aggregate gain in black death rates compared to whites reflects a younger population rather than a healthier one. Adjusted for age, black mortality rates were still one and a half times those of whites in 1969. Moreover, some black problems were getting worse, notably cirrhosis of the liver, homicide, and venereal disease.

Few health statistics are available for the past few years, obscuring recent trends and making it hard to estimate the impact of the recent explosion of subsidized health care. Health problems are far less subject to quick improvement even when substantial care is available. Good health is not simply a matter of treating the symptoms when they appear, but of establishing the nutritional, sanitary, housing, and environmental conditions which contribute to sound bodies. Until these conditions are equalized between the races, providing free medical care to all will not completely overcome the greater deterioration of black health compared to white.

But more income and better living conditions alone will not solve all black health problems where those are based on differing social practices. For example, further gains in the health of black mothers and babies must come in part from changes in patterns of pre- and postnatal care. Rather than simply relying on hospitalization and attendance by a physician, efforts need to be focused on education to encourage good nutrition, early visits to the doctor, and improved child care in the first year after birth. Similarly, the death rates from accidents, homicides, and cirrhosis of the liver, and possibly from heart disease, reflect differences in living patterns as well as inadequate care. As in the case of health during childbearing, part of the emphasis must be placed on education to change attitudes and social values as well as on the provision of more income and the delivery of various services.

7

LITTLE MORE THAN SHELTER

The quality, cost, and location of housing have major ramifications for the well-being of blacks. The relative quality of the home and its amenities is a major determinant of status and satisfaction. And, the location of residence affects access to schools and jobs and influences social contacts. No matter how solid a house, its value as a source of comfort or pride is diminished if it is located in a blighted neighborhood.

Improvements for the Ill-Housed

Substantial progress was made during the 1960s in improving conditions for the ill-housed, both black and white. Between 1960 and 1970 the number of dilapidated homes and those with inadequate plumbing which the Bureau of the Census classified as "substandard" fell by 44 percent. The number of nonwhite households in substandard units declined from 2.3 million to 1.4 million—or from 44 to 23 percent of all nonwhite households (table 7-1).

The "substandard" classification was not used in the 1970 decennial census, but the proportion of black-occupied units without adequate plumbing dropped from 41 to 17 percent between 1960 and 1970.[1] Some of the gain was related to the urbanization of the black population, but in rural as well as urban areas there was improvement. Outside metropolitan areas, 76 percent of black homes in 1960

Table 7-1. Substandard housing, 1950–1970

Race	1950	1960	1970[a]
Number of households in substandard housing units (thousands)			
All races	14,794	8,474	4,740
White	12,126	6,211	3,303
Black and other races	2,667	2,263	1,437
Percent of households in substandard housing units			
All races	35.4	16.0	7.4
White	31.8	13.0	5.7
Black and other races	73.2	44.0	23.0

Source: U.S. Office of Management and Budget, *Social Indicators, 1973* (Government Printing Office, 1973), p. 207.

[a] 1970 categories are White and Other races and black.

lacked adequate plumbing, but 49 percent were deficient in this regard in 1970.

To afford minimally adequate or even substandard units, many families have to crowd into small units. In 1960 only a tenth of white households had more than one person per room, compared with 28 percent of nonwhites. According to the 1970 census, the proportion for whites had fallen to 7 percent and for nonwhites to 19 percent. These significant gains, nevertheless, still left blacks ill-housed far more frequently than whites. In 1970 blacks were four times as likely to be in substandard units as whites, and three times as likely to be overcrowded.

The persisting problems are related to the low income of blacks, but this is not the only factor. In 1970 only 11 percent of the white households with an annual income of less than $5,000 lacked adequate plumbing, and 5 percent were overcrowded, compared with 25 and 17 percent of black households (table 7-2). If black households had the same income distribution as whites, the weighted proportion

Table 7-2. Housing units lacking plumbing and overcrowded homes, 1970

1969 family income	Percent households in units lacking plumbing		Percent households in overcrowded units	
	White and other races	Black	White and other races	Black
Total	4.4	16.2	6.7	19.4
Less than $2,000	14.0	29.9	3.5	12.3
$2,000–$2,999	10.0	24.2	4.5	18.4
$3,000–$3,999	8.1	21.4	6.4	22.8
$4,000–$4,999	6.8	17.8	7.5	24.0
$5,000–$5,999	5.6	14.0	8.3	23.8
$6,000–$6,999	4.3	11.0	8.6	23.0
$7,000–$9,999	2.6	7.7	8.5	22.3
$10,000–$14,999	1.2	3.9	7.5	19.8
$15,000 and over	0.7	2.3	5.4	17.4

Source: U.S. Bureau of the Census, *Census of Housing: 1970*, HC(2-1), September 1972, tables A-4 and A-14.

in substandard homes would still be 11.0 percent compared with the 4.4 percent for whites.

Of the other factors that contribute to the remaining differentials, larger black families are probably the most important. Standardization of this factor would reduce the difference, but would still leave a residual due to discrimination. According to a study for the President's Committee on Urban Housing, nonwhites in urban areas paid up to 30 percent more than whites to get minimally adequate housing in 1960 after adjusting for family size and other factors.[2]

Trickling Down and Moving Up

A "decent home and suitable living environment" means more than indoor plumbing and a roof that does not leak. The evidence suggests that while the quality of black housing has improved across-the-board,

Table 7-3. Housing characteristics, 1960 and 1970

Item	Nonwhite 1960	Black 1970	Total 1960	Total 1970
Total occupied (millions)	5.1	6.2	53.0	63.4
Median number rooms	4.2	4.6	4.9	5.0
Median number persons	3.2	3.0	3.0	2.7
More than one person per room	28.3%	19.4%	11.5%	8.0%
Single family house	67.0%	57.7%	76.3%	69.4%
Owner occupied	38.4%	41.6%	61.9%	62.8%
Median value	$6,700	$10,800	$11,900	$17,100
Renter occupied	61.6%	58.4%	38.1%	37.2%
Monthly rent	$58	$72	$71	$89
Structure built last 10 years	16.4%	15.8%	27.5%	24.8%
Percent lacking				
Clothes washer	50.2	49.3	26.3	28.9
Clothes dryer	97.8	88.2	82.9	58.3
Freezer	92.0	79.0	81.6	71.8
Air conditioner	96.0	82.0	87.6	69.0
Television	27.6	8.0	12.7	4.5

Source: Derived from data in U.S. Bureau of the Census, *Census of Housing: 1970,* HC(2-1), September 1972, tables 1–4; *Census of Housing: 1960,* Series PHC(1-1), 1963, tables 1-4.

there is still a substantial gap between blacks and whites which may not have been narrowed much, if at all (table 7-3). In 1960 the ratio of median rooms to median persons per household was 1.3 for non-whites, and it increased to 1.5 in 1970. At the same time, however, the rates for the total population increased from 1.6 to 1.9. In the latter year 26 percent of all occupied homes had more than one bath compared with only 12 percent of black homes. In terms of other amenities, blacks closed the "television gap," but they still lagged substantially in the proportions having clothes washers, dryers, and dishwashers.

Single family homeownership is the preferred living arrangement among those who can afford it, and there has been some absolute and very slight relative improvement for blacks. In 1970, 42 percent of black households were living in their own homes, building equity, and benefiting from the substantial tax subsidies granted to homeowners; this was an increase from 38 percent in 1960, but still left only two-thirds as many blacks as whites owning their homes. Moreover, though the median value of blacks' homes increased more rapidly than for whites, blacks' homes were still worth in 1970 only three-fifths as much as whites'.

The remaining black/white differences in homeownership are not easily explained. There is substantial regional variation in rates of homeownership; 47 percent of southern black households owned their own homes compared with 29 percent of those in the Northeast in 1970.[3] But these differences did not explain the overall gaps. In each income class and area of residence, whites more frequently owned their homes than blacks (table 7-4). For instance, among households in central cities with an income between $10,000 and $15,000, 62 percent of whites but only 52 percent of blacks owned their homes in 1970. The differences may result from the recency of black income gains which could not be translated immediately into equity, a prefer-ence for rental rather than purchase, a lack of "future-orientedness," or discrimination by banks and real estate agencies.

There is some evidence of a "trickle-down effect"—where whites move into newer units allowing blacks to upgrade into their vacated homes. This process is closely interrelated with the exodus of whites to the suburbs. Many central cities have declining populations and numerous abandoned but structurally sound homes.[4] Blacks appar-ently benefit from this slack. In 1970 only 14 percent of black renters lived in units built within a decade compared with 25 percent of whites; 70 percent of blacks but 59 percent of whites lived in units built in 1949 or earlier.[5] Among owner occupants, only 8 percent of blacks owned homes worth $15,000 or more and built after 1960, while 41 percent owned homes built before 1960 and worth less than $10,000 (table 7-5). The proportions among white owner-occupants were 22 and 18 percent, respectively.

Table 7-4. Percent of housing units owner-occupied, 1970

Race and residence	Total	Annual income					
		Less than $3,000	$3,000 to 4,999	$5,000 to 6,999	$7,000 to 9,999	$10,000 to 14,999	$15,000 or more
Black							
Total	42	33	34	38	47	57	70
Metropolitan areas	39	26	28	33	44	56	69
In central cities	35	23	25	30	40	52	66
Outside central cities	54	43	44	49	58	68	80
Outside metropolitan areas	52	46	48	56	63	70	77
White and other							
Total	65	53	53	54	63	74	82
Metropolitan areas	62	45	46	47	58	71	81
In central cities	51	35	37	38	49	62	72
Outside central cities	71	56	56	55	65	77	86
Outside metropolitan areas	72	65	65	66	72	80	87

Source: U.S. Bureau of the Census, *The Social and Economic Status of the Black Population in the United States, 1972,* Series P-23, no. 46, July 1973, table 62.

Table 7-5. Value and age of owner-occupied housing units, 1970

Year structure built	Total	Value of homes			
		Less than $5,000	$5,000 to 9,999	$10,000 to 14,999	$15,000 or more
Total black (thousands)	2,079	334	630	495	620
Total	100%	100%	100%	100%	100%
1969 to March 1970	2	1	1	2	3
1965 to 1968	6	4	4	6	10
1960 to 1964	10	7	8	10	14
1950 to 1959	22	17	20	24	26
1949 or earlier	59	71	77	57	47
Total white (thousands)	29,647	1,489	4,277	5,896	17,984
Total	100%	100%	100%	100%	100%
1969 to March 1970	2	1	1	1	4
1965 to 1968	10	3	2	4	13
1960 to 1964	14	5	5	9	18
1950 to 1959	29	12	17	29	34
1949 or earlier	45	80	75	57	32

Source: U.S. Bureau of the Census, *The Social and Economic Status of Blacks in the United States, 1972,* Series P-23, no. 46, July 1973, table 63.

Housing Costs

The quality of black-occupied homes is only half the picture; the related question is how much they pay and what they get for their housing expenditures. Despite the fact that they are more likely to be ill-housed at all income levels, and despite the fact that their homes on the average are smaller, less equipped, and less valuable, blacks pay a larger share of their income for the homes they buy and rent. In 1970 nearly a third of black homeowners, compared with less than a fifth of whites, reported paying more than 25 percent of their income for

Table 7-6. Homeownership and rental costs, 1970

Annual housing cost as percent of income	Homeownership		Rental	
	Black	White and other	Black	White and other
Number (thousands)	1,786	26,776	3,607	19,953
Percent	100	100	100	100
Less than 10 percent	14	20	23[a]	27[a]
10 to 14 percent	18	21		
15 to19 percent	14	18	15	17
20 to 24 percent	11	11	11	12
25 to 34 percent	13	9	14	13
35 percent or more	12	7	29	22
Not reported	19	14	8	9
Median	18	16	24	20

Source: U.S. Bureau of the Census, *The Social and Economic Status of the Black Population in the United States, 1972,* Series P-23, no. 46, July 1973, tables 64 and 65.
Note: Annual housing costs includes the sum of payments for real estate taxes, special assessments (if any), property insurance, utilities, fuel, water, ground rent (if any), and interest and principal payments on all mortgages (if property mortgaged), plus any other items included in the mortgage payment. Cost excludes taxes and insurance. Gross rent is the contract rent plus the estimated average monthly cost of utilities and fuel, if these items are paid for by the renter in addition to rent.
[a] Less than 14 percent.

housing, including utilities, interest, and principal (table 7-6). Among renter households, 43 percent of blacks compared with 35 percent of whites paid more than 25 percent. The primary reason for this differential is that there are more black low-income households whose rent inevitably takes a bigger slice of their income. When income classes are controlled, blacks spend less for housing than whites.

		Annual income			
	Total	Less than $5,000	$5,000 to 9,999	$10,000 to 14,999	$15,000 to 25,000	$25,000 or more
Black	$ 89	$77	$ 99	$115	$129	$121
White and other	112	90	112	135	162	208

The conventional wisdom is that because of discrimination, blacks pay more for less, but there is no good way to measure quality in order to determine what the black housing dollar will buy. Using the substandard classification, it was estimated in 1960 that black households paid more to get into "standard" units. But though blacks are more likely to be in substandard homes at any income level, they are also more likely to live in the South where substandard units are more prevalent. It is entirely possible that the flight of whites to the suburbs has reduced prices for blacks within the central cities, while migration out of the South has left more vacancies for remaining low-income blacks. There is enough doubt that the conventional wisdom should not be accepted uncritically, though in all likelihood blacks probably still do pay more.

One thing is certain—black housing outlays provide them with only a small share of the financial benefits which come with homeownership. A main reason for home purchase is investment and tax savings. It is estimated that by buying rather than renting, a four-person family with an annual income of less than $10,000 will save at least 1.7 percent of its income.[6] Blacks with incomes in this range are less than three-fourths as likely to own their own homes. Moreover, the value of blacks' mortgages is only two-thirds that of whites, averaging $14,800 in 1970.[7] Perhaps more critically, black-owned homes were concentrated in areas where appreciation in value is uncertain. Clearly, this is true in many central city areas where banks and mortgage companies refuse to loan on properties in "transition" neighborhoods because of the presumed risk. It is probably also true that low-value homes appreciate at a slower rate than those which are initially more expensive. Certainly, most newer homes hold or increase their value more often than older ones. For whites, homeownership is thus a less risky and more profitable investment.

Location: The Critical Issue

Whatever changes have occurred in the absolute or relative quality and value of black housing, there is one overriding and unequivocal development: residential segregation was accentuated in the 1960s. Continued migration increased the black share of central city populations from 16 to 22 percent, and the percent of blacks living there from 52 to 56 percent. At the same time, the black share in suburbia remained relatively constant, leaving the suburbs "lily-white" while the central cities became increasingly populated by blacks and other minorities.

These aggregate figures are mildly disturbing, but they mask the magnitude of the dichotimization. Census tract data reveal that in twenty large cities, the proportion of blacks in neighborhoods where they represented at least three-fourths of the population increased from 36 to 50 percent while the proportion in "mixed" neighborhoods with 25 percent or less blacks declined from 25 to 16 percent (table 7-7).

As one example of this process, the black share of the Newark, New Jersey population increased from 34 to 54 percent over the decade. In

Table 7-7. Percent of blacks living in census tracts by share of population, 1960–1970

Residence	75 percent or more	50 to 74	25 to 49	Less than 25
Average				
1960	36	25	14	25
1970	50	19	15	16
Baltimore				
1960	78	10	8	4
1970	83	8	4	5
Buffalo				
1960	35	47	6	12
1966	69	10	13	8
1970	70	13	6	11
Cleveland				
1960	72	16	8	4
1965	80	12	4	4
1970	81	13	4	2
Des Moines				
1960	—	28	31	41
1966	—	42	19	39
1970	—	41	30	29

Residence	75 percent or more	50 to 74	25 to 49	Less than 25
Evansville				
1960	34	27	9	30
1966	59	14	—	27
1970	53	17	11	20
Little Rock				
1960	33	33	19	15
1964	41	18	22	19
1970	64	13	10	13
Louisville				
1960	57	13	17	13
1964	67	13	10	10
1970	72	14	7	7
Memphis				
1960	65	26	5	4
1967	78	14	4	4
1970	81	12	2	5
Milwaukee				
1960	36	34	6	24
1970	58	30	4	8
Nashville				
1960	55	14	16	14
1970	61	14	11	14
Newark				
1960	46	30	14	11
1970	77	13	5	5
New Haven				
1960	—	33	19	48
1967	16	19	27	38
1970	37	12	33	18
Phoenix				
1960	19	36	24	21
1965	18	23	42	17
1970	14	28	34	24

Table 7-7. (continued)

Residence	75 percent or more	50 to 74	25 to 49	Less than 25
Table 7-7. (continued)				
Providence				
1960	—	23	2	75
1965	—	16	46	38
1970	—	—	66	34
Raleigh				
1960	86	—	7	7
1966	88	4	2	6
1970	80	3	5	12
Rochester				
1960	8	43	17	32
1964	16	45	24	15
1970	38	25	17	20
Sacramento				
1960	9	—	14	77
1964	8	14	28	50
1970	5	28	19	48
San Diego				
1960	7	30	33	30
1970	19	24	10	47
Shreveport				
1960	79	10	7	4
1966	90	—	6	4
1970	90	—	6	4
Trenton				
1960	26	9	48	17
1968	24	55	13	8
1970	21	58	16	5

Source: U.S. Bureau of the Census, 1960 and 1970 Census Tract Reports; and *The Social and Economic Status of Negroes in the United States, 1969,* Series P-23, no. 29, 1970, p. 11.

1970 only 10 percent of all blacks lived in tracts which were less than half black. Though the black population grew from only 13 to 19 percent of the entire metropolitan area, there was a substantial increase in segregated living patterns. Most of the tracts which were predominantly white at the beginning of the decade remained so, while those in which blacks came close to being proportionately represented in 1960 became heavily black in 1970. For instance, tracts which were less than 5 percent black in 1960 (averaging 0.9 percent) averaged a 4.4 percent black population in 1970. Those between 15 and 20 percent black (averaging 18.2 percent black) changed dramatically to a 46.9 percent black population by 1970 (figure 7-1).

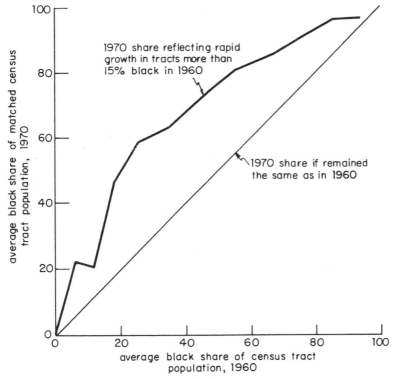

Figure 7-1. Black census tract population share in 1970 by population share in matched tracts in 1960, Newark metropolitan area.

Source: Derived from data in U.S. Bureau of the Census, *Census Tracts, Part 6,* Series PHC(1), 1963, Newark, New Jersey; and *Census Tracts, Newark, New Jersey,* Series PHC(1)146, April 1972, table 1.

Viewed in another way, a fifth of the tracts with less than 2.5 percent blacks in 1960 had a declining black population and in only a tenth did the black population rise by 5 percentage points or more. In tracts with a 1960 black population between 20.0 and 49.9 percent of the total, the black share rose 20 or more percentage points in two of every three cases (table 7-8). Every tract in which blacks made

Table 7-8. Probability of given increase in black percentage in census tract, based on Newark experience, 1960–1970

Census tracts by 1960 black share	Decline	0–4.9% increase	5.0–9.9% increase	10.9– 19.9% increase	Increase 20% or greater
0–2.4%	19%	71	4	3	3
2.5–4.9	36%	46	4	7	7
5.0–9.9	26%	22	19	11	22
10.0–19.9	10%	27	7	33	23
20.0–49.9	5%	5	5	18	67
50.0–89.9	0%	0	14	52	34
90.0–100.0	0%	50	50	0	0

Source: Derived from data in U.S. Bureau of the Census, *Census Tracts, Part 6,* Series PHC(1), 1963, Newark, New Jersey; *Census Tracts, Newark, New Jersey,* Series PHC(1)-146, April 1972, table 1.

inroads did not suddenly shift in composition. But the sensitivity to abrupt change increased with the percentage of black population. The aggregate evidence of increased segregation suggests that the patterns of change in the Newark metropolitan area are widespread.

While the evidence of segregation is unequivocal, the implications are not. Increased segregation means that fewer blacks have contacts with white neighbors and vice versa. In 1970 a national sample found that only 29 percent of blacks reported contact with a white neighbor. Almost as many (24 percent) had contact with white policemen, while the most interaction took place with employers or supervisors (68 percent).[8] Thus blacks' principal social dealings are with blacks, while their contacts with whites are more often with supervisors or authority figures.

The racial alienation and antipathy fostered by increasing segregation may be less harmful than the effects which ghetto isolation may have on black upward mobility. Some writers have argued that housing segregation locks in the black middle class so that their sons and daughters cannot be isolated from lower income elements, forcing each generation to fight its own battle against the "vicious cycle of poverty." The road to upward mobility for most ethnic groups has been suburbanization, and this remains largely foreclosed for blacks. Whether or not this view is valid, sociopsychological evidence suggests that where contact can be made between groups of equal economic status who are in some degree interdependent, racial attitudes of both blacks and whites will improve.[9]

The economic impacts of the central city concentration of blacks may have been overstated, however. Suburban penetration is far from an open sesame to improved income and earnings. The suburbanization of employment has been frequently cited as a cause of the employment problems of central city residents, but despite a faster rate of employment growth in the suburbs, total jobs in the largest central cities have increased more rapidly than their populations. While the employment mix has changed, the evidence indicates that low-wage and low-skill jobs have not declined as a proportion of the total. This suggests that disadvantaged central city residents may be no worse and perhaps better off in terms of their contiguity to jobs.[10]

This judgment is supported by an analysis comparing blacks with similar characteristics residing inside and outside the central cities. Nonwhites living in the suburbs do not have significantly higher earnings or less unemployment than those with equivalent education in the central city.[11]

Whether or not blacks are worse off in segregated communities, there is no doubt that obstacles to overcoming racial inequality are intensified. While significant advances were made toward integrated jobs and education, the doors to white neighborhoods remain barred. Blacks are apparently moving toward "equal but separate" housing, a development which threatens to undermine progress elsewhere.

Attitudes Toward Housing

Thus, the overall picture is one of a significantly improved physical environment for ill-housed blacks, a more gradual improvement across-the-board, and a deplorable dichotomization of the population into black and white neighborhoods. Whether blacks are better or worse off depends on how the question is defined and who is supplying the answers. Attitude surveys indicate that the quality of housing remains a crucial concern to blacks. Ironically, though blacks recognize that gains have been made, they are increasingly dissatisfied with conditions. In 1970, 41 percent of a national black sample felt that they were better off than three years before, as did 43 percent in 1966 and 1963; only one in ten in each of these years felt they were worse off. Yet only half were satisfied with their housing situation in 1969 compared with three-fifths in 1949 (table 7-9). As income increases,

Table 7-9. Satisfaction with housing situation, national opinion samplings, 1949–1969

	Satisfied		Dissatisfied		No opinion	
	White	Black	White	Black	White	Black
	(percent)					
1949	67	59	28	32	5	9
1963	76	43	21	54	3	3
1965	77	29	20	66	3	5
1966	77	51	19	44	4	5
1969	80	50	18	48	2	2

Source: Thomas F. Pettigrew, "Attitudes in Race and Housing: A Social-Psychological View," in Amos Hawley and Vincent Rock, eds., *Segregation in Residential Areas* (Washington: National Academy of Sciences, 1973), pp. 47–48.

satisfaction with housing increases among both blacks and whites but the degree of satisfaction is much lower for blacks at all income levels and rises much more slowly.[12] Only among the small numbers of young, very high income blacks does housing satisfaction improve sharply.

One reason may be that poorer black neighborhoods receive inferior quality and quantity of governmental services. In a 1970 fifteen-city study, 21 percent of blacks, but only 8 percent of whites, felt that their neighborhoods had worse city services than other parts of the city and proportionately fewer blacks than whites indicated satisfaction with specific services.

Satisfaction with:	Black	White
Quality of schools	42 percent	48 percent
Parks and playgrounds	30	50
Police protection	46	67
Garbage collection	68	81

Source: Campbell, *White Attitudes*, p. 98.

Another probable source of dissatisfaction is that many blacks feel that they pay more for less housing than whites. In 1963, 53 percent felt that they would pay more rent for a given unit than whites and only 30 percent felt they would pay the same. A 1968 survey found that more than three-fourths believed that they were missing out on good housing buys because of discrimination.[13]

The evidence is mixed whether the level of discrimination is increasing or declining. On the one hand, whites are apparently becoming more and more open to the *idea* of residential integration. When asked whether it made a difference if a black with the same income and education moved into their block, 62 percent of a national sample of whites objected in 1942, 46 percent in 1956, 39 percent in 1963, but only 21 percent in 1968. Forty-six percent in 1958 claimed they would move if a black family moved in next door, but only 35 percent felt this strongly in 1967. On the other hand, seven out of ten whites in a 1971 national sample claimed that they would move if blacks entered in "great numbers" into their neighborhoods, only a slight decline from 77 percent in 1958. More than two-fifths of whites in 1970 felt that they should have a right to exclude blacks from their neighborhoods.[14] A majority of whites still apparently oppose federal laws forbidding discrimination in housing against blacks. In other words, while whites are more frequently willing to agree in principle to the goal of equal opportunity in housing, they continue to resist infringements on their property rights and assumed threats to their property value.

The claims that blacks do not want to live in integrated neighborhoods and that a desire for separatism is on the rise are unsubstantiated. Three-fourths of a 1969 sample of black households claimed they would prefer to live in a mixed rather than an all black neighborhood if housing were available that they wanted and liked; only 16 percent preferred an all black area. The proportion favoring mixing had increased from 64 percent in 1963, and those for segregated neighborhoods had declined from 20 percent.[15]

Despite the improving income and education of blacks, and despite the fact that both blacks and whites claim to be more amenable to residential integration, there is increasing segregation. This paradox may be explained in part by the disparity between attitudes and action. But another factor is differing definitions of an integrated neighborhood. Attitudinal data and statistics such as those for Newark demonstrate that whites tend to abandon a neighborhood if it gets over 15 to 20 percent black. Only 1 percent of blacks in a 1968 survey preferred mostly white neighborhoods, with 48 percent desiring about "half and half" mixtures.[16] Thus, as blacks move into mixed neighborhoods seeking an "ideal" racial mixture, they may trigger white flight even before a "racially balanced" neighborhood is achieved.

The Housing Inventory

Changes in the housing conditions of blacks have, thus, been a mixed bag. Any judgment concerning the net impact of the last decade's developments depends on the weight given to absolute as opposed to relative gains, and to structural size and soundness versus location and amenities.

There is no doubt that blacks are living in better homes. The percentage of black households in Bureau of the Census-classified substandard and overcrowded units declined markedly in the 1960s. In 1970 blacks lived in larger and better equipped homes and they were more likely to own these homes.

Despite this improvement, the relative status of black housing improved very little, if at all. The proportion of white households in substandard and overcrowded units fell faster than the proportion of blacks. The number of rooms per person increased in black homes, but the average number among whites rose more and white gains in amenities and appliances have apparently outstripped black improvements. The relative gains in homeownership were slight.

Offsetting this progress is the fact that black housing is now more segregated than it was a decade ago. Though a majority of both blacks and whites claim that they would prefer or at least accept integrated neighborhoods, there has been a massive white exodus in area after area where blacks have penetrated in any number. Anecdotal literature supports the statistical evidence that the black middle class has tried to move into more stable mixed neighborhoods only to have them become all black. Claims that residential segregation has foreclosed jobs for blacks are often overstated, but there are major sociological and political implications of residential polarization.

Whatever the balance of change, black housing problems remain serious. A fourth of all blacks still live in homes which are severely deteriorated or lack adequate plumbing. A fifth contain more than one person per room. Blacks at all income levels are less likely to own their homes; when they do, the value is much lower and probably less secure than for homes owned by whites. Black homes are older and have fewer amenities on the average, yet they may cost more than those occupied by whites. Worst of all, blacks do not have equal opportunity to choose where and how they want to live.

8

BLACK POWER

A decent income, a well-paid job, an adequate education, a stable home, and good health and housing are necessary but not sufficient conditions for individual well-being. Other less tangible factors determine the quality of life—a sense of dignity resulting from individual responsibility and self-determination, and security resulting from stability and influence over the future. The rallying cry in the 1960s was "black power." While such power must be ultimately based on inner strength and conviction, it is also related to position, institutional attachments, and control over resources. Meaningful black power can only be achieved when blacks occupy decision-making jobs in the public and private sectors, when they have a voice in unions, and federal, state, and local politics, and, finally, when they own businesses and financial assets.

Responsible Jobs

The most direct and visible positions of power and control are in government, in large corporations, and increasingly in nonprofit institutions, where decisions are made concerning the uses of the nation's resources. Despite gains in education, occupation, and earnings, blacks are still largely excluded from such positions. In 1970, 616,000 blacks held professional and technical jobs, 5.4 percent of such workers. There were 166,000 black managers and administrators, 2.2

162

percent of the total. Though the proportions of blacks had advanced from 3.7 percent of professionals and 1.6 percent of managers in 1960, blacks were still woefully underrepresented.[1]

Discrimination in managerial employment appears to be worse in the private sector. Of all private sector wage and salary managers and administrators in 1970, only 1.7 percent were black. Though blacks were higher percentages of health administrators (4.5 percent), restaurant managers (3.7 percent), and school administrators (4.6 percent), there were almost no black office managers (0.8 percent), nonretail sales managers (0.6), or durable goods manufacturing managers (0.8 percent).[2] Moreover, the blacks who have become managers are still likely to be confined in the least paid, least responsible jobs. Only a third of black managers make as much as $10,000 compared to two-thirds of white managers (table 8-1).

Table 8-1. Managers and administrators, 1970

Income	Blacks as percent of managers and administrators with earnings	Distribution of white managers and administrators with earnings	Distribution of black managers and administrators with earnings
Total	2.2%	100%	100%
Annual income			
Under $6,000	5.3	11	28
$6,000–9,999	3.1	27	40
$10,000–14,999	1.5	31	22
$15,000 and over	0.7	31	10

Source: U.S. Bureau of the Census, *Earnings by Occupation and Education,* PC(2)8B, tables 1 and 2.

Even high salary may be no guarantee of real authority for blacks. A 1971 Department of Labor survey of 500 black male professional and managerial workers in the private sector revealed that despite the median salary of $14,000, their authority was limited. Most were in service fields, research, or marketing, with only 16 percent in finance,

4 percent in production, and 9 percent in general management where the most significant corporate decision-making occurs. Less than one-fourth were supervisors and only 4 percent had control over other supervisors. Also, average earnings tended to level off after eight to nine years of service, suggesting that blacks were outside the track leading to the highest paying management positions. Not surprisingly, 38 percent found their progress up through the company ranks unsatisfactory, and three-fifths thought the companies did not offer blacks the same opportunities as whites.[3]

While blacks in business are not exclusively pigeonholed into show piece jobs, it does appear they are less likely to get into positions of real authority. They are more likely to get into staff rather than line jobs, and this hurts their chances for advancement. This apparent side-tracking of black executives in peripheral management functions does not augur well for blacks soon achieving a real representation in the topmost ranks of business. Until recently there were hardly any blacks in top corporate positions. As late as 1958 a survey of the fifty largest United States corporations found that there were only 3 black senior officers or directors out of 3,185.[4]

This situation has changed some, especially since the scramble for black executives in the late 1960s. Still, by late 1973, though blacks sat on the boards of such giants as GM, Standard Oil, and IBM, there were only 72 black directors of major United States corporations out of a total of more than 14,000.[5] Similarly, a survey of top corporate law firms in 1972 could find only 13 blacks and only 1 partner among 2,225 lawyers.[6] And a 1969 survey of large accounting firms turned up only 136 blacks among the 100,000 certified public accountants, and only 1 black among 3,139 firm partners.[7] As one reviewer of black status in corporate enterprise lamented, "The number of blacks who have keys to the executive suite is so small that most know each other personally."[8]

Blacks have relatively more responsible positions in the public sector, but they are still grossly underrepresented. The number of blacks employed by all levels in government in 1970 was 1.6 million, an increase of 90 percent over the preceding decade, while the number employed by the federal government rose by a third between 1962 and 1972. In 1972, 15 percent of all federal employees were black, yet blacks held only 3.0 percent of the jobs at the GS-12 level and above ($17,500 per year minimum in October 1973). Among the supergraders above GS-16, blacks were only 2.3 percent of the total. In the postal services, blacks were only 5 percent of those above grade 12 and 2.6 percent of those in grade 16 and above. Similarly, in the military the number of blacks above the rank of captain jumped from 765 in 1962 to 2,513 in 1972, or from 0.8 percent to 2.2 percent. But in 1972 blacks were still virtually excluded from the top ranks, making up 0.9 percent of generals and admirals, and 0.8 percent of colonels and navy captains (table 8-2).

This absence of black faces at the top of federal bureaucracies is paralleled by their prominence at the bottom. Blacks are 19 percent of federal workers below grade 6 (annual salary below $9,000) and 14 percent of enlisted soldiers below sergeant. So far, the trends toward greater equality in federal employment have hardly changed the status quo: black workers obeying white managers.

At the state and local level the story may be even worse. About two-thirds of all black government employees work at the state and local level, and the numbers of these workers have doubled since 1960.[9] However, a study of state and local employment in the South found that substantial black quantitative gains were less spectacular from a qualitative point of view. In North Carolina, equal opportunity efforts were pursued aggressively, and 17 percent of state employees in 1968 were black (compared with 25 percent of the state's population). But two-thirds of white employees were in skilled or white-collar jobs compared with less than a third of blacks, and of this minority three in eight worked in predominantly black institutions. Thirty-nine of 106 agencies had no blacks in white-collar jobs, and 13 only one; in 96 there were no black supervisors. In Virginia, 102 of 151 state agencies had no black supervisors in 1969, and another 20 had only one; on the other hand, the 9 which were predominantly black employed three-fifths of all black white-collar workers.[10] In northern states, and especially in the central cities, the situation may differ in degree but probably not in substance, with blacks concentrated in the agencies serving largely black clienteles, such as welfare and manpower offices, neighborhood health centers, and civil rights offices. Increased control over the programs affecting blacks is important, but the continued growth of "black jobs" in the social welfare area depends on increased funding. In the public as in the private sector, blacks have gained only

Table 8-2. Blacks in federal employment, 1962 and 1972 (numbers in thousands)

	1962		1972	
Classification	Number	Percent of all employees	Number	Percent of all employees
Total civilian	293.1	13.0	387.7	15.1
General schedule	96.5	9.1	153.4	11.5
GS 1–4	65.9	18.1	66.3	21.7
GS 5–8	23.3	7.7	59.0	15.0
GS 9–11	5.9	2.6	18.8	5.9
GS 12–18	1.4	0.8	9.3	3.0
Wage board	105.7	18.6	102.8[a]	20.4[a]
Less than $4,499	44.7	43.0	31.8	49.0
$4,500–$6,499	56.3	16.9	34.8	33.1
$6,500–$7,999	4.5	4.2	23.5	18.1
$8,000 and over	0.2	0.6	12.5	6.9
Postal field service	86.9	15.2	127.3[b]	18.6[b]
PFS 1–4	81.9	16.6	111.6	19.6
PFS 5–8	4.8	7.7	14.5	15.6
PFS 9–11	0.1	1.2	1.0	5.8
PFS 12–20	—	0.4	0.3	6.4
Other pay systems	4.0	8.1	4.2	1.4
Military officers	6.1	2.0	7.9	2.4
WO–01	2.0	3.4	1.7	3.0
02–03	3.3	2.3	3.7	2.4
04–05	0.8	0.9	2.4	2.4
06 and above	—	0.1	0.2	0.8
Enlisted	193.8	9.2	270.5	13.5
E–1–E4	133.0	9.6	168.7	14.0
E5–E7	59.8	8.8	97.8	13.0
E–8–E9	1.0	2.6	4.0	7.4

Source: United States Civil Service Commission, *Minority Group Employment in the Federal Government, May 31, 1972* (Washington: Government Printing Office, 1973), tables 1-9; *Study of Minority Group Employment in the Federal Government, 1966* (Washington: Government Printing Office, 1967), tables 1-4; U.S. Department of Defense, *The Negro in the Armed Forces: A Statistical Fact Book*.

[a] Due to changes in Wage Board salary scales, the 1972 figures are not strictly comparable. Wage Scale 1–3 are included in the first category, 4–6 in the second, 7–9 in the third, and 10 or above in the last.

[b] Due to changes in Postal Field Service reporting in 1972, the first group includes PFS 1–5, the second PFS 6–9, the third PFS 10–12, and the fourth PFS 13 or above for 1972.

limited control over the reins of power even though they have advanced into higher paying and higher status jobs.

One of the most important areas of public employment in which blacks are still very underrepresented is law enforcement. The Kerner Commission investigating the riots of 1966 and 1967 found that friction between ghetto residents and predominantly white police forces was one of the chief causes of black anger and frustration. Since the riots a major effort has been made to recruit black policemen. Few police forces, even in the deep South, are any longer entirely white, and overall blacks have increased from 3.7 percent of public police officers in 1960 to 6.4 percent in 1970, nearly tripling their numbers. By 1970 blacks were 7.5 percent of federal, 7 percent of local, and 2.3 percent of state officers. But these overall gains still leave most cities in both the North and South with police forces which are considerably whiter than their populations (table 8-3). On the courthouse side of the judicial system, the situation is the same. Overall, blacks are only 1.3 percent of all lawyers. They are only 2.3 percent of publicly employed state and local prosecutors, and 2.3 percent of state and local judges. Though all of these figures represent nearly double the percentages in 1960, they still do not mean more than token public legal authority for blacks.

Blacks and Unions

Membership in unions and influence on union policies are important factors affecting black employment status. As Martin Luther King observed in a 1961 address to the AFL-CIO: "Negroes are almost entirely a working people. There are pitifully few Negro millionaires and few Negro employers. Our needs are identical with labor's needs."[11]

This community of interest between blacks and organized labor was strained by the changes of the 1960s. Hiring quotas instituted in the construction crafts were highly controversial and bitterly opposed by the trade unions. In the late 1960s, according to some reports, blue-collar workers and union members were embittered by the inroads of blacks, and had shifted their political orientation to the right. These

Table 8-3. Blacks in police force, 1970

	Black population	Police
Atlanta	51 percent	10 percent
Baltimore	46	12[a]
Buffalo	20	2
Chicago	33	16
Cleveland	38	7
Dallas	25	2
Detroit	44	13
Hartford	28	13
Los Angeles	18	5
Miami	23	11
Milwaukee	15	3
Minneapolis	4	1
Newark	54	14
New York	21	9
Oakland	35	7
Philadelphia	34	20[a]
Phoenix	5	2
St. Louis	29	15
Washington	71	37

Source: William B. Gould, "Labor Relations and Race Relations," in Sam Zagoria, *Public Workers and Public Unions* (New York: Prentice-Hall, 1973), p. 149.
[a] "Civil Service—Does the Merit System Work?" *Black Enterprise* (April 1972), p. 31.

controversies obscured the truth that, despite discrimination, unions continued to be of vital importance to blacks—representing them in bargaining for better jobs and higher pay, assuring them more equal treatment in the labor force, and working in the political arena for a variety of civil rights causes.

Blacks are slightly more likely to be union members than whites. In 1970 nonwhites constituted 11.7 percent of the labor force, 12 percent of all union members, and an estimated one-third of all new union members.[12] Three of ten employed nonwhite males and 14

Table 8-4. Labor union membership, 1970 (in thousands)

Number in unions	All workers	White-collar workers	Blue-collar workers	Service workers
Total	17,192	3,865	11,893	1,409
Nonwhite	2,130	425	1,395	304
White	15,062	3,440	10,498	1,105
Male	13,506	2,305	10,244	935
Nonwhite	1,496	204	1,119	167
White	12,009	2,100	9,125	769
Female	3,687	1,560	1,648	474
Nonwhite	634	221	276	137
White	3,053	1,339	1,372	337
Percent unionized				
Total	20.4	9.8	39.3	10.9
Nonwhite	21.8	16.6	35.5	10.8
White	20.2	9.3	39.8	10.9
Male	27.8	12.5	42.1	20.1
Nonwhite	29.0	20.7	36.7	19.9
White	27.6	12.0	42.8	20.2
Female	10.3	7.4	27.8	5.7
Nonwhite	13.8	14.0	3.5	6.9
White	9.8	6.9	27.1	5.3

Source: U.S. Bureau of Labor Statistics, *Selected Earnings and Demographic Characteristics of Union Members, 1970,* Report 417 (Washington: Government Printing Office, 1972), table 1.

percent of females were unionized compared with 28 and 10 percent, respectively, among white workers (table 8-4). In part, this greater incidence is explained by the occupational distribution of blacks: two-fifths of nonwhites compared with 34 percent of whites are in blue-collar jobs, which account for 70 percent of all union membership. Yet among males, 43 percent of white, compared with only 37 percent of nonwhite, blue-collar workers are unionized. On the other hand, nonwhite professionals, managers, clerical, and sales workers are much more likely to be organized than their white counterparts. Blacks are also more likely than whites to be union members in durable goods manufacturing, wholesale and retail trade, and personal and medical services, but they are slightly underrepresented on the rolls of railroad, construction, and postal clerks unions.

Unions and unionized jobs are an upward mobility route for blacks. Nonwhite males in unions in 1969 earned an average of 31 percent more than those not in unions, while white male union members earned 2 percent less than those not in unions. For nonwhite females, unionized workers earned 19 percent more, compared with an 8 percent differential among whites. Within most occupational groups, the nonwhite union/nonunion earnings differential is larger than for whites (table 8-5).

While increasing union membership has been beneficial to blacks, it has not resulted in commensurate control over union policy. Blacks represent one in eight union members, one in nine teamsters, one in six steelworkers, and one in three autoworkers; but they have nowhere near this representation at the executive level. The teamsters, for instance, employed one black in a key post in 1972. This lack of representation brought complaints to the Equal Employment Opportunity Commission that the union was assigning lower paying local jobs rather than long hauls to black truckers. In 1968 blacks picketed the United Steelworkers' convention protesting a lack of adequate representation in union leadership positions. They claimed that of the fourteen departments in the union, only two had black personnel; of the thirty districts, there were no black directors and only one subdirector. Four years later only the civil rights department had a black director, although large locals in Baltimore, Chicago, and Gadsden, Alabama had black presidents.[13]

The United Autoworkers Union has the highest black membership, the most progressive civil rights stance, and the most blacks in top positions of the major unions. There is a black vice president and a black regional director, and blacks head a number of locals. Yet, in 1969 a "National Ad Hoc Committee of Concerned Negro UAW Members" demanded that blacks get a proportionate share of the International's jobs, where they allegedly held only seven of one hundred key staff positions. Independent black unions such as the Dodge Revolutionary Union Movement and the League of Revolutionary Black Workers sprang up at many plants and in several cases

Table 8-5. Median earnings of year-round, full-time wage and salary workers, by occupation and labor union membership, 1970

Occupation	White males			Nonwhite males			White females			Nonwhite females		
	Union	Non-union	Union Non-union	Union	Non-union	Union Non-union	Union	Non-union	Union Non-union	Union	Non-union	Union Non-union
Total	$ 9,285	$ 9,478	0.98	$7,732	$5,906	1.31	$5,890	$5,467	1.08	$5,363	$4,496	1.19
White-collar	9,923	11,542	0.86	8,883	8,330	1.07	6,840	6,008	1.14	6,526	6,254	1.04
Clerical	8,886	8,657	1.03	8,715	7,137	1.22	6,218	5,572	1.12	5,973	5,531	1.07
Blue-collar	9,175	7,802	1.18	7,772	5,469	1.42	5,095	4,327	1.18	4,387	4,116	1.07
Craftsmen and foremen	10,245	8,820	1.16	8,874	6,702	1.32	—	—	—	—	—	—
Operatives	8,663	6,865	1.26	7,512	5,493	1.37	5,011	4,319	1.16	4,350	4,087	1.06
Nonfarm labor	8,048	5,627	1.43	7,192	4,690	1.53	—	—	—	—	—	—
Service	8,682	6,929	1.25	6,335	5,319	1.19	4,888	3,797	1.29	4,950	3,366	1.47

Source: U.S. Bureau of Labor Statistics, *Selected Earnings and Demographic Characteristics of Union Members, 1970*, Report 417 (Washington: Government Printing Office, 1972), table 6.

waged wildcat strikes demanding proportionate representation for blacks in both the union and company management.

The absence of power is perhaps best illustrated by issues where the interests of black and white union members diverge, for example, in the disputes over quotas in the building trades. Despite the AFL-CIO's strong stand on most national civil rights legislation, it has opposed the imposition of affirmative action and quota hiring plans by the federal government. The federation preferred instead voluntary apprenticeship programs and exhortation of recalcitrant building trade unions. This stance led militant black unionists to organize new unions and in several instances to stage wildcat strikes in support of their demands. These developments suggest that the limitations on black power found elsewhere are not completely absent in unions despite their contributions to blacks in the work place.

Wealth and Business Ownership

Positions of elective, appointive, and bureaucratic authority are the most visible but perhaps not the most influential seats of power. In the United States as in other countries, the wealthy have great leverage over the course of economic and political affairs. Blacks, as might be expected from a history of second-class status, have little such leverage because they control almost none of the nation's income producing and business assets.

In 1972 blacks received an income from dividends, interest, rents, royalties, estates, and trusts estimated by the Census Bureau at $295 million, or 1.0 percent of such receipts. Though this return was larger than the $229 million blacks received five years before, the black share of such income had not changed at all.[14] Moreover, much income from these sources is not reported, and capital gains and imputed rents (the rent which would have been paid by homeowners) are not counted. If these factors were added to the tallies, the black share might be even less.

This tiny proportion of income from capital reflects, of course, the small fraction of business and personal equity held by blacks. Comparisons of net worths of black and white families reveal that non-

Table 8-6. Net worth of families, 1966

Net worth	White	Nonwhite	Nonwhites as percent of asset class
Total	100%	100%	11%
Debt of $500 or more	6	11	25
Debt of $1 to $499	5	19	30
No Assets	2	14	46
$1 to $999	10	17	16
$1,000 to $2,999	10	11	11
$3,000 to $4,999	8	6	9
$5,000 to $9,999	15	10	7
$10,000 to $14,999	11	5	5
$15,000 to $24,999	14	4	4
$25,000 and over	18	3	2
Average	$18,332	$4,489	—

Source: Unpublished data from the U.S. Bureau of the Census.

white families average less than $4,500 or a fourth of the net worth of whites. Blacks are more than two-fifths of families with no net worth but less than 2 percent of those with assets above $25,000 (table 8-6).

Even this ratio may overstate the proportion of income producing assets held by blacks. The first few thousands of net worth usually represent equity in a car, home, or furnishings, thus most of the major assets owned by blacks are consumer durables and homes, and even in these cases whites are much better off. In July 1972, 55 percent of black households owned one or more cars, compared with 83 percent among whites. The average age of black owned automobiles was 5.4 years compared to 4.4 for whites.[15] Black homes are also older and less valuable. Forty-two percent of black households owned the homes they occupied in 1970, compared to 69 percent of whites. The median value of black homes was $10,900 compared to $17,500 for whites.[16]

But even though fewer blacks own cars and homes, and their value is less than those of whites, these types of depreciable assets represent larger proportions of blacks' net worth. The total estimated value of black homes and cars in 1966 represented as much as four-fifths net worth, while these assets comprised slightly more than half of white worth. Thus, the spread between white and black ownership of the types of capital likely to produce revenue was even wider than the net worth differences.

One type of asset is profoundly important to the acquisition of power in America—business ownership. Besides giving the owner a sense of independence and a chance to determine his own fate, entrepreneurship has provided a major route of upward mobility for immigrants. Businesses can provide, in addition to income, assets which can be passed on to heirs.

Blacks own an infinitesimally small—and during the 1960s, declining—share of all businesses. In 1960, 4.6 percent of self-employed workers were black; by 1970 blacks made up only 3.9 percent of those working for themselves. The shift away from self-employment was especially dramatic among managers and proprietors. While the number of black managers rose during the decade, self-employed blacks in these positions declined by more than 15,000. White self-employment also fell, but blacks' fell faster so that the black share declined from 2.8 percent in 1960 to 2.4 percent in 1970 (table 8-7).

A special census of businesses in 1969 found that blacks owned or controlled only 2.2 percent of the 7.5 million nonfarming proprietorships, partnerships, and corporations (table 8-8). Less than a fourth of the black owned businesses had any paid employees. Black firms

Table 8-7. Self-employment, 1960–1970 (numbers in thousands)

	1960			1970		
	Total	Black	Black percent	Total	Black	Black percent
Total	64,647	6,087	9.4	76,805	7,403	9.6
Self-employed	7,923	368	4.6	7,146	278	3.9
Managers and proprietors	5,408	88	1.6	6,387	166	2.6
Self-employed	1,983	55	2.8	1,664	40	2.4

Sources: U.S. Bureau of the Census, *1960 Census of the Population*, Series PC(2)7F, Tables 7 and A-5; and *1970 Census of the Population*, Series PC(2)7A, tables 43-44.

Table 8-8. Black owned businesses and their receipts, 1969

Industry	Number of firms (thousands)			Receipts (millions)		
	Number of all firms	Number black firms	Blacks as percent of all firms	Receipts of all firms	Receipts black firms	Blacks as percent of all receipts
All industries	7,489	163	2.2	$1,497,969	$4,474	0.3
Contract construction	856	16	1.9	92,291	464	0.5
Manufacturing	401	3	0.8	588,682	303	0.1
Transportation and other public utilities	359	17	4.7	106,040	211	0.2
Wholesale trade	434	1	0.2	213,196	385	0.2
Retail trade	2,046	45	2.2	320,751	1,932	0.6
Finance, insurance, and real estate	1,223	8	0.6	86,670	288	0.3
Selected services	1,803	56	3.1	61,858	663	1.1
Other industries and not classified	367	17	4.5	28,481	228	0.8

Source: U.S. Bureau of the Census, *Minority-Owned Businesses: 1969*, MBI August 1971, table 1.

employed a total of 152,000 persons, or less than one person per enterprise in addition to the owners, compared with an average of eight employees per white firm. Altogether, these businesses employed only 0.2 percent of all private wage and salary workers.[17]

With total receipts of $4.5 billion—0.3 percent of the receipts of all firms in 1969—black-owned enterprises grossed an average of $27,400, or a tenth of the national average. Even if black businesses had the same profit margins (6.2 percent of net receipts) as all businesses, black firms averaged a miniscule $1,600 per firm in 1969. Moreover, black businesses are more often proprietorships and partnerships than corporations, and the latter have lower profit margins than corporations.

Most black firms, then, are very marginal enterprises. In the construction industry there were 16,000 black owned businesses in 1969, but only a quarter had any employees, and most consisted of an individual craftsman selling his labor on a contract basis. Of the less than 3,000 black owned manufacturing firms, 43 percent were logging operations typically comprised of one or two individuals contracting to cut and saw timber. Impressive sounding "transportation and public utilities firms" were mostly single taxi cab drivers and truckers, averaging less than one employee for every two firms. Retail and service establishments which accounted for two of every three black owned firms, but averaged only one employee per firm, consisted mostly of mom and pop grocery stores, barber and beauty shops, and one-man building and maintenance firms.

The still insignificant position of blacks in the nation's business establishment was born out by a 1973 survey of the largest black businesses conducted by *Black Enterprise* magazine. Of the top 100 black corporations, only 26 had 1972 sales of more than $5 million. With total sales of $450 million, all 100 companies *combined* would have placed 284th on the *Fortune* 500 list of the nation's top businesses. Although these figures for ownership of "large" black businesses reflect great gains over the decade—seven of ten of these black businesses did not exist ten years ago—they reveal also that whites still own almost all business enterprises.[18]

Apparently, most black owned businesses might be better described as labor contracting establishments, whose products are a little more than the sweat of the entrepreneurs. Undercapitalized and usually in highly competitive fields, these firms have little chance for growth and limited resources to command or build on. The frequently cited success stories—H. G. Parks, Johnson Publishing Company, North Carolina Mutual Insurance, and Motown Enterprises—are notable exceptions to an otherwise bleak picture.

Political Power

Constitutionally and practically, elected office is the seat of the most concentrated power in the United States. Until recently, except for a brief period during Reconstruction, blacks have won few positions at the ballot box. In 1955 there were only two black congressmen representing the ghettos of Chicago and New York. Not until 1967 did a black win the mayor's office of a major city—Carl Stokes in Cleveland.

This failure to win elected positions was a result not only of black minority status and the prejudice of white voters against black candidates, but of low rates of registration among black voters. During the late 1960s, concerted organizational drives raised the numbers of registered black voters dramatically. In the southern states, the proportion of registered voting age nonwhites rose from 29 percent in 1960 to 62 percent in 1971.[19] Though there was little change in the percentage of blacks registered in the North and West (where the proportions actually fell from 72 percent to 67 percent between 1968 and 1972), black gains in the South raised the overall black registration rate to nine-tenths that of whites by 1972.[20] These registration gains were important to the realization of black political power in the more than one hundred southern counties in which blacks constituted a majority.

At the same time that voter registration was changing the political complexion of the rural South, migration to urban areas was increasing black leverage in many cities. By 1970 blacks were majorities in thirteen cities, including Newark, Gary, Atlanta, and Washington, D.C., and more than two-fifths of the population in twenty-two others, including Baltimore, Detroit, and St. Louis. Black voting strength in these areas was somewhat weakened because blacks were less likely to register, and to vote, and because more blacks were under voting age. But continuing concentration of blacks in urban areas, coupled with the exodus of whites, assured the election of many new black city officials.

A crucial factor in converting numbers into power was the cohesiveness of black voters. More than whites and other minority groups, blacks tended toward block voting. At the national office level, the concentrated black vote sometimes tipped the balance of close elections, as in 1960 when Kennedy's plurality was only 119,000 votes and his 4 to 1 margin in the black community was crucial.[21] At the local level, block voting made possible the election of a number of black officials. For example, Mayor Carl Stokes won his reelection bid in Cleveland in 1969 by polling 95 percent of black voters but only 25 percent of whites (who represented 62 percent of registered voters).[22] In Atlanta, Maynard Jackson won with 30 percent of the white vote but 95 percent of blacks.[23] In Los Angeles, where blacks represented only 18 percent of the population, Tom Bradley was elected mayor with less than half of the white, but more than 90 percent of the black vote (and a similarly large percentage of Chicano voters).[24]

Increased registration and concentration combined with cohesive voting have resulted in substantial gains in Congress, state houses, and city halls. In 1973 there were 254 black legislators at the federal and state level, compared with only 40 in 1960 (table 8-9). Thirteen states had at least 100 black elected officials, led by Michigan with 179, New York with 164, Mississippi with 156, and Alabama with 149.

But while these gains are noteworthy, it is questionable whether they represent any fundamental change in black political leverage. Between 1968 and 1973 elected black local officials rose by 150 percent, but by 1973 they still made up only 0.5 percent of the more than 500,000 elected officials in the United States. Most of the gains were local positions of limited power. Of the 1,500 new black officials elected since 1968, two-thirds were city and county councilmen or school board members. In 1973 blacks were 11.5 percent of the population, but only 1 percent of U.S. senators, 2.3 percent of state senators, 3.5 percent of U.S. representatives, and 5.7 percent of state representatives. None of these proportions is sufficient to give blacks

Table 8-9. Elected black officials, 1960–1973

Office	1960	1969	1973
Total	NA	1,125	2,624
U.S. Congress	4	10	16
Representatives	4	9	15
Senators	—	1	1
State legislatures	36	172	238
Senators	6	27	42
Representatives	30	145	196
Mayors	NA	29	127
County councilmen, commissioners, and others	NA	86	211
City councilmen, aldermen, and others	NA	398	928
School board members	NA	304	744
Judges and Magistrates	NA	46	154
Constables, sheriffs, and marshalls	NA	33	115

Source: *Congressional Quarterly,* "Black Elected Officials," July 14, 1973, pp. 1887–1888, and "Detroit Win Reflects Growing Black Political Strength," September 12, 1969, pp. 1681–1684.

any real voice in public policymaking, let alone a representative share. And these dismal national averages do not disguise areas and states in which blacks are fairly represented. In 1970 only one state—Ohio— and one city—Jacksonville, Florida—had percentages of blacks on their lawmaking bodies even roughly proportional to the number of blacks in their populations.[25]

If the political changes which have occurred to date are less than momentous, the future does not promise radical advances. Though blacks will certainly continue to gain more equal representation and greater control in the areas in which they are concentrated, it is likely that they will soon reach a ceiling on their national and state-wide political power.

Despite the notable exception of Senator Edward Brooke in Massachusetts, blacks are still elected almost exclusively in areas in which they are a majority or a near majority of the voters (or as in Los Angeles, where they allied with another sizable minority voting block). Except for a few liberal communities such as Berkeley, California and Raleigh, North Carolina, most whites (and blacks) are still likely to vote along racial lines when choosing between a white and a black candidate. Thus, in 1972 of the fifteen black candidates who were elected to Congress, fourteen came from districts in which blacks made up at least 42 percent of the population. Only Ronald Dellums of California came from a district in which blacks were a relatively small minority—26 percent in 1972. On the other hand, of the black candidates who lost to whites in 1972, nine of eleven were in districts in which blacks were less than 35 percent of the population.[26]

At least as of 1972, blacks were seldom able to win area-wide political office if they were less than two-fifths of the population. Unless such racially antagonistic voting patterns change, the necessity for such large concentrations of black voters places severe limitations on the number of blacks who can be elected to Congress. Eleven of the fourteen congressional districts in which blacks make up 45 percent or more of the population are already represented by black congressmen. Though as many as twenty other districts have nearly two-fifths black population, fourteen are in the South where black voter registration and participation are lower.

It is unlikely that the requirement of near majority status among the voters can be met by increases in voter registration and participation. The rapid voter registration gains in the South in the 1960s will not be duplicated, and further reductions in the black/white registration gap will be difficult. Attempts to increase black registration before the second election of Mayor Stokes in Cleveland resulted in less than 2,000 additions at a cost of over $20 each.[27] Also, since voter participation is correlated with age and education, it is not likely that black voting rates will soon match those of whites. It is not even clear that black voting interest can be maintained. In 1964, 58 percent of the black voting age population cast their ballot, compared with 52 percent in 1972. While white voting also fell 7 percentage points from 71 to 64, the black share of the total declined.[28] Appar-

ently, the enthusiasm of the 1960s and the hopes of bringing about
change through the ballot box have given way to highly tempered
expectations in the 1970s. More blacks have come to believe that in
national elections their votes do not matter: according to a 1969 poll,
almost a fourth of black voters felt that it really did not make a
difference who was elected.[29]

Even in local elections, the maintenance of high levels of black
participation is not guaranteed. After the novelty of the "black takeover" of city hall has been replaced with the deadening realities of
intractable municipal problems, the maintenance of enthusiastic support in the black community may become more difficult. Never having
had city-wide political power, blacks in many cities may have overestimated its promise. For example, in the 1969 Newark mayoralty
election between Addonizo (white) and Gibson (black), 65 percent
of blacks thought they would be better off with a black mayor,
compared to 46 percent of whites believing they would be better off
with a white mayor.[30] After a few years of black rule, blacks may find
these hopes unfulfilled. One consequence may be declining voter
participation. After two years in the Cleveland mayor's office, Carl
Stokes discovered that declining numbers of black voters were likely
to go to the polls. As a result, he was forced to moderate his political
stance to attract additional white votes. Though this strategy succeeded in 1969, Stokes was replaced by a white in 1971.

Besides these specific difficulties in garnering the votes to put blacks
in elected positions, there are other clouds on the horizon of black
political gains. The continuing concentration of blacks in central cities
clearly insures increasing numbers of black mayors and congressmen,
but this concentration may have other less favorable ramifications.
State and national policymakers outside black dominated areas may
find it easier to ignore black interests. Increasingly, the battle between
state houses and city halls over the allocation of revenues and taxes
may take on racial overtones. This may lead to the anomaly of more
black representatives with less leverage to "bring home the bacon" to
their constituents.

One particularly touchy issue is metropolitization. To solve central
city problems, there will have to be increasingly close coordination
with surrounding suburban areas. Reorganization into metropolitan-

wide governmental units may be the only way to overcome class and racial differences. Yet black control may be diluted in the broader units. Blacks in central cities may be faced with the Hobson's choice of either struggling on their own without the power and the funds to solve their problems, or expanding the boundaries of their cities and thus diluting their power base. Studies in Cleveland, St. Louis, Miami, and Nashville have shown that black leaders are consistently opposed to metropolitization. As Julian Bond put it, "If there were no racial considerations, metropolitization would be desirable, but black people have to fight until they can get certain guarantees of equitable representation."[31]

Revenue sharing may be another threat. Any shift of authority from the federal government to the states is likely to diminish the leverage of blacks, since they are only a minority in any state and since few states have historically displayed as deep a commitment to black needs as the federal government. Though revenue sharing formulas provide for bypassing state governments to grant funds directly to municipal and other local governments, this mechanism does not assure more money and control for blacks in central cities. On the contrary, the allocation formulas proposed to date have tended to shift funds to the suburbs. If aid is to be passed out to every area rather than concentrated in those with the greatest needs (as categorical programs have tended to do in the past), blacks will get a reduced share.

Thus, though the numbers of black politicians in high elected offices are certain to keep rising for the next few years, it appears that these gains will fall short of providing blacks with equal representation. Voting patterns divided along racial lines and lower rates of black registration and participation mean that blacks outside the areas of greatest racial concentration will be unable to elect black officials, and that the blacks who are elected will be too few to have much leverage over legislative bodies. Moreover, trends toward residential separation of the races, metropolitization, and revenue sharing suggest that even the representation that is obtained will not result in much increase in the ability of black politicians to demand the programs and platforms which will benefit black people.

Limited Black Power

Expanded voting rights, higher income, and better jobs have given blacks more control over resources and more decision-making authority than in the past, but these gains have not been deep-rooted. In the labor market, blacks increased their share of better jobs, including professional and technical occupations, but less extensively in managerial and administrative positions. Blacks who rose to executive positions more often than not found themselves in staff rather than line positions, frequently involved in civil rights or community affairs. In the public sector, black gains have been concentrated in the agencies delivering services to a predominantly black clientele.

Union membership has expanded, but blacks remain grossly underrepresented among policymakers. Unions have generally supported black interests in national politics, but more because of common interests and a liberal ideology than because of black participation in decision-making. When black demands threaten union solidarity as in the case of quotas, union policymakers have been reluctant to support the minority.

Though black income has risen absolutely and relatively, there has been little change in the distribution of wealth. Blacks own little beyond low-cost homes and consumer durables. Business ownership, in particular, is limited. Black owned firms in 1969 accounted for only 0.3 percent of total receipts, with most being one or two man operations where net revenues were simply wages paid on a contract basis.

It is not surprising that increases in power and control have lagged behind the gains in income, occupation, voting rights, and union membership. It takes more time to change institutions than to help individuals, and longer to wrest power away from those who have built up control over the years. Yet the transfer of power and control is not automatic, and the lag may prove permanent.

It is very doubtful that rising income will ever result from or produce black business ownership on a large scale. Blacks will advance as they prove themselves on the job and there will be a gradual transfer out of staff and civil rights positions into general management. Black gains in unions are likely to be substantial as a result of governmental pressures, increasing representation, the aging of present leadership, and the threat of dual and competing unions. But in politics, the most decisive arena for the exercise of power, the future of black power is a question mark. More blacks are likely to gain elective positions, but their leverage may be limited and the rate of gain may be slow.

9

RACE AND SOCIAL CLASS

In most dimensions of socioeconomic status, blacks progressed dramatically during the 1960s. They doubled their real income; they moved into higher status occupations and higher paying jobs; they graduated from high school more regularly and went on to college more often. Yet some problems intensified. Buffeted by change, the black family deteriorated, dependency became widespread as more black men left the labor force, and black crime rates reached their highest levels ever.

One interpretation of these divergent developments is that blacks are increasingly divided into two groups—those who have succeeded and those who have been left behind. There seems to be a large group of blacks whose problems are becoming more severe and more intractable, an "underclass" locked in a vicious cycle of poverty or a "secondary labor market." Persons in this class share the characteristics of low income, poor health, unstable families, ghetto living environments, and dependence on welfare. They presumably share attitudes of alienation, "present orientedness," and apathy. Rising welfare, crime, and family deterioration are taken as evidence that this underclass has grown, or at least that its problems have intensified. At the other end of the spectrum, it is argued, stands the emerging black middle or upper class. Persons with higher incomes and education, and white-collar or craft jobs, are approaching equality with whites, and are presumed to share positive attitudes, a work orientation, a saving ethic, and a desire for upward mobility. Income, education, and employment gains all document that the number of those "making it" by any absolute standard is increasing.

These simultaneous, contradictory trends have been accepted as evidence of a growing polarity in black society along class lines. Rather than a basically homogeneous group set off by color and shared socioeconomic status, it has been assumed that blacks may now be composed of varied groups whose conflicting class interests are as important as their common racial ties.

This is a testable hypothesis. Data can be analyzed to determine whether there is a bipolarity in the patterns of socioeconomic change, with an elite or upper class advancing faster than those at the end of the line. Information can also be assessed to suggest whether dislocations have occurred among the less advantaged which have exacerbated or intensified their problems. Though the evidence on this issue is not unanimous, it provides little support for the theory of sharply diverging class lines within black society.

The Distribution of Income, Education, and Job Gains

Income, employment, and education are the crucial determinants of social class. Increasing bipolarity might be manifested in a shifting distribution of black income toward greater inequality, more rapid employment gains at the upper end of the labor queue, the evolution of an educated elite far removed from other blacks, or the geographical separation of black social classes. None of these patterns has emerged. Much of the evidence, in fact, suggests the opposite—that the gains in income, employment, and education were more rapid at the back of the line, resulting in greater rather than less equality among blacks.

1. *Income*. Since 1950 the distribution of income among blacks and whites has become slightly more equal, with a greater share going to those at the bottom and proportionately less to those at the top (table 9-1). Though black income is still less evenly distributed than that of whites, the patterns are converging. The average income of the top fifth of black families narrowed from 11.5 times the average of the bottom fifth in 1959 to 9.4 times in 1971. The ratio for whites fell from 7.4 to 7.1 (table 9-2).

Table 9-1. Percentage share of aggregate income received by each quintile of families, 1950–1971

Income rank	1950	1960	1971
Nonwhite			
Lowest fifth	3.5	3.8	4.7
Second	10.2	9.7	10.3
Third	17.6	16.5	16.4
Fourth	25.2	25.3	24.5
Highest	43.5	44.7	44.2
Top 5 percent	16.6	16.1	15.2
White			
Lowest fifth	4.8	5.3	5.8
Second	12.2	12.4	12.2
Third	17.3	17.6	17.4
Fourth	23.1	23.3	23.6
Highest	42.5	41.4	41.1
Top 5 percent	17.6	16.7	15.2

Source: U.S. Bureau of the Census, *Money Income in 1971 of Families and Persons in the United States,* Series P-60, no. 85, December 1972, table 14.

The distribution shifts are even more substantial when dollar figures are considered. The mean incomes of black families in all income classes rose rapidly during the decade, but the gains were greatest for the lowest income groups. Although blacks in the lowest quintile averaged only about one-sixth as much as the mean for all groups, their real incomes rose by 85 percent between 1959 and 1971, which was faster than for any other group—white or black. As income rose, the absolute gap between the top and bottom increased for both races, but this effect was less for blacks than for whites.

Most of the gain at the bottom of the income distribution came from increases in nonearned income. In 1959 unearned sources, mostly from welfare and social security, accounted for 26 percent of the income of nonwhite families making less than $3,000. By 1969 nonwhite families with less than $4,000 (roughly comparable to

Table 9-2. Mean income of white and nonwhite family quintiles, 1959 and 1971 (1971 dollars)

Income rank	1971				1959			
	Nonwhite	Ratio[a]	White	Ratio[a]	Nonwhite	Ratio[a]	White	Ratio[a]
Mean	$ 8,101	0.70	$12,005	1.04	$ 5,290	0.57	$ 9,638	1.05
Bottom fifth	1,904	0.16	3,482	0.30	1,032	0.11	2,651	0.29
Second fifth	4,172	0.36	7,324	0.63	2,541	0.28	6,072	0.66
Third fifth	6,642	0.57	10,445	0.90	4,366	0.47	8,579	0.93
Fourth fifth	9,922	0.86	14,167	1.22	6,640	0.72	11,277	1.22
Top fifth	17,901	1.55	24,672	2.13	11,880	1.29	19,663	2.13
Top 5 percent	24,666	2.13	34,102	2.94	17,359	1.88	31,040	3.36

Source: Derived from U.S. Bureau of the Census, *Money Income in 1971 of Families and Persons in the United States*, Series P-60, no. 85, December 1972, tables 3, 4, and 14; and Decennial Census, *Sources and Structure of Family Income, 1960*, Series PC(2)4C, tables 1 and 7.
[a] Ratio to the mean for all families.

$3,000 in 1959) received 42 percent from the unearned sources. If in-kind aid were added to these figures, the rise in unearned sources would be even more noticeable. Although the average earnings of these poor families actually fell during the decade, their overall incomes increased. The advances in income of the bottom quintile were thus achieved as a result of rising dependency rather than improvement in employment and earnings. There are, therefore, grounds for arguing that the sources rather than the level of income are important in assessing the rise of the underclass.

It should be noted, however, that an even sharper shift toward nonearned income occurred among white low income groups, whose earnings fell from 54 percent to 40 percent of their incomes. Thus, both whites and blacks have become more dichotomized into upper income quintiles of earners and in the bottom segment of dependents. The difference, of course, is that whites in the lowest fifth are older and more likely to be social security recipients, while blacks tend to be female family heads on welfare. But except for prevailing beliefs concerning the acceptability of the two kinds of dependency, there seems little justification for designating black, but not white, non-earners as an underclass.

2. *Labor market changes.* Although the greatest attention has been focused on blacks moving into professional, technical, and managerial jobs, the more extensive gains during the 1960s came at the lower end of the labor market as blacks moved out of unskilled labor and farm work and into semiskilled operative and clerical jobs. If the black occupational distribution had not changed since 1960, there would have been 400,000 fewer working in professional, technical, and managerial jobs in 1972, but 1.5 million more performing unskilled labor, farm, and service work. Upgrading at the bottom affected almost four times as many blacks as the entrance into upper echelon job classifications.

These employment gains by the less advantaged resulted in greater equality among blacks in the labor market. One measure which sug-gested this trend was the rising median to mean ratio of black earnings, which indicated that the middle and bottom of the labor force was improving its position more rapidly than the top. In 1960 the median earnings of nonwhite males age twenty-five to sixty-four

was 93 percent of the mean (compared with 87 percent for whites).[1]
By 1970 this ratio for black males was 98 percent (compared with 89
percent for whites), indicating that black earnings spread narrowed
more than that of whites.

If this evidence casts doubt on the hypothesis that there is a growing
dichotomy between blacks with good jobs and those without, a closer
look at the relatively few blacks who are "making it" in the labor
market further dispells this notion of polarity. The occupations of
blacks with high earnings indicate that, far from an emerging professional, technical, and managerial elite, almost half of black men
earning more than $10,000 are operatives, laborers, clerical, or
service workers. High earning black males are twice as likely as whites
to be in service, operative, or laboring occupations, and much less
likely to be in sales, craft, or managerial positions (table 9-3). In
addition, a much smaller share of blacks have high income; the
$10,000 to $15,000 income bracket which is middle class for whites is
upper class for blacks. Twelve percent of white males earned $15,000

Table 9-3. Occupation of males age 25 to 64 years earning more than
$10,000 in 1969

Occupation	$10,000–14,999		$15,000 or above	
	White	Black	White	Black
Total	100.0%	100.0%	100.0%	100.0%
Professional and technical	22.1	18.1	34.4	37.0
Managerial	16.4	8.3	31.8	18.1
Sales	7.6	2.5	11.5	4.6
Clerical	5.7	8.0	3.0	5.2
Crafts	28.0	22.0	11.4	13.5
Operatives	8.3	16.2	2.0	6.0
Transport operatives	4.8	9.0	1.6	5.3
Laborers.	1.7	6.8	0.6	3.9
Service	3.7	8.7	1.4	5.5
Farmers	1.5	0.2	2.3	0.6
Farm laborers	0.2	0.2	—	0.2
Private household workers	—	—	—	—

Source: U.S. Bureau of the Census, *Earnings by Occupation and Education*, Series
PC(2)8D, January 1973, tables 1 and 2.

or more in 1969, about the same as the 13 percent of blacks earning above $10,000. Comparing these top groups, two-thirds of whites were professional workers or managers compared with only a third of blacks; operatives, laborers, and service workers accounted for 37 percent of black males but only 6 percent of whites.

More detailed occupational data document the fact that many blacks are "making it" by earning good money in less than glamorous jobs. In 1970 out of the 324,000 black males earning more than $10,000, 3 percent were engineers, 5 percent were teachers, and 2 percent were physicians or dentists (table 9-4). While these jobs

Table 9-4. Selected occupations of black men age 25 to 64 years earning more than $10,000 in 1969

Laborers	20,534
Construction craftsmen, except carpenters	14,015
Truck drivers	12,460
Teachers	11,594
Salesmen	9,228
Engineers	7,348
Mechanics, except auto	7,303
Metal workers	6,637
Physicians and dentists	6,555
Policemen and detectives	6,305
Auto mechanics	5,887
Public officials and administrators	4,667
Engineering science technicians	4,396
Bus drivers	4,119
Carpenters	3,353
Printers	1,839
Health technicians	1,541
Taxi drivers	1,458
Farmers and farm workers	1,329
Firemen	1,201
Other technicians	921
Barbers	841

Source: U.S. Bureau of the Census, *Earnings by Occupation and Education*, Series PC(2)8D, January 1973, tables 1 and 2.

correspond to the conventional image of success, there were more high-earning black male construction workers than teachers, more mechanics than engineers, and more truck drivers than physicians and dentists. So far, at least, the emerging black middle class is not composed exclusively of a white-collar elite, but of a relatively broad cross-section of well-paid workers in all occupations.

3. *Educational improvement.* Between 1960 and 1972 the college enrollment of blacks grew nearly 400 percent, and the economic status of blacks with college training also improved. Young (age twenty-five to thirty-four) black males with at least a year of college had an average income nearly half again as high as black high school graduates, and nine-tenths that of whites with the same education.

But most of the aggregate improvement in the educational (and economic) status of blacks came from the greater frequency of high school graduation rather than increased college attendance. If black college attainment had not improved during the 1960s, there would have been 590,000 fewer nonwhites with some college education. If the high school completion rate were the same, however, there would have been 3 million fewer blacks with a diploma. In 1969 the mean income of nonwhite high school graduates was 29 percent higher than among dropouts, and 28 percent lower than of those with some college education. Because average individual gains were similar, high school graduation was about five times as important a factor in economic gains as college attendance since five times as many individuals were involved.

If an educated elite were developing, it might be reflected in growing disparities between the incomes of highly educated and unschooled blacks. But though the percentage gap between the incomes of white high school and elementary school graduates nearly doubled from 1958 to 1972, the differential for nonwhites changed only modestly (table 9-5). Throughout the period, the income of white and nonwhite men with one or more years of college has remained between 25 and 34 percent higher than that of high school graduates. The comparatively small group with the least education is being left slightly further behind, but the dichotomization according to this measure is less among blacks than whites.

Table 9-5. Differences in median annual income by years of school completed for white and nonwhite men age 25 years and over, 1958–1972

Year	High school and elementary school		College and high school	
	White	Nonwhite	White	Nonwhite
	(percent difference)			
1958	42	29	25	23
1961	43	35	24	26
1963	49	40	22	27
1964	58	23	28	28
1966	53	41	28	24
1967	51	46	28	31
1968	52	35	27	29
1969	58	43	25	25
1970	62	47	34	34
1971	66	39	31	31
1972	74	37	26	22

Source: U.S. Bureau of the Census, *Current Population Reports,* Series P-60, annual issues.

There is contrary evidence suggesting that the most educated blacks are more rapidly improving their earning status relative to whites. From 1959 to 1969 black men with at least four years of college education raised their earnings from 55 to 71 percent of similarly educated whites. For those who had not reached high school, the black/white proportions rose from 62 to 70 percent. Apparently, opportunities are opening up fastest for those with college degrees.

Despite these greater gains for the most educated, the predominance of college graduates among the black elite is cast in doubt by closer analysis of the education of blacks with high earnings. Among nonwhites earning $10,000 or more, high school dropouts are the most numerous of any education cohort, although individually, of course, dropouts are much less likely to reach this earnings level (table 9-6). On the other hand, 53 percent of black male workers with a college education earned $10,000 or more, but these better educated males accounted for only 22 percent of black high earners.

In terms, then, of the fundamental measures of socioeconomic status and the traditional parameters of class, there is no evidence of a

Table 9-6. Education of males age 25 to 64 years earning $10,000 or more, 1969

Years of education	Percent of all earning over $10,000	
	Black	White
11 or less	35.9	22.6
12	28.4	31.6
13 to 15	13.7	15.7
16	8.7	14.7
17 and over	13.2	15.3

Years of education	Likelihood of earning over $10,000	
	Black	White
11 or less	5.6	22.5
12	12.1	37.5
13 to 15	19.5	49.0
16	31.8	68.1
17 and over	53.0	70.9

Source: U.S. Bureau of the Census, *Earnings by Occupation and Education,* Series PC(2)8B, January 1973, tables 1 and 2.

bifurcation among blacks. Those groups which were best off at the start of the decade advanced significantly in income, education, and employment, but those who were worse off advanced even more. If anything, equality increased.

Problems Despite Progress

Despite these across-the-board gains and basically unaltered class patterns, several developments may have offset these improvements, especially among the more disadvantaged groups.

1. *Deteriorating family status.* Higher incomes and better jobs might have been expected to lead to more stable black families, but in fact the opposite development occurred. From 1960 to 1970 the percentage of black families which were husband-wife units fell from 75 to 69 percent, and the percentage of children who were in families with both parents declined from 75 to 64 percent.[2]

Since the growing numbers of black female family heads were unable to participate in the labor force, the employment gains of the 1960s passed them by. As a result, most of the deterioration in the black family status coincided with low or at best middle income status.

| Year | Total | Nonwhite families with husband and wife present | | |
		Bottom 3 income deciles	Middle 3 income deciles	Top 4 income deciles
1960	75 percent	59 percent	80 percent	87 percent
1970	69	47	71	87

At the very bottom of the income scale broken families with children became the predominant group in poverty. Females headed six of every ten poor families in 1970, double the rate a decade earlier.

Stable husband-wife families advanced most rapidly. In 1972 they had attained a median income 75 percent of white husband-wife families, an increase from 64 percent in 1966. Most of the advance was due to increasing employment by wives. In 1959, 65 percent of the wives in nonwhite husband-wife families worked; by 1969 the proportion rose to 77 percent. The median income of black families with a working wife was three-fifths greater than for those with one breadwinner, compared with a third higher in 1959. To an increasing degree middle and upper income families are those which have the husband and wife present, with the latter contributing significantly to the higher standard of living.

There is a similar dichotomization when marital and educational patterns are considered. In 1960 the average education of black husbands was about the same as that of unmarried men. But in 1970 the husbands tended to have better than average school attainment, suggesting that those with lesser education and lesser earning potential were the ones who were failing to establish stable marriages.

2. *Rising crime rates.* Violent black crime increased sharply in the 1960s in both absolute and relative terms. In 1950 blacks were arrested five times more often than whites for robbery.[3] By 1972 blacks in urban areas were twenty times more likely than whites to be charged with this offense (table 9-7). From 1964 to 1972 black arrest rates for rape, murder, robbery, and homicide increased 73 percent while rates for whites rose 63 percent (table 9-8).

It has been suggested that these statistics, which are based on FBI

Table 9-7. Arrests for violent crime in urban areas, 1972 (rate per 100,000 population)

Arrest	Black	White
Murder and nonnegligent manslaughter	80	5
Rape	83	7
Robbery	592	29
Aggravated assault	595	68

Source: Derived from U.S. Department of Justice, *Uniform Crime Reports 1972* (Washington: Government Printing Office).

Table 9-8. Arrest rates for violent crimes,[a] 1964–1972 (urban arrest rate per 100,000 population)

Year	White	Black
1964	67	780
1965	70	855
1966	72	841
1967	77	960
1968	84	1,057
1969	86	1,174
1970	97	1,191
1971	99	1,310
1972	109	1,353

Source: Office of Management and Budget, *Social Indicators 1972* (Washington: Government Printing Office, 1973), p. 70.
[a] Homicide, robbery, aggravated assault, rape.

compilations, overstate the relative incidence of black crime because they reflect arrests rather than the actual commission of crimes. Selective enforcement and prejudice by white police officers, it is argued, inflate the figures. While it is plausible to use this rationale to dismiss much of the higher black rates for prostitution, carrying concealed weapons, and gambling, the predispositions of the police can have much less effect on arrests for robbery and murder.

Obviously, the higher incidence of violent crime is related to the age and economic status of blacks. Violent crime is far more likely among the young, and property crime is much more likely among the poor. Since more than half of all black men are under twenty-two and a third of all blacks are in poverty, demographic factors alone would be expected to raise the incidence of crime.

But poverty and youth by themselves are insufficient explanations for violent black crime. Those arrested for the crimes most associated with poverty,—property crimes—are no more likely to be black (31.5 percent) than the black proportion among the poor (31.5 percent). But blacks were 56 percent of those arrested for violent crimes in 1971. Moreover, if poverty were the key factor underlying black violence, there would be no explanation for rapidly increasing crime rates during a period of socioeconomic progress.

Several studies have found that even if poverty and other factors are taken into account, black rates would still be as much as three times higher for violent crimes.[4] For example, Puerto Ricans are a similar proportion of the population of New York City as blacks (15 percent compared to 20 percent). The socioeconomic status, ghetto living environments, and youthful population of the two groups are also quite comparable. Yet in 1972 blacks were 63 percent of those arrested for violent crimes, while Hispanics were only 15 percent.[5]

3. *Increasing dependency and declining male labor force participation.* Blacks are overrepresented among recipients of welfare and in-kind assistance, even when their higher incidence of poverty is considered. Forty-three percent of all welfare families in 1971 were black, as were 41 percent of food stamp recipients, and 47 percent of families in public housing, exceeding in each case the 29 percent of the poor who were black. The black share of welfare dollars has not increased in recent years; however, the rapid growth of welfare has raised the number of blacks dependent on public assistance. In 1961, 8 percent of black families were welfare recipients; a decade later this proportion had risen to 21 percent.

At the same time as dependency was rising, black male labor force participation was declining, again more rapidly than among whites. Although some of this drop was due to increased school attendance and earlier retirement, participation by blacks of prime working ages between twenty-five and fifty-four also fell from 95 in 1960 to 90 percent a dozen years later. This compared with a drop from 97 to 96 percent for whites. While some of this drop may have resulted from greater disability coverage, part of it, no doubt, reflects the greater availability of welfare support.

Is There an Underclass?

The rise in black crime, dependency, nonparticipation in the labor force, and broken families all give cause for concern. But merely to catalogue these problems and to demonstrate that they are more prevalent among blacks with low income, education, and inadequate employment and earnings does not prove the existence of an underclass. Identification and substantiation are, in fact, very difficult.

At the very outset the definition of the "underclass" is elusive. Is it the less than 1 percent of blacks who are criminals or the 10 percent of prime working age males who do not participate in the labor force? Does it include the 21 percent of blacks who are on welfare or the 36 percent who are not in husband-wife families? Moreover, since there are more whites in every category than blacks, why is it a black underclass? Do blacks become underclass when the relative incidence of some problem or condition reaches a level, say, 50 percent greater than that of whites? The arbitrariness of these definitions casts doubt on attempts to isolate presumed members of the underclass.

If the definition of an underclass is difficult to pin down, a theory explaining its existence is even more difficult to construct. The concept of an underclass rests on the notion that its members are in some way trapped in their condition. Terms such as the "vicious cycle of poverty," "dependency syndrome," and "secondary labor market" seek to describe the pernicious interaction of social and institutional factors which prevents blacks at the bottom from escaping upward. Not merely the isolated impacts of segregation in housing and discrimination in employment and education are involved. The evidence indicates that, on the average, blacks do not end up with the same income even when they have the same education and training and live in the same regions. Rather, the interaction of many factors multiplies effects, with poorer schools leading to poorer jobs, and less income leading to poor neighborhoods and poorer schools. The impacts may be long run or less direct. Attitudes and self-confidence may be affected by insensitive teachers, parents with low expectations, or a lack of success models to emulate. Criminal records may foreclose future options and a childhood spent on welfare may nurture attitudes of dependency and despair.

But though the existence of pervasive institutional mechanisms continues to insure the failure of many disadvantaged blacks, it is doubtful that these debilitating impacts got worse during the past decade. If earnings and income gaps other than those related to education, age, and other factors are indications of the barriers holding blacks back, then the absolute and relative gains of those more disadvantaged suggest that some of the barriers fell during the decade. There has never been any evidence of a "welfare ethic" transmitted from one generation to another, and the broadly improving social and economic status of blacks indicates that the compounded impacts of disadvantages must be slackening. Even the damaging influence of a criminal record may have lessened as laws and practices have changed.

The difficulty of establishing a firm statistical definition of the underclass and the insufficiency of "trapping" as a complete explanation for worsening problems leads to a focus on attitudes and values. The assumption is that the common denominator of the black underclass is a sense of alienation from accepted middle class values—such as stability, investing in the future, and the male responsibility to provide for a family. It may be argued that though middle class values are the natural outgrowth of most white children's experience, they may be less obvious to blacks whose upbringing is aimed at "getting by" rather than "getting ahead." Among blacks who have been denied control of property and the right to invest in their own futures, the inclination to save for a rainy day may be less developed. Though society's prevailing ethic has been one of male dominance, black men have frequently been excluded from jobs with wages sufficient to support families, let alone from positions of power and control. The apparently quicker acceptance of a dependent status in society, the higher incidence of violent crimes, and the unstable family patterns which are evident among a minority of blacks might be the product of a hard-to-change set of values which have been produced by years of having no stake in society.

The presumption of broad differences in attitude must be made with caution. Surveys of black welfare mothers find that they want no less for their children than whites.[6] Black students have as high or higher academic goals than others.[7] Among disadvantaged black males there is such a variance in work ethic that averages may be misleading.[8] Still, the higher incidence of crime, dependency, and family deterioration among some blacks suggests that attitudes and values as well as socioeconomic status are involved.

The impact of the alienated values of some groups within black society may have been multiplied by the increased social and physical isolation of blacks. The negative spillover effects may also be increased because blacks are a more homogeneous group forced together by the common experience of discrimination. The ethic of an entire group can be determined or changed when a certain "critical mass" of beliefs or attitudes is established. In schools where many students shun homework or disparage academic excellence, such attitudes affect all but the most dedicated students. In a ghetto in which the most envied successes are streetwise hustlers or rebellious "badmen" who use physical force to overcome white oppression, it should be expected that attitudes toward trickery and violence would be more tolerant. In areas where illegitimate childbirth, welfare dependency, or crime are common, such behavior may be less likely to be condemned. Similarly, recent analyses of drug addiction have shown that epidemics of drug abuse follow a pattern of social contagion—in a group or society in which it is "cool" to use drugs, virtually everyone will try them.

Thus, the effects of a critical mass of alienated beliefs may be more damaging to black society as a whole, simply because the have-nots in the central cities outnumber the haves. This problem of a dominant ethic established by the large percentage in the lower class may be exacerbated by the lack of alternatives for rising blacks to physically and perhaps psychologically separate themselves from the others. Those who are able to overcome housing discrimination to live in the suburbs are criticized for abandoning their race. Yet the value system in the ghetto often seems intractably opposed to middle class values, so that to be "truly black" and to be middle class is perceived by some as a contradiction in terms.[9]

The questions remain: Why have these attitudes become more pervasive during a decade of evident progress? Why is dependency and family deterioration more prevalent today than a decade ago despite income and employment gains which should have facilitated greater marital stability? Why should the socialization process for men—the pattern of accepting adult responsibilities, including education, jobs, and marriages, and of giving up the "wild oats" of teenage years—be lengthening as the barriers to black men entering and sharing in society are falling? Several factors may have been involved.

First, the growth of society's wealth made dependency or nonworking status far more feasible. Pension benefits, unemployment insurance, welfare payments, and a variety of other income supports expanded. Among whites, the growth of dependency was manifested in longer support for children's educations, earlier retirements, and the expansion of institutional nursing care for the elderly. Among blacks it has appeared not only in these areas but also in increased welfare dependency and lower male labor force participation. Even the growth of hustling and street life in the ghettos may be traced in part to the increase of society's wealth: there is simply more "fat" in society off which to live.

Second, the economic developments of the past generation have outstripped the capacities of some uneducated and unskilled individuals to contribute to society. It should be no surprise that blacks, who were overrepresented in the shrinking areas of employment and underrepresented in the expanding post-industrial jobs, have had greater difficulty weathering this transition than whites. More have been left with little to contribute to society and no alternatives but dependency.

Third, paternal government policies have tended to place black men in a dependent status. Because political consensus is easiest to achieve in support of programs designed to help women and children, most government social aid has been funneled through women. The infinitely more difficult job of equalizing the footing of black male providers has received less attention. At the same time, the status of black females in the employment market has been steadily equalized with whites, again because this involves no difficult compromises (equality among those in inferior status being easy to grant). From this perspective, the growth of institutionally supported dependency among blacks and the possibly attendant deterioration of family stability is not a symptom of pathology but the result of rational decision-making by blacks in reaction to economic realities created by well-intentioned but ill-conceived governmental efforts.

Fourth, the increase in racial concentration has probably augmented the spillover effects of alienated values, and as a result the spread of these values may have achieved a momentum independent of socio-economic change or government policy. Although legal efforts to desegregate the schools and to end housing discrimination were pushed by government, they did not counterbalance the more powerful trends toward residential separation of the races.

The answer to the question, "Is there a black underclass?" must be equivocal. If an underclass is taken to be a specific group of individuals who have been forced by society into positions of inferiority, then the answer to the question would be a qualified "no." Though society already discriminates against all blacks and thus raises their chances of failure, there is no *single* set of individuals who can be identified as those who have been held at the bottom of black society by insidious institutional mechanisms.

On the other hand, if underclass is understood as meaning a vague but pervasive set of nonmiddle class values which have developed among greater numbers of blacks as a result of centuries of enforced second class status, then the answer would seem to be "yes." Though such differences in values and attitudes may be small and difficult to document, they do offer some explanation for the simultaneous trends of progress and pathology. Certainly, if such a set of values exists, its spillover impacts would be greatest among blacks.

If attitudes developed among those denied opportunities may explain part of the negative developments of the decade, it appears that their impacts have been magnified by a combination of economic trends, governmental policies, and continuing racial isolation. The issue is whether deterioration may continue as a result of these factors or whether it may be reversed. Government has limited leverage over the technological developments which will continue to create specialized occupations and growing numbers of nonworkers supported by society's great productivity. On the other hand, public policy may have profound impacts on racial equality and racial separation. If federal social welfare efforts should shift from "treating the symptom" by increasing welfare benefits to "treating the cause" by equalizing the status of black men as providers, the impacts might be dramatic. If income supplements to the working poor were adopted, welfare reform might become a moot issue. Similarly, governmental policy effectively committed to integrating housing and schooling might have impressive long-run effects. Not only might the spillover effects of racial isolation be mitigated, but the pervasiveness of discrimination in employment might be eased.

Even if such intervention is unsuccessful, however, there are grounds for optimism. Ultimately, progress toward equality in income, education, and employment should dissolve the legacy of alienated values fostered by centuries of racism. Gradually, the growing numbers of black successes in the middle and upper classes will become models, influencing the aspirations and attitudes of coming generations. Though there may be a lag between changes in socioeconomic status and those in values, progress toward equal opportunity must eventually be reflected in all aspects of social development.

PART 2

BLACKS AND THE GOVERNMENT

10

SUPPLEMENTING INCOME

There has been a massive expansion of income maintenance programs over the last decade. In 1960, $26 billion was paid out under social security, public employee retirement, veterans', unemployment, and workmen's compensation, public assistance, and several smaller programs (table 10-1). By 1973 these cash payments had increased almost fourfold to $96 billion.

Black Benefits and Beneficiaries

Blacks were among the primary beneficiaries of these expanding transfer programs. More frequently unemployed, injured on the job, disabled, and most of all poor, they were more often eligible for social welfare benefits addressed to such problems. In 1971 a fourth of black families and a fifth of unrelated individuals reported receiving welfare or public assistance; 18 percent of families and 27 percent of unrelated individuals got social security payments; a seventh of families and a tenth of individuals received either unemployment benefits, workmen's compensation, government employee pensions or veterans' benefits (table 10-2). The $6.1 billion reported from these sources (which understates the amount actually received) accounted for 13 percent of all black income.

Black income maintenance recipients tend to be younger, to have more children, to live more often in female-headed families, and most

207

Table 10-1. Public income maintenance programs, 1960 and 1973

Program	Benefits (millions)		Percent total 1972	1970 benefits 1960 benefits
	1960	1973		
Total	$25,873	$95,931	100.0	3.7
Social security	11,081	51,130	53.3	4.6
Public employee retirement	2,598	14,627	15.2	5.6
Public assistance	3,263	11,396	11.9	3.5
Veterans' pensions and compensation	3,437	6,439	6.7	1.9
Unemployment compensation (including railroad)	3,025	4,554	4.7	1.5
Workmens' compensation	860	3,600	3.8	4.2
Railroad retirement	942	2,565	2.7	2.7
Temporary disability benefits	368	803	0.8	2.2
Lump-sum benefits	300	696	0.7	2.3
Training allowances	—	120	0.1	—

Source: *Social Security Bulletin* (June 1974), p. 25.

of all to be poorer than white beneficiaries. In 1971 over one-third of all black family heads receiving social security benefits were women, compared with less than a fifth of whites. There was an average of one child in each black family receiving social security, two and one-half times as many as among white recipient families. Perhaps most significantly, a third of black families receiving social security were poor, three times the rate for white families. Under the public assistance program, similar patterns prevailed (table 10-3). Three-fifths of black recipient families were poor compared to less than half of whites and two-thirds were headed by females compared with 43 percent among whites.

Table 10-2. Black beneficiaries of income maintenance programs, 1971

Program	Number black beneficiaries (thousands)	Blacks as percent of all beneficiaries	Average annual benefit of black recipients	Black average as percent of overall average benefits	Estimated total benefits to blacks[a] ($ millions)
Social security, government, and railroad retirement					
Families	930	9	$1,733	81	$1,612
Unrelated individuals	507	8	1,185	84	601
					2,213
Public assistance					
Families	1,301	37	1,838	113	2,391
Unrelated individuals	398	30	1,133	110	451
					2,842
Unemployment compensation, workmen's compensation, government pensions, veterans' benefits					
Families	699	8	1,249	82	873
Unrelated individuals	197	9	1,109	76	218
					1,092

Source: U.S. Bureau of the Census, *Money Income in 1971 of Families and Persons in the United States*, P-60, no. 85, December 1972, table 42.
a. Income receipts from transfer payments are less than estimated payouts under transfer programs because of underreporting.

Table 10-3. Characteristics of families and unrelated individuals receiving public assistance income in 1971

Selected characteristics	Total		Male head		Female head	
	Black	White	Black	White	Black	White
Families						
Total (thousands)	1,301	2,156	421	1,219	880	936
Percent of all families	25	5	12	3	54	21
With related children under 18 years (thousands)	1,067	1,471	266	722	801	748
Mean number of related children under 18 years	2.84	2.46	3.11	2.58	2.75	2.35
Median age of head	40.7	43.7	54.1	49.7	35.8	38.2
Percent with head 65 years and over	17	20	31	26	10	13
Median family income	$3,353	$4,117	$4,750	$4,947	$2,997	$3,298
Percent below poverty level	61	45	42	36	70	57
Unrelated Individuals						
Total (thousands)	398	910	110	265	288	645
Percent of all unrelated individuals	21	6	12	5	29	7
Median age	65+	65+	54.6	62.2	65+	65+
Percent 65 and over	50	58	30	43	58	65
Percent below poverty level	75	66	85	66	72	66

Source: U.S. Bureau of the Census, *The Social and Economic Status of the Black Population in the United States, 1972*, Series 23, no. 46, July 1973, table 24.

Increasing Welfare (AFDC) Dependency

A dramatic rise in welfare dependency was one of the significant developments for blacks during the 1960s. In 1971 there were an estimated 1.1 million black families receiving Aid to Families with Dependent Children (AFDC), triple the number a decade earlier (table 10-4). While the AFDC caseload rose at only a slightly slower

Table 10-4. AFDC beneficiaries, 1961 and 1971 (numbers in thousands)

	1961	1971	Percentage increase
Number of families	823	2,524	207
White	425	1,220	187
Black	357	1,093	207
Other	42	211	406
Number of children	2,457	7,015	185
White	1,198	3,184	166
Black	1,134	3,199	182
Other	125	632	406

Source: U.S. Department of Health, Education, and Welfare, Welfare Administration, *Study of Recipients of Aid to Families with Dependent Children, November-December 1961: National Cross-Tabulations,* August 1965, tables 2 and 53; and U.S. Department of Health, Education, and Welfare, Social and Rehabilitation Service, *Findings of the 1971 AFDC Study, Part I. Demographic and Program Characteristics,* December 22, 1971, table 2.

rate for whites, its base as a percentage of the white population was much lower and the aggregate impact much less consequential. Fewer than three in every hundred white families was supported by AFDC in 1971, compared with one in five black families. In 1971 one of every twenty white children was in a family on welfare, compared with two-fifths of black youths.

Legislation, court decisions, and administrative actions extending and liberalizing eligibility were largely responsible for the dramatic growth of public assistance payments.[1] Some of these changes opened

AFDC to groups which included large numbers of blacks. For example, the provisions which allowed benefits for families with unemployed heads were important for blacks, since almost a third of poor unemployed family heads are black. Similarly, the 1968 Supreme Court decision which struck down the "man in the house" rule (which had held the male in an AFDC home responsible for the children's support) may have permitted many black households to continue to receive welfare payments. The courts' invalidation of residency requirements may also have helped more black migrants to obtain welfare eligibility.

While these legal and administrative changes made welfare more readily available, other developments increased the need for and reliance on it, especially among blacks.

1. Differential changes in the universe of need contributed somewhat to the faster growth of dependency among blacks. The number of white children under eighteen years increased by 11 percent between 1960 and 1970, compared with 25 percent among nonwhites. More crucially, the number in poverty declined by one-third of whites, while it fell less than a fourth for blacks.

2. Changes in marital and family patterns also swelled the number of potentially dependent families. Between 1960 and 1971 the proportion of all black families headed by women rose from 22 to 32 percent. More detailed data for the period from 1967 to 1971 reveal that the number of black female family heads rose by 361,000 (table 10-5). A large proportion of the 540,000 growth in black welfare families could thus have been the result of rising numbers of families headed by women. It is important to note, however, that the incidence of dependency increased among all female family heads, so that it is not just a question of break-ups causing or being caused by relief.

3. The growth of black dependency may also have resulted from the increased acceptability or inevitability of welfare. The National Welfare Rights Organization and antipoverty community action agencies asserted black rights to welfare and informed potential clients. More widespread dependency itself probably reduced the onus connected with welfare. In central city ghetto areas where dependency is frequent, where the black middle class is limited, and where there is little contact with white society, welfare may be as acceptable as tax

Table 10-5. Total black females, black female family heads, and AFDC recipients, 1967 and 1971

Year and age	Total (thousands)	Family heads (thousands)	Mothers receiving AFDC (thousands)	Numbers receiving AFDC as percent of	
				All women	Family heads
1971					
Total	8,428	1,633	1,093	13	67
14 to 19 years	1,575	227[a]	95	6	145[b]
20 to 24 years	1,085		234	22	
25 to 34 years	1,520	423	374	25	88
35 to 44 years	1,305	381	238	18	62
45 years and over	2,943	602	120	5	22
1967					
Total	7,461	1,272	553	7	43
14 to 19 years	1,368	103[a]	31	2	111[b]
20 to 24 years	865		83	10	
25 to 34 years	1,321	316	198	15	63
35 to 44 years	1,273	306	147	12	48
45 years and over	2,634	574	71	3	13
Increase 1967–1971					
Total	868	361	540	—	—
14 to 19 years	207	124[a]	64	—	—
20 to 24 years	221		51	—	—
25 to 34 years	199	107	176	—	—
35 to 44 years	32	75	91	—	—
45 years and over	209	55	59	—	—

Source: U.S. Bureau of the Census, Series P-60, nos. 59 and 85, and unpublished data based on studies conducted by the U.S. Department of Health, Education, and Welfare.

[a] 14 to 24 years.

[b] Greater than 100 percent because many younger female recipients live in subfamilies.

avoidance among affluent whites. On the other hand, the lack of earning opportunities for black women in the ghetto may have led to deepening feelings of resignation and increased willingness to go on welfare. Generally, low income blacks are more likely to be on welfare than similar whites. In 1961, 21 percent of poor black families with children under eighteen were on AFDC rolls; white recipients represented only 11 percent of the white poor. By 1971 the comparable proportions had increased to 87 and 51 percent.

Problems With the Welfare System

By the end of the 1960s, taxpayers and policymakers were becoming increasingly concerned with the mushrooming cost of AFDC. The fundamental issue was money, but other problems were apparent. First, with welfare benefits rising more rapidly than average earnings, and frequently comparable to the wages available to unskilled and deficiently educated female heads, the incentives to get off welfare were often lacking, particularly where welfare could be supplemented with earnings without losing AFDC payments. Moreover, welfare payments in combination with in-kind aid frequently created notch problems in which full-time employment could actually cause a drop in real income. As a result of these factors dependency was often a long-term affair, especially for blacks.[2] Nearly two of every five black families on welfare in 1971 had been on the rolls three years or more (compared with a fourth of white families) (table 10-6). That 28 percent of black recipients in 1971 have been on the rolls less than one year, and 62 percent less than three years, was less a testament to rapid turnover than to the near doubling of the caseload between 1968 and 1971. While welfare was not a one-way street, recipients once qualified tended to remain on the rolls as long as they were eligible.

Second, the welfare system apparently contributed to family deterioration, especially among blacks. In almost three-fourths of black recipient families, compared with two-fifths of the white families, the father was not present in 1971 because of separation, desertion, or other reasons. Half of black welfare mothers reported not knowing where the father resided, compared with 30 percent among white

Table 10-6. Length of time since the family joined the AFDC rolls, 1961 and 1971

Length of time	White families		Black families	
	1961	1971	1961	1971
Total (thousands)	425	1,220	357	1,093
Percent	100.0	100.0	100.0	100.0
Less than 6 months	20.1	21.2	13.2	13.4
6 months to 1 year	16.3	20.0	15.1	15.1
1 to 3 years	26.3	33.1	29.0	33.5
3 to 5 years	14.1	12.2	18.3	15.2
5 to 10 years	15.4	9.1	17.1	14.8
Over 10 years	7.8	4.3	7.2	7.8
Unknown	—	0.3	—	0.3

Source: U.S. Social and Rehabilitation Service, Department of Health, Education, and Welfare, *Study of Recipients of Aid to Families with Dependent Children, November-December 1971: National Cross-Tabulations,* August 1965, table 34; and *Findings of the 1971 AFDC Study* (unpublished table).

recipients. In a fourth of all white welfare families, but only a tenth of black households, the father was present, usually either incapacitated or unemployed. Roughly half of all the black children on welfare were born out of wedlock, compared with less than a fifth of whites.[3]

While the impacts of welfare on work behavior and family patterns are uncertain, and while any negative effects must be balanced by the benefits of increased income, charges that expansion had gotten out of hand, especially among blacks, became increasingly widespread during the late 1960s and early 1970s. A number of reforms were suggested. One proposal was the Family Assistance Plan (FAP) offered by President Nixon in 1969. FAP would have been structured to offer greater work incentives and would have been available to male-headed families, hopefully forestalling the breakup of families. But instead of welfare reform such as FAP, Congress enacted legislation requiring all able welfare recipients to register for work and providing funds for job creation subsidies. In a number of cases, aggressive efforts were launched to purge the relief rolls of cheaters. In some cases benefits levels were reduced.

The result was a slowdown in the growth of benefits and beneficiaries.

Year	Caseload growth	Average benefit increase
1967–1968	17 percent	4.0 percent
1968–1969	23	4.7
1969–1970	36	6.8
1970–1971	14	1.6
1971–1972	6	0.1

Source: *Social Security Bulletin* (August 1973), table M-25.

Between 1971 and 1972 the average AFDC payment per family remained almost constant (declining in real terms) while the caseload grew by only 6 percent.

Future welfare policies are uncertain, but unless there are dramatic changes it is unlikely that the number of dependent blacks will grow as it did in the 1960s. Work opportunities have continued to expand, while the number of poor black female family heads not on welfare has continued to decline. On the other hand, any modifications which would provide income supplements to low-wage earners would have a disproportionate influence on blacks. In March 1972 three of every ten black male labor force participants had inadequate employment or earnings. More than 850,000 were household heads with earnings in the previous year which were inadequate to lift their families out of poverty, and they accounted for a fourth of all male heads with employment and earnings problems.[4] Income supplements might help to stem the tide of marital deterioration but would increase the already high levels of dependency among blacks.

Aid to the Aged, Blind, and Disabled

In addition to families with dependent children, three other needy groups are assisted by Social Security programs: poor persons age sixty-five and over under Old Age Assistance (OAA); those with severe visual impairment under Aid to the Blind (AB); and the disabled under Aid to the Permanently and Totally Disabled (APTD). Needy persons not eligible for one of these federally-subsidized programs or for AFDC may receive state and locally-funded General Assistance (GA). Even combined, these other programs aid only about a third as many persons as AFDC and blacks tend to get a smaller share of benefits than under AFDC; but their total impact is significant. If it is assumed that blacks received payments proportionate to their share of clients, total benefits equaled over $1.2 billion in 1971 (table 10-7).

Table 10-7. Black share of aid to the blind, disabled, aged, and general assistance, 1972

Type of aid	Percent total recipients	Estimated number of black recipients (thousands)	Total money payment (millions)	Estimated payment going to blacks (millions)
Total	29	1,056	$3,939	$1,157
Aid to the blind	30	24	101	30
Aid to the permanently and totally disabled	29	320	1,189	345
Old age assistance	24	486	1,888	453
General assistance	43[a]	226	761	327

Source: *Social Security Bulletin* (May 1973), tables M-25 and M-26; and U.S. Department of Health, Education, and Welfare, *Trend Report,* October 6, 1972.
[a] Estimated as the black share of AFDC.

The number of Old Age Assistance recipients has remained relatively stable in recent years because of the increased availability of regular contributory social security (OASDI), which now covers all persons seventy-two and over and reaches more than nine-tenths of those over age sixty-five. About half of the nearly 2 million OAA recipients also get OASDI benefits. The number of elderly poor also declined from 5.6 million in 1959 to 4.3 million in 1971. Yet the number of nonwhite elderly poor increased from 774,000 in 1965 to

786,000 in 1971, accounting in the latter year for one of every five of the aged in poverty. It is not surprising, then, that blacks increased from an estimated 21.6 percent of OAA recipients in 1965 to 24.4 percent in 1971.[5]

Blacks represented 30 percent of disabled and blind beneficiaries in 1971. They are clearly overrepresented relative to their share among the completely disabled—16 percent of males and 18 percent of females. But disabled blacks are less likely to receive aid under workmen's compensation, OASDI, or private programs, and their needs are greater. Their median income was under $2,000, as compared with $4,500 for completely disabled whites. Where a third of severely disabled white married males were poor, 70 percent of blacks lived in poverty.[6] These data indicate that blacks are probably not as overrepresented relative to their true proportion of those in need.

Social Security

While the growth of welfare dependency among blacks has been the object of attention and concern, the rapid expansion of black benefits and beneficiaries under the Old Age, Survivors and Disability Insurance (OASDI) has gone largely unnoticed. Welfare caseloads and payments leveled off in the 1970s, but social security payments continued their rise, with an increasing share going to blacks.

OASDI is essentially three separate social insurance efforts financed by a tax on the wages of covered workers. Those who retire after age sixty-two, or those who become disabled are eligible for benefits, provided they have paid social security taxes for a sufficient number of quarters. Payments are also available to dependents of deceased workers.

Nine of every ten jobs were covered by the social security system in 1972, when 93 percent of persons reaching age sixty-five were eligible to receive OASDI benefits. Approximately 95 percent of all children and their mothers would receive benefits if the father or husband were to die.

OASDI is nominally an insurance program financed out of taxes paid by employers and employees in covered employment. But benefits have been raised and eligibility criteria liberalized, so that current recipients are getting back more than they put in. Current taxes rather than accumulated funds provide for benefits—thus the program is an income transfer from workers to retirees, survivors, and the disabled.

There is also a transfer from higher to lower earners. A retired worker receives 109 percent of his average monthly earnings if they were only $110, but 55 percent if they were $470. Persons age seventy-two and over may receive benefits no matter what their prior work experience. Finally, disability is more frequent among the low-paid, so that they are likely to get a disproportionate share of benefits.[7]

Overall, blacks represented nearly one in ten OASDI recipients in 1971 (table 10-8). Because blacks have shorter life expectancy, they

Table 10-8. Black share of OASDI benefits and beneficiaries, 1971

Beneficiary	Black recipients (thousands)	Percent of all recipients	Average monthly benefit of blacks	Average black benefit as percent of white
Total	2,595	9.5	—	—
Retired workers	1,044	7.5	$106	79
Disabled workers	238	14.4	127	85
Wives	184	6.1	46	68
Children	805	18.7	67[a]	69[a]
Widows	295	7.7	86	72
Parents	3	10.7	101	88
Age 72 and over	18	3.8	48	100
Disabled widows and widowers	8	14.5	75	81

Source: *Social Security Bulletin, Annual Statistical Supplement, 1971*, table 67.
[a] Children of deceased workers.

accounted for only 7.5 percent of all retired workers receiving benefits, which was nearly equivalent to their 7.9 percent share of the elderly population (age sixty-two and over). Under the survivors' segments, 7.7 percent of widows receiving benefits were black. While 14.4 percent of all disability benefit recipients were black, this was less than the black share of the disabled population and less than the proportion receiving public assistance for the disabled. In all categories recipient black families were more likely to have children than whites. Blacks accounted for 5.8 percent of widows without children, but 18.8 percent of widowed mothers. Overall, 18.7 percent of children receiving survivors' benefits were black.

Because of lower prior earnings and fewer quarters of covered employment, the average monthly benefit for retired blacks in 1971 was four-fifths that of whites. Blacks also elected early retirement more frequently, resulting in reduced benefits. In 1971, 53.4 percent of black retired workers started receiving benefits between age sixty-two and sixty-four, compared with 47.5 percent of whites.[8] In other segments of the program the average benefits of blacks were also less than for whites, but since black recipients were more likely to have children and thus to receive supplements to their own benefits, the average payment per family was equalized somewhat. Blacks received one-tenth of all benefits in 1971 and represented roughly the same proportion of all beneficiaries, including children.[9]

The black share of benefits and beneficiaries has been increasing. Nonwhites received 10.6 percent of all benefits in 1971, compared to 8.2 percent in 1967, with their share increasing in all components as a result of liberalized eligibility criteria and economic changes.

	1967	1971
Retired workers	8.1 percent	8.4 percent
Children	19.1	20.9
Disabled workers	15.3	15.5
Wives	6.6	7.2
Widows	5.7	6.5

Formerly concentrated in irregular or uncovered agriculture and domestic service jobs, blacks currently reaching retirement age or qualifying under the disability provisions are more likely to have had steady work experience in the covered sectors. As black income and earnings increase, and as more blacks reach retirement years with extensive work in covered employment, their share of OASDI should continue to rise.

Greater reliance on social security is preferable to dependency on public assistance, but the OASDI system is not without some drawbacks.

1. There is no adjustment in the social security tax for family size. With more mouths to feed, black families are harder hit by the regressive tax than whites. Moreover, the wages of both husbands and wives are taxed and proportionately more black than white wives work. Married couples get the same benefits whether or not the wife has worked.

2. While the social security tax may be "progressive" if the distribution of future benefits is considered, this does little to alleviate the pressure on younger workers who will not receive payments for many years. Blacks in the work force tend to be younger than whites so that the intergenerational transfer burdens fall more heavily on them. Moreover, black life expectancies are considerably shorter than whites, meaning that blacks are paying into a system which is less likely to benefit them in later years.

3. Income from rents, royalties, or dividends are not offset in calculating benefits, yet payments are reduced 50 cents for each dollar of earnings above $3,000. Since whites more frequently have accumulated wealth than blacks, they may receive higher income in addition to their social security.

One approach which could correct some of these problems would be to supplement payroll taxes with contributions from general revenues. To the extent that income taxes are more progressive and that blacks have lower incomes, they would benefit.

Other Income Maintenance Programs

OASDI insures against income loss due to old age, death, and disability, but not against the failings of the economic system; that is the purpose of unemployment compensation. Under this federal-state system, benefits are financed by a payroll tax. States determine the level and duration of payments, the eligibility of covered workers, and the tax rate for employers, with the federal government determining coverage and other broad guidelines. In 1972 an average of 1.85 million persons—less than two-fifths of the unemployed—received weekly benefits averaging $54 for fourteen weeks. In 1969 one-fourth of the work force was not covered by unemployment compensation, including 1.8 million domestics, 1.2 million agricultural workers, and 7.8 million state and local employees. Since covered workers must have minimum periods of employment and earnings in order to qualify, low-wage earners, who are most susceptible to unemployment, are the least likely to be protected.

Since blacks are twice as likely as whites to be unemployed, they are overrepresented among compensation recipients. But because they more frequently work in noncovered employment, receive lower wages, and have had previously interrupted employment, proportionately fewer blacks than whites receive unemployment benefits. In 1972 blacks accounted for a fifth of the unemployed, but only a seventh of all unemployment insurance recipients.[10] Their chances of receiving help during periods of idleness were therefore considerably less. It is young and female blacks who are most frequently ineligible because of entry or reentry into the labor force, but the very limited evidence suggests that unemployed black male heads are also less likely to receive benefits than whites. In 1970 only half of the black central city male family heads experiencing some unemployment received unemployment compensation.[11] Nationally, about three of every four males who were unemployed got benefits.[12]

There is little support for the contention that a significant segment of blacks quit work to get unemployment compensation or remain on the rolls rather than seeking a new job. Disadvantaged workers less frequently qualify for unemployment compensation and if they do, tend to receive low benefits for short durations. Recipients must be available to work and registered with the employment service, which may find it easier to place unskilled manual or domestic workers than, for instance, unemployed white professionals. The proportion of all unemployed who have been out of a job fifteen weeks or more and may be "malingering" has declined from 28 percent in 1962 to 24 percent in 1972, and the black share of these long-term unemployed has fallen from 26 to 19 percent.[13] The real problem is not that blacks are turning away from jobs to get or stay on unemployment compensation, but that they are frequently unable to get jobs or to qualify for benefits.

There is much less evidence about the status of blacks in other income maintenance programs. One which may be of particular importance is workmen's compensation, which provides cash and medical costs for covered workers who are permanently or temporarily disabled on the job. This program has grown in recent years, to an estimated $3.7 billion in 1972, but there are no records on the characteristics of clients. It is reasonable to assume, however, that the program is of some significance to blacks. In central city poverty areas, the number of families reporting receipt of workmen's compensation was 60 percent as large as those reporting unemployment compensation.[14]

Another set of programs of probable importance to blacks are veterans' compensation and pensions, with a total disbursement of $6 billion in 1972.[15] Racial breakdowns are not available, but blacks are underrepresented in the veteran population—equaling 7.2 percent of veterans over age twenty as opposed to 10.7 percent of the total civilian noninstitutional male population over twenty years old.

In 1970 black veterans were more frequently unemployed and out of the labor force than whites, and their median incomes were less than two-thirds those of whites. Twenty-six percent of black veterans compared to 12 percent of whites had incomes below $3,000.[16] These data suggest that a disproportionate percentage of black veterans would qualify for need-based support.

The Government as a Provider

Black income is supplemented under a wide range of federal programs, and though the details are complex, they suggest several conclusions.

1. Transfer programs have a massive impact on the well-being of blacks, especially the poor, more than half of whose income comes from sources other than earnings.

2. Blacks are overrepresented in the needs-based programs and

underrepresented in the social insurance programs. Yet the latter are growing in importance as blacks are becoming eligible under blanket coverage and are more frequently qualifying because of their improved employment status.

3. Dependency on welfare is a widespread phenomenon among blacks. While the income provided has been beneficial to recipients, the welfare system has been poorly structured, discouraging work and contributing to family instability.

11

PROVIDING GOODS AND SERVICES

For many years the federal government has provided in-kind assistance to selected groups among the needy. Low-income public housing and the school lunch programs date from the New Deal; health care to veterans is almost as old as the nation. Recently, a growing share of federal social expenditures have been channeled into these direct forms of assistance. The government's concept of its responsibilities has broadened to include all the needy, rather than only the "deserving" poor. Moreover, in selling domestic welfare programs, it has proved more feasible to supply the "sick, hungry, and homeless" with goods and services rather than to simply dole out welfare dollars.

Consequently, the scale of these programs has increased substantially. Expenditures for federal in-kind aid rose from approximately $2 billion in 1960 to $24 billion a dozen years later. Because blacks are overrepresented in the needy populations targeted for this assistance, they benefit disproportionately. In 1972 blacks received an estimated $5.4 billion (valued at cost) of in-kind aid, an increase from less than half a billion dollars in 1960. Health care accounted for two-thirds of the 1972 amount (table 11-1). Because of the rising outlays for Medicare, a program serving the aged population of whom 92 percent are white, the black share of in-kind assistance has fallen from 27 percent in 1960 to 22 percent in 1972—despite the fact that blacks have become a larger proportion of the poor. In 1972 blacks received about 6 percent of the nearly 9 billion Medicare dollars. On the other hand, they shared roughly two-fifths of food stamps and housing assistance.

Table 11-1. Estimated federal in-kind assistance, 1972 (amounts in millions)

Assistance	Total	Black share (percent)	Blacks
Total	$24,440	22	$5,450
Health	19,600	19	3,710
Medicaid[a]	7,600	33	2,480
Medicare	8,810	6	510
Veterans health	2,360	16	390
Other health including: Maternal and child health, crippled children, community health centers	820	40	330
Food	3,530	34	1,190
Food stamps	2,000	41	820
Food distribution	350	27	100
School lunch and associated programs	1,190	24	280
Housing	1,310	42	550
Public housing	890	47	420
Homeownership	250	22	60
Rent supplements	90	63	50
Interest reduction	90	20	20

Note: Totals may not add due to rounding.
Source: Derived from statistics compiled by the Departments of Agriculture, Health, Education, and Welfare, and Housing and Urban Development, and the Office of Management and Budget.
[a] Includes state and local contributions.

Health Care

A number of federal programs supply free or reduced-price medical care to those who cannot afford private services. Public health service and veterans hospitals have been federally supported for many years. In 1965 Congress undertook to provide health care for all the aged and poor under the Medicare and Medicaid programs. As a result of these new programs, federal health expenditures expanded rapidly, reaching $20 billion in 1972, of which blacks received about $3.7 billion.

1. Medicaid is by far the most important health program for blacks, supplying them an estimated $2.5 billion in care during 1972. Under the state administered program, those receiving federally supported cash assistance are provided free medical care and the federal government reimburses the states 50 to 83 percent of the costs. Approximately half of the states also extend benefits to the "medically indigent" with incomes less than one-third above the level needed to qualify for cash assistance. Medicaid benefits cover costs of hospitalization, outpatient and nursing home care, physicians and home health services, and laboratory and x-ray tests. In addition, states may provide medical screening and diagnosis for children and youths under age twenty-one, including dental care, eyeglasses, and hearing aids. These provisions potentially allow comprehensive medical care for all poor children.

Because the medical care needs of the aged and disabled are greatest most Medicaid dollars are spent on these populations. Younger, nondisabled welfare families are a majority of beneficiaries, but receive less treatment per person. Blacks make up 43 percent of recipients of Aid to Families with Dependent Children, but less than three-tenths of those receiving Aid to the Blind, Old Age Assistance, or Aid to the Permanently and Totally Disabled. If it is assumed that blacks share in benefits in proportion to their eligibility, then they receive a third of all outlays (table 11-2). But this estimate may overstate black utilization of services. For one thing, nearly a quarter of all Medicaid recipients do not receive public assistance because they are either in publicly supported institutions or have incomes too high to qualify for cash aid. This group is disproportionately white, female, and aged. Second, if Medicare usage patterns are any indication, eligible blacks utilize available medical services less frequently than whites. One sampling of Medicaid recipients in states with the highest numbers of blacks listed a third of those reporting as "other races." If the percentages are adjusted to include nonreporting states, blacks may represent as little as 27 percent of Medicaid recipients.[1]

Table 11-2. Medicaid benefits to blacks, 1971

Category	Total outlays (millions)	Costs per person	Esti-mated per-cent black	Black recipients (thou-sands)	Total black share (millions)
Total	$5,939	$258	39	7,500	$1,960
Age 65 and over	2,227	618	24	880	540
Blind	47	386	30	40	14
Disabled	1,235	823	29	440	360
Children under 21 years	1,093	132	43	3,820	470
AFDC adults	1,117	238	46	2,040	510
Other adults	220	200	27	300	60

Source: Derived from U.S. Department of Health, Education, and Welfare, *Medicaid and Other Medical Care Financed from Public Assistance Funds*, 1971 (SRS) 73-03154, NCSS, Report B-5 (FY 71), November 1972 (Washington: Government Printing Office, 1972), tables 1 and 2; and U.S. Bureau of the Census, *Statistical Abstract of the United States, 1972* (Washington: Government Printing Office, 1972), tables 487 and 491.

Note: Details do not add to totals due to rounding.

No matter what the actual usage figure, it is clear that blacks benefit proportionately less from Medicaid than from cash public assistance. Possibly the combination of white-staffed hospitals and unavailability of medical care facilities discourages greater use. Another important factor may simply be the complexity of the Medicaid form. In a 1970 Harris survey, a third of whites and half of blacks failed to fill out the Medicaid form correctly, compared to only 3 and 8 percent, respectively, who had difficulty with the public assistance application. Apparently, a system ostensibly aimed at delivering care has been tied to a form which is complex and difficult to answer.[2]

2. Medicare includes two programs which provide federally subsidized assistance to those age sixty-five and over. Under the Hospital Insurance Plan (HI), those eligible for social security or railroad retirement are covered for all costs from the second through the

sixtieth day of hospitalization and received a reduced rate through the ninetieth day. A second program—Supplementary Medical Insurance (SMI)—provides physicians' care, diagnostic tests, and medication to any citizen over sixty-five who has elected to pay the small monthly premium ($4.60 in 1972). HI is by far the more expensive, with a price tag of $6.7 billion in 1973 compared to $2.5 billion for SMI.

In 1970 blacks accounted for 8 percent of the population over age sixty-five and 8 percent of those enrolled in both Medicare programs. But despite the fact that the health of older blacks is generally worse than that of aged whites, they make less use of Medicare benefits. Only 16 percent of eligible nonwhites used HI in 1968, compared to 21 percent of whites; for SML the rates were 30 percent for eligible nonwhites and 40 percent for whites (table 11-3). As a result, only 6 percent of Medicare beneficiaries are black. In addition to this lower frequency of usage, blacks receive less intensive care. Nonwhites were slightly more likely to use out patient services but less likely to

Table 11-3. Utilization of medicare (percent of those enrolled)

Category	Nonwhite	White
Total	28.2	38.3
Hospital insurance	16.2[a]	20.8[a]
Inpatient	15.4	20.1
Outpatient	1.0	0.7
Extended care	0.9	2.1
Home care	0.7	0.8
Supplementary medical insurance	30.4[a]	40.3[a]
Physician and other medical care	27.9	39.5
Outpatient	9.0	7.2
Home care	0.7	0.7

Source: U.S. Department of Health, Education, and Welfare, *Medicare, 1968,* Publication No. SSA 7311704, May 30, 1973, tables 1-11.

[a] Details do not equal totals due to multiple usage.

become hospitalized, to receive extended care, or to use physicians' services. Blacks received an average of $652 worth of care each, compared with $671 for the average white recipient, reducing their share of dollar benefits to 5.8 percent (table 11-4).

Table 11-4. Medicare benefits, 1968 (millions)

Category	Persons enrolled	Persons receiving benefits	Reimburse-ments
Total	21.1	7.9	$5,283
White	19.4	7.4	4,974
Nonwhite	1.7	0.5	309
Nonwhite percent of total	8.0	6.0	5.8

Note: Details may not add due to rounding.
Source: U.S. Department of Health, Education, and Welfare, *Medicare 1968*, Publication No. SSA 7311704, May 30, 1973, table 1.9.

As in the case of Medicaid, the underutilization may be due in part to the unavailability of facilities. But discrimination may also play a part. Though participating hospitals are forbidden to exclude eligible patients on the basis of race, southern hospitals have apparently sidestepped this requirement. In 1968 nonwhite usage in the South (where three-fifths of eligible blacks lived) was 15 percent compared to 22 percent for whites. In all other areas the rates were 17 and 20 percent respectively.[3]

Another possible explanation for lower nonwhite usage may be the cost of Medicare, which discourages the poor, including a disproportionate number of blacks. SMI users must pay a monthly charge, and HI beneficiaries are charged for first day of hospitalization and approximately one-fourth of the costs from the sixtieth day to the ninetieth day. To help defray these costs and thus make health care more available to the poor, the federal government allows the states to use Medicaid funds to pay the SMI premium for the poor. To date forty-six states have elected to "buy into" the Medicare program in this way. These "buy in" plans have had an important impact in bringing Medicare to poor nonwhites. "Buy ins" represented about 10 percent of white SMI enrollees in participating states, but about 35 percent of nonwhite SMI enrollees. Nonwhites comprised 19 percent of "buy ins" but only 4 percent of self-purchasing SMI participants in 1969.[4]

3. Veterans' health care programs provided $2.4 billion worth of institutional medical treatment in 1972 to 811,000 former servicemen with war injuries or with incomes too low to pay for private care. The Veterans Administration operates 167 hospitals and a number of nursing homes, domiciliaries, and out patient clinics.

The VA's criterion of need is lenient—the veteran must only certify that he is unable to defray hospitalization costs. Consequently, two-thirds of all recipients of VA medical care qualify on the basis of need rather than service-connected disability. This explains the overrepresentation of blacks in veterans hospitals. Blacks constituted 8 percent of all veterans in 1972, but accounted for 14 percent of low-income (below $4,000) veterans and 17 percent of hospital patients (table 11-5). The apparently higher usage of veterans' medical care (com-

Table 11-5. Veterans hospital and medical care, 1972

Type of service	Total cost (millions)	Percent black	Black benefit (millions)
Total, including overhead	$2,363	16.4	$387
Total services	1,951	16.4	320
Hospital care and outpatient care	1,822	16.9	308
Domiciliaries	43	8.2	4
Nursing care	86	8.9	8

Note: Details may not add due to rounding.
Source: Veterans Administration, unpublished data, and U.S. Congress, Joint Economic Committee, *Handbook of Public Income Transfer Programs*, 92d Cong., 2d Sess. (Washington: Government Printing Office, 1972), p. 199.

pared to Medicare and Medicaid) among blacks may be due to several factors. VA hospitals apparently have fewer discriminatory barriers than other public hospitals, particularly in the South. VA care can be obtained with relative ease and is completely free. And there is little stigma attached to accepting assistance, a condition which may not be true of Medicaid.[5]

4. Other health programs operated by the Department of Health, Education and Welfare are important for blacks. Federal funds support a number of comprehensive health centers located in ghettos or rural areas remote from other facilities. These clinics, often subsidized with Medicare or Medicaid funds, frequently serve black or Spanish-speaking clienteles. Given the apparent underutilization of both Medicare and Medicaid, the success of these centers in finding more effective models for health service delivery could be important.

One example of such clinics is the maternal and child health program which subsidizes states to provide clinics and visiting nurses for mothers as well as medical, dental, and diagnostic care for children. Because many clinics serve predominantly black, low-income urban and rural areas, they may have contributed to reducing maternal and infant mortality among blacks. Part of the maternal and child care money goes to support family planning assistance. Recently, as moral and technical barriers have fallen, these programs have expanded. Beginning with the expenditure of $16 million in 1968, family planning funding reached $166 million by 1972.

The documented relationship of poverty and large families and the greater incidence of both conditions among blacks, plus the evidence that lower income black women more often practice ineffective birth control, suggests that assistance can have substantial benefits to blacks.[6] And because federal family planning programs are primarily directed at the poor, their clientele includes a disproportionate number of blacks. Thirty-one percent of the 1.6 million patients who visited clinics in 1972 were black.[7] This higher usage by minorities also reflects the fact that federal family planning aid is primarily delivered through organized clinics rather than by private physicians. Lower income black women more often rely on clinics, while higher income white women tend to use private physicians.[8]

Despite this greater usage by lower income poor women, comparatively few family planning clients are Medicaid or welfare recipients. Only 26 percent of AFDC mothers were provided any family planning services in 1971, of whom 58 percent were black.[9]

It is debatable whether the recent decline in the number of children per family among blacks in poverty may be attributed to the increased federal emphasis on family planning. But there is little doubt that the federally supported family planning clinics reach many blacks who might not have obtained birth control counseling or prescriptions from private physicians.

The Impact of Federal Health Expenditures

Though federal health expenditures are double welfare outlays, it is more difficult to weigh their impacts, especially upon blacks. The evidence suggests that federal outlays have expanded medical care not merely subsidized it. Between 1962 and 1970 both personal and government expenditures for medical care increased. Federally-financed care grew from a small proportion of total per capita expenditures in 1962 to as much as 60 percent of all black health care in 1970.

Though the gains are clear in terms of dollars, it is nearly impossible to measure the impact upon the health of blacks. In a few areas, notably the steady improvement in maternal and infant death rates during the last five years, federally supported health care may have had a significant effect. It seems reasonable to assume that other health problems, particularly those caused by neglect or procrastination, may have been improved by expanded federal programs. On the other hand, the emphasis of the federal programs on health care for the poor and the aged may have limited the impact on blacks. In all income classes, blacks spend less on health care than whites, and their health tends to be poorer at all ages except fifteen to twenty-four. Though dollars alone cannot insure health, a national health insurance plan for all age and income groups might be more effective in narrowing the remaining gaps between the health of blacks and whites.

Federal Food Programs

The Department of Agriculture operates three food programs: food stamps, commodity distribution, and school lunches. The food stamp program is by far the most important and most expensive. Food stamps are available to all public assistance recipients and to other families who meet federal low-income standards. Participants pay from $0 to $152 (depending on family income) to receive stamps worth from $36 to $192 (depending on level of need and size of family).

The original food stamp program was oriented more toward buying farm products than feeding the hungry. The stamps represented small subsidies, the program was understaffed and unpublicized, and few certification offices were available. As a result, a limited number of people were reached at first. Recognition of the administrative problems led to liberalization of the pay-in requirements and a greater effort to make the program available to the poor. Public participation and program costs subsequently multiplied at a rapid pace. From $33 million to help 425,000 people in fiscal 1965, the food stamp program expanded to reach 3.2 million people in fiscal 1969, and an estimated 13.2 million people in fiscal 1973, when the price tag reached $2.2 billion.

Blacks receive a large percentage of this food aid. Slightly more than two-fifths of food stamp recipients were black in 1972 with the nearly 4.6 million black beneficiaries receiving food aid worth approximately $900 million. Since most of this went to poor families, it represented a substantial supplement to the incomes of black poor, whose total cash income was only about $5 billion in 1972.

The commodity distribution program also provides food to the poor, delivering up to thirty-nine pounds per person per month of various foodstuffs to public assistance recipients and others certified as needy. These commodities include butter, cheese, flour, egg mix, shortening, canned meats and vegetables, and dried beans, milk, potatoes, and fruit.

The great increase in food stamp funding has curtailed the growth of direct food distribution. From an all time high in 1965 of 5.8 million people the number of recipients declined to an estimated 3 million in 1973. Costs, too, have fallen slightly to approximately $350 million in 1972. Racial breakdowns of recipients indicate that blacks make up a smaller proportion of those receiving commodities than food stamps. In 1972 blacks represented about 27 percent of commodity recipients, receiving approximately $95 million worth of free food.

The school lunch program is a third program which grafted the laudible aim of "safeguarding the health and well-being of the nation's children" with the pragmatic goal of providing relief to farmers. Originally oriented toward all school children, the program was modified to provide special assistance in poverty areas and free or reduced price lunches to poor children. A school breakfast program was added in 1966 providing a second meal to children in low-income areas. Food assistance is also available for children in day care centers, neighborhood houses, and recreation centers. The federal government supplies both cash and surplus commodities to school systems under the program.

In 1972 federal payments totaled nearly $800 million under the school lunch program which helped provide 2.7 billion lunches to 25.2 million children. Of this amount approximately $320 million was allocated for free or reduced-price lunches to nearly 8 million needy children. Blacks who represented 14 percent of students and 37 percent of children in poor families received an estimated 570 million lunches in 1972 worth approximately $185 million.

There have been few national studies of the incidence and severity of nutritional deficiencies, despite the publicity generated by the discovery of "hunger in America" in the late 1960s. It is not possible to declare with certainty that the food distributed to the poor has significantly improved their nutrition as opposed to merely subsidizing food costs. There is no doubt, however, that the food and the billions of school meals have been important supplements to poor families and children who once did without this help. Blacks, whose nutritional problems have been shown to be more severe because of their aggregate income deficit, have been prime beneficiaries of this aid.

Subsidized Housing

The Housing Act of 1949 set as a national housing goal the "realization as soon as feasible of a decent home and a suitable living environment for every American family." To this end the federal government has taken a major role in two areas: encouraging the flow of funds into mortgage financing in order to facilitate home purchase and construction and subsidizing units for lower income families.

The mortgage programs of the Federal Housing Administration (FHA) and the Veterans Administration (VA) provide government guarantees on loans made by private institutions. With risks covered, the loan-to-value ratio can be higher than otherwise and lower down payments and longer repayment periods are possible. In 1970, 29 percent of all new nonfarm housing starts were financed through FHA, and 4 percent through VA; these programs accounted for 21 and 13 percent, respectively, of all mortgage credit outstanding.[10] The FHA program is self-supporting from premiums; its major purpose is to make loans more readily available rather than to subsidize cost. The VA program charges no premiums and subsidizes the loans.

The record of the FHA and VA in providing loans to minorities has not been good. Until 1948 both agencies tolerated and sometimes encouraged restrictive covenants barring resale of homes to minorities. Through the early 1960s they tended to lend only on projects in predominantly black or white areas, on the assumption that property values in transition neighborhoods were unstable. After the passage of the 1968 Civil Rights Act, loans to blacks increased.

Before the 1960s blacks tended to get only a small share of all loans and these were usually for smaller amounts and more often for existing rather than new homes. By April 1973 this pattern had improved with blacks representing 8 percent of those moving into new units and 20 percent of those moving into existing homes. Under the FHA program providing housing for those displaced by urban renewal, 14 percent of new home buyers and a third of existing homebuyers in April 1973 were black.[11] Blacks still hold a very small share of all outstanding FHA and insured loans, since compensatory efforts are relatively recent. If government efforts continue, however, equal opportunity mortgage financing may be a very important factor in opening homeownership to blacks.

Using a variety of funding mechanisms, housing assistance programs provide substantial subsidies for the purchase, rental, renovation, and construction of units for occupancy by low-income families. The programs grew dramatically in the late 1960s, accounting for a fourth of the nation's housing starts in 1971. By the end of fiscal 1972 blacks occupied about 700,000 subsidized units, over a third of all such housing (table 11-6). Nearly a fifth of black families with incomes between $1,000 and $4,000 lived in subsidized units, and

Table 11-6. Estimated black occupants in federally-assisted housing units, June 30, 1972

Program	Number occupied (thousands)	Percent black
Total	2,005	36
Public housing	1,019	47
Rent supplements (alone)	69	63
Homeownership (235)	323	25
Interest subsidizing on rented units	104	20
Elderly housing (202)	42	4
Rehabilitation loans and grants	54	25
Farmers Home Administration programs	394	18

Source: Derived from unpublished tabulations provided by the U.S. Department of Housing and Urban Development.

overall about one in eight black households were subsidized (table 11-7). Estimates of the average subsidy per unit vary, but they are usually in the neighborhood of $750 to $1,000.[12] Assuming the lower figure, the housing assistance programs represented an aggregate income supplement for blacks of over one-half billion dollars in fiscal 1972.

After four years of accelerated activity under these programs, a freeze was placed on new commitments in late 1972. The cost had proved to be more than expected, and a number of problems had emerged. In some cases, the programs were not reaching those with the greatest need and when they did, projects were beset by high default rates, vandalism, and crime. The programs also failed to provide much beyond minimally adequate and less costly shelter. Subsidized housing was administered under severe cost limits implemented to insure that there were no "frills." More critically, however, little racial integration or dispersal of subsidized projects was achieved outside the confines of central cities.

An example is the rent supplement program begun in 1965 and

Table 11-7. Percent of households served by HUD subsidy programs by income and minority group, as of December 31, 1972

Gross income	Total U.S.	Black
$0–$999	1	2
1,000–1,999	7	19
2,000–2,999	7	20
3,000–3,999	6	18
4,000–4,999	6	17
5,000–5,999	5	14
6,000–6,999	4	11
7,000–7,999	3	7
8,000–9,999	1	4

Source: Department of Housing and Urban Development, *Housing In The Seventies* (Washington: Government Printing Office, 1973).

Note: Excludes programs administered by the Farmers Home Administration. Subsidized households are as of December 31, 1972. Total households are as of the 1970 census.

initially envisioned as a substitute for public housing. The government paid the difference between one-fourth the tenant's income and the market rent in privately-owned units. Since any type of rental unit could be subsidized, it was hoped that low-income families could be integrated into projects where middle and lower-middle income families resided. In fact, however, little mixing was achieved. Unsubsidized families did not want to live in subsidized projects, and affluent communities refused to accept concentrations of poor, especially when they were blacks with large families. Overall, less than an eighth of subsidized rental units other than public housing, and an even smaller percentage of public housing, were located in the suburbs.

An alternative approach initiated in 1968 subsidized the purchase of homes by low-income families, providing interest subsidies to lenders, thus reducing the monthly payment for low-income purchasers. This program accounted for the production of 350,000 units through fiscal 1972. Though 21 percent of new home buyers and 43 percent of those purchasing existing units were blacks, an intensive study in four metropolitan areas revealed that the homes bought by blacks were more likely to be old and to have serious structural problems. With a lower purchase price, the subsidies were also less. Most important of all, the black homes were almost exclusively in black or transition neighborhoods. Local FHA officials tended to let market institutions operate the program, and the result was a pattern of discrimination by brokers, lenders, and sellers, effectively excluding minorities from white areas.[13]

The failure of housing programs to break through the barriers of racial and class segregation can be blamed on several factors. The lack of legislative mandate and administrative commitment to use the housing programs as leverage to combat housing discrimination continued to be a deterrent to successful implementation. The Department of Housing and Urban Development generally played a passive role, relying on private institutions which often continued their discriminatory practices. Local public housing authorities were reluctant to pick sites outside the central city. Suburban whites and affluent central city blacks were able to stall many low-income projects, confining publicly supported housing to blighted and urban renewal areas.

The subsidized housing programs have made a substantial contribution to improving the physical quality of shelter for ill-housed blacks, significantly reducing housing costs for those lucky enough to benefit. But progress toward providing a truly "decent home and suitable living environment for every American family" has been slow, and steps toward breaking the patterns of racial isolation have been halting.

The Cornucopia

Though there is little concrete evidence that low-income blacks are healthier, better fed, and better housed as a result of in-kind assistance, these conclusions are surely justified. The most obvious measures of the importance of the programs are the lines of individuals queuing up to receive benefits. Utilization has expanded most rapidly under open-ended programs, such as Medicaid and food assistance, and long waiting lists attest to the popularity of programs whose supply is rationed, such as public housing. If in-kind assistance did not improve the status of low-income families, it would not be utilized.

Clearly, the programs have significantly boosted the real incomes of the black poor and near poor. In 1972 they had a cash income of approximately $9 billion. As much as $4.5 billion of the estimated $5.4 billion of in-kind benefits going to blacks was directed specifically to the poor. In-kind aid may have, therefore, raised the real income of black poor by as much as 50 percent. Even if part of this aid is unnecessary, underutilized, or "lost in the pipeline," federal in-kind aid has clearly been important in improving the status of blacks at the bottom of the income scale.

12

DEVELOPING HUMAN RESOURCES

Public and private investments in education and training have risen more rapidly than any other major outlay—from $9 billion in 1950 to $25 billion in 1960 and $86 billion in 1972. Blacks have historically been denied their full share of these investments, both because their lower incomes would not allow equal personal expenditures for education and because public policy usually slighted black needs. During the 1960s some progress was made toward equalizing investments in black education and training. Federal compensatory education and vocational training programs were key factors in these improvements.

Investments in the Schools

Though public education is primarily the responsibility of states and localities, the federal government has provided various kinds of support to the nation's schools and colleges for nearly two centuries, beginning with the reservation of public land for township schools in 1787. In the years following World War II, federal programs provided support for veterans' education, for "impacted" schools with many children of federal workers, and for school lunches, student housing, research fellowships, and loans to college students. During the 1960s, the federal emphasis shifted from the training of more scientists and engineers to the Great Society's egalitarian ideals of providing more educational opportunity to the poor. Under the Economic Opportunity Act of 1964, the federal government began to focus its efforts on those whom the educational system had failed.

As a result of this shift in objectives, the black share of federal education outlays grew enormously during the decade. In 1960 blacks were receiving less than 10 percent of the $1.2 billion in federal aid to education because most of this money went for fellowships, support of science education, aid to impacted areas, and veterans' education stipends. By 1972 direct federal education expenditures increased to $8.1 billion of which an estimated $1.6 billion aided blacks.

This increasing share resulted from the expansion of programs for the disadvantaged. The federal attempt to equalize educational opportunity covered every level of education: programs for disadvantaged preschool children aimed at narrowing the initial gaps in their cognitive development; grants to elementary and secondary schools tried to stem the progressive decay in the educational achievement of poor children; and finally, aid to colleges and students sought to improve the quality of higher education and to make it more available to youths from low-income families. These multiple goals led to the establishment of a number of programs which, by 1972, affected 10 million disadvantaged students and 3 million blacks and cost more than $3.1 billion (table 12-1).

Equalizing Early Schooling—Head Start and Follow Through

The Head Start Program, which provides schooling for disadvantaged preschool children, is the most heralded and the most expensive (per child) of the federal programs for the educationally disadvantaged. The early childhood years have been shown to be critically important for future cognitive development, and poor children entering school are already educationally behind their peers. To try to put them on an equal footing, Head Start created new primary educational institutions by funding local community action agencies. The Head Start agencies provide educational, nutritional, and health care for three to six-year-old children in families below the poverty level. In 1972 approximately half of the 356,000 children enrolled in the program were black.

Table 12-1. Federal education programs for the disadvantaged, 1972

	Obligations for fiscal 1972 (millions)	Participants (thousands)	Average federal cost per participant	Percent[a] black
Early childhood				
Head Start				
Full year	$ 376[b]	270	$ 1,118	51
Summer		86	230	37
Elementary and secondary education				
Follow Through	63	90	700	50
ESEA, Title I	1,570	6,200	250	33
College				
Direct student loans	317	614	670	17
Guaranteed student loans	231	1,256	125	17
College work-study	272	600	640	21
Educational opportunity grants	210	304	670	30
Upward Bound	30	25	1,078	60
Talent Search	5	125	40	54
Special Services for Disadvantaged	14	49	291	56
Support to developing institutions	52	556[c]	93,000	60

Source: U.S. Department of Health, Education, and Welfare.
[a] Data for fiscal years 1969 through 1972.
[b] Full year and summer.
[c] Institutions (actual number).

Most of the Head Start programs concentrate on general child development and social competency, although a small proportion act as day care centers and a few seek to develop language or quantitative skills. Programs range from full-year centers averaging eight hours a day for eleven months, to eight week, part-day summer sessions for children about to enter first grade. Recently, several alternative approaches to preschool child development have been tried, including experimental teaching programs, health care for poor children outside Head Start, and training of parents to provide stimulating environments in the home. Recognizing that successful child development cannot occur without the full participation of the parents, Head Start projects have also attempted to enlist parents as paid and volunteer workers. In 1972 Head Start provided full- or part-time employment to 64,000 workers, of whom approximately 42 percent were black.[1]

Preschool programs have provided important benefits to blacks. By 1972 black preschool children were as likely to be enrolled in "school" between the ages of three and five as white children. Moreover, though the jobs created by Head Start have often been short-term, low-wage "aide" positions, they have provided employment in many of the most disadvantaged sections of the black community.

However, the cognitive gains of children in Head Start have not fulfilled initial, and perhaps inflated, expectations. Head Start children tend to gain faster than similar nonparticipants, but apparently these gains are not retained through the first years of grade school. By the third grade, there are few significant differences between Head Start students and control groups, and both lag a year behind nondisadvantaged students on achievement tests.[2]

Of the few significant cognitive improvements the researchers found, black children from central cities showed some of the greatest gains. Also, Head Start children in the follow-up study received higher subjective evaluations from teachers, even though their tests showed little improvement. Moreover, the emphasis on lasting achievement gains has obscured other benefits such as health and medical care for children, day care services for working mothers, and parental and community involvement.

Evidence that initial gains made by Head Start children were not retained after they left the program encouraged attempts to continue compensatory education through the early years of grade school. In

1967 Congress funded Follow-Through, an experimental program aimed at determining the best ways of educating disadvantaged students in grades 1 through 3. In 1972 Follow-Through spent $63 million for over 90,000 children at 617 schools. Approximately 60 percent of the students were black.

Unlike the categorical grants to all school districts under the Elementary and Secondary Education Act, Follow-Through has been an experimental program concentrated in selected school districts. Program sponsors—who may be university educators, community groups, research corporations, or public schools—are given grants to design and implement new educational strategies. Sponsors provide technical assistance, training for teachers and parent advisers, and program guidelines, but the actual implementation of the programs is left to teachers in the public schools. Sponsors are encouraged to seek innovative approaches and are expected to involve, consult, and utilize parents and community groups.

Preliminary comparisons of 1969 to 1971 Follow Through children with control groups suggested that the program had some small positive impacts on children's academic performance and attitudes toward school and learning. Gains appeared greatest for children from poor families and tended to increase the longer the children were in the programs. Structured academic approaches had the largest effects on achievement test scores, while more child-centered "cognitive discovery" efforts stimulated the most improvement in children's attitudes. Parents and teachers appeared to be more involved with the children's education and to react more positively under Follow Through programs.[3]

Program effects, though positive, did not push performance close to middle class standards. Policymakers felt the results did not warrant the cost, and the program is being phased out.

Improving Elementary and Secondary Education

Blacks and other disadvantaged students tend to fall farther behind with each year of school. To correct this situation, the federal government began in 1965 to distribute assistance to school systems based on the percentages of children from institutions or from low-income or welfare families. Under Title I of the Elementary and Secondary Education Act (ESEA), the schools have the options to add staff, serve breakfasts or lunches, establish kindergartens, attempt innovative programs, purchase equipment, or whatever other supplemental assistance they feel may improve the performance of disadvantaged students. In 1972, $1.6 billion in grants went to 13,900 school districts reaching 6.2 million students. This included 2.2 million blacks or 30 percent of black students age five to seventeen.

The actual benefits of Title I expenditures are unclear, in part because the apparently large sums expended nationally for Title I were spread over large numbers of disadvantaged children, diluting the amount of compensatory services each received. In 1972 expenditures averaged $250 per pupil, compared with average total expenditures of $1,100. Even where funds were concentrated, they were not often sufficient to equalize, much less compensate for, the disparities between wealthy suburban and poor urban districts. For example, though California did a good job of concentrating its resources on the most disadvantaged, the nearly $400 of ESEA money per pupil in 1972 could hardly overcome the $2,000 gap between the richest and poorest districts in the state. Thus, though the concept of compensatory education is often criticized, to a large extent compensatory education supported by truly compensatory resources has not been tried. Moreover, the federal government has provided little guidance as to how the billions of compensatory education aid should be spent. The ESEA and subsequent administrative clarifications specified that the money should not supplant regular funding or be used to benefit advantaged students, and that it should not be diluted by trying to reach too many students or spent primarily on "hardware." But there were few positive instructions how the money should be used.

Lacking guidelines, the program was initially severely abused. In 1966 more than a third of all funds were spent on hardware and construction.[4] Reports covering 1965 to 1969 indicated that Title I money bought everything from swimming pools to football uniforms, that districts had indiscriminately used funds to support all students, and that the grants had gone to beef up black schools in support of continuing segregation.[5]

Although stricter guidelines have corrected these flagrant abuses, there is evidence that much of the aid still goes to nondisadvantaged students. School districts with the highest concentrations of disadvantaged students generally have the lowest per pupil expenditures and lowest Title I allocations. Moreover, academic instruction, for which most students have the greatest need, has been slighted, while health and food programs have been overemphasized and often delivered to nonneedy students. Also, the aim of concentrating resources has often been overlooked. The majority of Title I elementary school children received less than one hour per day of compensatory instruction.[6]

Finally, Title I programs have frequently failed to enlist the support and active participation of the community. Though the Department of Health, Education, and Welfare required that parent advisory councils be formed to participate in planning, operation, and evaluation of Title I programs, these councils were often nonexistent, rubber stamps, or figureheads. The conflict between entrenched educational bureaucracies and concerned parents was not resolved by these groups.

Possibly as a result of these problems in implementation or the insufficiency of funding, or simply because of the difficulties of overcoming educational disadvantages, the ESEA has had little impact on the cognitive achievements of disadvantaged students. National totals for 1968 and 1969 showed that neither disadvantaged participants nor nonparticipants made any significant gains in reading achievement.[7] These reports confirmed an earlier analysis of the school year 1966–1967 which reported that "a child who participated in a Title I project had only a 19 percent chance of a significant achievement gain, a 13 percent chance of a significant achievement loss, and a 68 percent chance of no change at all."[8]

Despite the disappointing results from national samples, a number of programs (particularly smaller ones) have reported impressive gains. One research review cited forty-one successful projects of which three-fourths served primarily black clienteles.[9] The researchers identified several attributes which seemed common to most successful programs, including sound planning, teacher training, instruction in small groups, intensive treatment, and active parental involvement. More recent data have revealed similar patterns, with some projects and some states reporting improvement. For example, 61 percent of a large 1970–1971 California sample made reading achievement gains greater than expected.[10]

In general, however, even the reported successes have not achieved improvements great enough to allow disadvantaged children to keep up with middle class students, let alone make up for their early handicaps. Most assessments of success are based on gains greater than the predicted average monthly learning rate for disadvantaged students (0.7 months of achievement for a calendar month of instruction). Since the norm is one month achievement per month of instruction, even "successful" compensatory programs may result in students falling farther behind. For example, in the California programs (which appear to be the best run and most successful in the country), three-fourths of disadvantaged children did not improve enough to reach the level of one month gain for one month's instruction.

Nevertheless, a great deal of subjective data has accumulated which indicates that the noncognitive benefits to students may be substantial, especially in terms of student health, nutrition, and social and personal development. Teacher evaluations of participating students have often been more favorable than those of nonparticipants.[11]

Evaluations of compensatory elementary and secondary education programs suggest that, at the level of funding which has prevailed, they have been unable to equalize educational opportunity on a national scale. Even the most successful projects show only small gains, and the most common finding is "no change." While it has been possible to isolate important factors contributing to successful projects, the problem of translating local success into nationally effective policy remains. Federal money, even in much greater quantities and with tighter guidelines, is of little use without well-defined, tested, and predictably effective programs. Given the wide variations in local resources, conditions, and needs, such structured federal programs are unrealistic.

Thus, it may be expected that federal aid to disadvantaged students will have little effect independent of the local initiative and enthusiasm which are harnessed to the federal dollars, and that aggregate national totals will continue to show disappointing results unless some nationwide grass roots commitment to revamp education occurs. It was unrealistic to hope that a few years and a few billion dollars would show dramatic changes in an amorphous, $40 billion, two-hundred-year-old educational system. Yet the fact that success can be achieved in some situations, even if great financial and human resources are needed, is grounds for hope. Though evidence of limited gains is often marshaled to prove that compensatory education is a nationwide failure, the success stories indicate that the problems are not insoluble and that given sufficient commitment (not merely in congressional appropriations, but in local initiatives) substantial improvements can be made.

Aid to Disadvantaged College Students

The federal commitment to education for the disadvantaged extends past high school graduation under a variety of programs which seek to enable and encourage students from poor and minority backgrounds to pursue higher education. In 1972 more than $1.1 billion was spent to aid nearly 3 million college students, of whom approximately 650,000 were black.

The oldest program, first enacted as the Defense Education Act in 1958 and later incorporated into the Higher Education Act of 1965, provides for direct low-interest loans of up to $5,000 to students whose parents have less than $15,000 annual income. Initiated in the wake of the "sputnik crisis," as part of a federal effort to close the imagined gap between the American and Russian production of college-trained professionals, the program's emphasis later shifted to supplying funds to those priced out of the higher education market. Although the $15,000 annual income ceiling has tended to orient the program toward lower middle class whites, 16.5 percent of recipients were black in 1972.

In contrast to the original national defense goals of direct loans, the college work-study program initially sought to equalize educational opportunities, authorizing grants to colleges and nonprofit institutions to pay up to 90 percent of the wages of part-time jobs for poor students. Later the program was expanded, making students from all income brackets eligible, and the federal share was reduced to 80 percent. Participants increased from 150,000 in 1965 to 600,000 in 1971, while the percentage of families with less than $3,000 income declined from one-half to one-fourth. Representation of minority students in the program, however, has continued at a high level: more than a fifth of part-time work-study jobs were held by blacks in 1970.

Educational opportunity grants authorized under the 1965 Higher Education Act are a third source of federal funding for poor students. The grants provide up to $1,500 per year to qualified high school graduates with exceptional financial need and must be matched by the educational institution. In 1972 approximately 300,000 students received grants averaging $670 per student; three of ten recipients were black in 1969 and almost three-fourths were from families with an annual income of less than $6,000.

In addition to the funding efforts that seek to support poor students through college, the federal government also operates three programs to encourage poor students to attend college, and to help them succeed once they are there. The most individually expensive program is Upward Bound, in which colleges, using their campus facilities during summer recess, provide remedial programs and counseling to selected tenth and eleventh grade students from low-income backgrounds. With costs of over $1,000 per participant, the $30 million program was able to serve 25,000 students in 1972, three-fifths of whom were black.

Upward Bound has enjoyed apparent success. Approximately 97 percent of Upward Bound students finish high school and about one-half go on to college. Moreover, high percentages remain in college. Of those who entered in the fall of 1970, 60 percent were still there in 1972. But it is unclear whether this success represents the positive impacts of the training or the fact that only 7 percent of those eligible are "creamed" for the program.

A second program seeking to encourage poor and particularly minority students to attend college is Talent Search. Conducted by educational institutions and public agencies under federal grants, the program is designed to identify poor students with exceptional potential and to make them aware of sources of financial assistance. In 1972 Talent Search spent $5 million to reach 125,000 youths; more than half of those recruited were blacks.

Special Services for Disadvantaged Students, first funded in 1970, seeks to help poor students to remain in college once they get there. The program funds schools to provide services including counseling, tutoring, and student personnel services. In 1972, 420 projects helped approximately 49,000 students, of whom 56 percent were black.

Although the Trio programs, as these three encouragement measures are called, were nominally designed to serve all poor and educationally disadvantaged high school students, most clients are from minority groups. In 1972, only one-fourth of Trio participants were white, despite the fact that three-fourths of those eligible were white. Apparently, educational institutions, most of whom are under federal pressure to equalize their minority enrollment ratios, are using the federal support presumably provided for all poor students to recruit black and other minorities to meet their goals.

In addition to support for black students, the federal government also aids black colleges. Under the Support for Developing Institutions program the Office of Education provides grants to colleges for teaching fellowships and professorships, visiting scholars, and cooperative arrangements such as shared curriculums and student exchanges and joint use of library and laboratory facilities. In 1972, $52 million was spent under the program at 556 institutions—three-fifths of which were predominantly black colleges.

It is difficult to gauge the overall impact of the federal effort to equalize opportunities for higher education. Funding has been limited in comparison to the potential need, and many students would undoubtedly have attended college even without the aid. But the over-representation of blacks in the programs may indicate that the assistance has been of greater importance to them. To the extent that lower college enrollment ratios have been the result of unawareness of or inability to afford college rather than inadequate preparation, the combination of federal aid to students and federal pressure on institutions to equalize enrollments may have been key factors in black enrollment gains during the 1960s.

General Educational Aid

Many other federal education programs, though not specifically for disadvantaged or black students, offer them substantial benefits. For example, children of social security recipients are eligible for federal payments if they are attending college and are between the ages of eighteen and twenty-two. This program, enacted in 1965, paid $700 million in student support during 1972, of which 14 percent went to blacks. Other large federal programs reach blacks because they are represented among the eligible population, including aid to the handicapped, vocational education, aid to impacted school districts, and veterans' educational benefits (table 12-2).

Table 12-2. Federal education programs which benefit blacks, 1972

Program	Outlays (millions)	Estimated black share (percent)	Estimated black share (millions)
Aid to impacted school districts	$ 649	12.9	$ 84
Veterans benefits	1,758	8.5	149
Vocational education	547	14.9	82
OASDI student benefits	704	14.0	99
Education for the handicapped	110	14.4	16

Source: U.S. Office of Management and Budget, *Special Analyses of the Budget of the United States Government, 1974* (Washington: Government Printing Office), p. 107, and unpublished data.

Blacks, who make up about 13 percent of all federal and civilian and military workers, may be estimated to receive about the same proportion of federal aid to impacted areas. Similarly, blacks, who are 14 percent of disabled social security beneficiaries, receive about the same amount of educational aid to the handicapped.

Of all the large federal educational programs, the lowest rate of black participation is in veterans' education readjustment benefits. This program, under which veterans receive monthly support while enrolled in college or vocational training, includes less than 9 percent black students because few college-age veterans are black (9.1 percent). Also, black veterans have less education on the average than whites, and thus use the college-oriented program less frequently.

Remedial Education and Training

For those who have failed in or been failed by the schools, a second chance is provided by remedial education and training programs. Outlays for these jumped from $235 million in 1962, largely expended for vocational rehabilitation, employment services, and aid to veterans, to $5.2 billion for these and dozens of other national programs in 1972 (table 12-3). These provided such diverse services as

Table 12-3. Federal outlays for manpower programs, fiscal 1961, 1967, 1973 (millions)

	1961	1967	1973 (estimated)
Total	$235	$1,770	$5,236
Institutional training	4	573	889
On-the-job training	2	55	524
Vocational rehabilitation	66	234	757
In-school work support	—	183	388
Post-school work support	—	262	1,439
Job placement	129	292	518
Employment-related child care	26	53	517
Administration	8	118	205

Source: Sar A. Levitan, Garth L. Mangum, and Ray Marshall, *Human Resources and Labor Markets: Labor and Manpower in the American Economy* (New York: Harper and Row, 1975), table 12-1 (revised by the Center for Manpower Policy Studies, George Washington University, April 1, 1974).

counseling and testing, on-the-job and institutional training, work experience, remedial education, sheltered employment, job creation, and placement. Their common goal was to help workers to effectively compete in the labor market by providing them with education, skills, positive work attitudes, experience, and credentials.

Even when allowance is made for their overrepresentation among the disadvantaged, blacks receive a disproportionate share of aid under these federally assisted manpower programs. Of 1.4 million new enrollees in the major programs (assuming no double counting) in fiscal 1973, 630,000 or 45 percent were black (table 12-4). Reflecting their critical teenage unemployment, the black concentration was greatest in the youth oriented programs, the Neighborhood Youth Corps and the Job Corps. Excluding these, the blacks represented a third of all new enrollees in fiscal 1973. Even this total is more than

Table 12-4. New black enrollees in federal manpower programs, 1973

Program	Blacks as a percent of all new enrollees	New black enrollees (thousands)
Neighborhood Youth Corps (in school and summer)	48	268
Neighborhood Youth Corps (out of school)	44	33
Public Employment Program	26	46
Manpower Development and Training institutional	30	36
Work Incentive program	45	106
Concentrated Employment Program	58	40
JOBS	41	21
Jobs-optional program	22	17
Job Corps	59	26
Public Service Careers	45	28
Operation Mainstream	20	7

Source: *Manpower Report of the President, 1974* (Washington: Government Printing Office, March 1974), p. 367.

the proportion of blacks with employment problems. Blacks represented less than a fifth of the unemployed in 1972, 22 percent of those with inadequate employment and earnings, and 16 percent of labor force participants with less than a high school education.[12] Judged by these benchmarks, it is apparent that manpower assistance is oriented toward overcoming racial as well as economic disadvantages.

Programs for Youths

The Neighborhood Youth Corps (NYC) serves more blacks than any other manpower program. The in-school and summer segments, which had more than 265,000 black new enrollees in fiscal 1973, aimed to provide part-time jobs for students to give them useful work experience and a source of income that might help them stay in or return to school. In fact, however, summer NYC has been expanded each year largely as a means of keeping youths off the streets. Training never developed as an important component and the ability to provide useful work experience was hampered by the short term of employment. In both the in-school and summer segments, youths were put to work as recreation aides, clerks, maintenance personnel, and at other low-skill jobs requiring little supervision or overhead, therefore providing limited on-the-job training.[13]

Nevertheless, there is evidence of some positive long-run effects. A study of NYC participants found that they earned an average of $831 more during the eighteen-month follow-up period than a carefully selected control group. For blacks the differences were greater, $1,182 for males and $1,217 for females, mostly the result of more steady employment. These income gains were statistically significant and outweighed the costs of the program. The probability of black youths completing high school was also increased, while for whites it remained unchanged.[14]

Whether or not black participants benefit in the longer run, they are certainly better off in the short-run. In August 1972 there were an estimated 418,000 nonwhite youths working in NYC. In the same month there were 304,000 unemployed sixteen- to nineteen-year-old nonwhites out of 1.2 million labor force participants. It is difficult to guess what would have occurred in the absence of NYC, but if all participants had been unemployed, the nonwhite teenage unemployment rate would have been increased from 26 to 62 percent. More conservatively, if participants had the same employment status as all nonwhite youths in August 1972, the unemployment rate would have still been raised by a fifth.[15] The Neighborhood Youth Corps is obviously very important in mitigating the summer job crisis for black youths.

Despite these positive impacts and popularity of the NYC summer and in-school program, the Nixon administration tried to impound the funds for the 1973 summer program as a budget-cutting measure. The courts declared this to be illegal, and the usual summer allocation was released so that enrollments came close to reaching the level of the previous summer. But no NYC appropriations were requested for fiscal 1974, on the assumption that they could be financed from a block manpower appropriation under the proposed revenue sharing plan.

The out-of-school NYC and Job Corps programs work with more disadvantaged youths and are far more costly than summer and in-school NYC. In the Job Corps, where three-fifths of 1973 enrollees were black, nine of every ten had less than a high school education and seven out of ten were from families with less than $4,000 annual income. In the out-of-school segment, which was two-fifths black, almost all participants were dropouts and from poor families. There has been limited success in helping this hardcore, especially blacks. A one-year follow-up of 1966 Job Corps terminees found that the average hourly wage gain of whites employed eighteen months after termination was 75 cents more than their pre-enrollment average; for blacks it was 62 cents more.[16] A follow-up study of the Neighborhood Youth Corps out-of-school enrollees in Indiana—three-fourths of whom were nonwhite—found that on the average they earned only $136 more than controls over the two-year period, a statistically insignificant difference.[17] Even if there is no positive lasting impact, however, these programs do provide an alternative to unemployment and street life.

Apprenticeship programs serve a much more qualified group of youth, helping them to get into better paying blue-collar jobs. Beginning in 1963, Apprenticeship Information Centers were established in several cities to provide comprehensive information concerning apprenticeship opportunities. AICs helped place over 7,500 individuals during fiscal year 1972, bringing the program's five-year total to 36,330. One-quarter of these placements were from minority groups. More significantly, 120 Apprenticeship Outreach Programs operated jointly by local building and construction trades councils, the National Urban League, and the Workers' Defense League, provided preapprenticeship training and placement in apprenticeship for 17,000 minority group members through fiscal 1972, primarily in the building and construction trades. Despite these efforts, only 9 percent of registered apprentices in 1970 were minority youth.[18]

Training and Other Pre-employment Assistance

There are a number of programs which provide primarily adult clienteles with training and other pre-employment assistance. Institutional training under the Manpower Development and Training Act (MDTA) dates back to 1962 and is remedial in its orientation, providing vocational training, basic education where needed, and an allowance. MDTA was initially intended for the technologically displaced, but was altered to stress the needs of those with socioeconomic handicaps. From fiscal 1963 to 1968 the black share of participants rose from 21 to 45 percent. By 1973, however, it had fallen back to 30 percent.

Blacks have had mixed success under MDTA. A 1970–1971 survey of 1969 terminees revealed that blacks with at least one job in the interim earned $1,438 above pretraining averages, compared with a $1,678 gain for whites.[19] A more detailed study of MDTA enrollees in Michigan also found that white participants gained more than black ones; but the social benefits were greater in the case of blacks because transfer payments were reduced by more.[20] The most extensive study which has been done, following up 57,000 1964 institutional enrollees for five years, indicated that black females gained more than any other group of participants, while black males experienced smaller but still positive increases which tended to decline over time.[21]

The Work Incentive Program (WIN) provides pre-employment services and training to persons on welfare, mostly mothers. Initiated in 1967, it offers basic education, vocational training, child care, and counseling, as well as placement services and some subsidized jobs. As a work incentive, participants are able to keep the first $30 of monthly earnings plus one-third of the remainder without offsets from welfare payments. In 1972, to encourage greater use of the program, funds were allocated for job creation and tax incentives were provided to cover the costs to private employers of hiring recipients. Mandatory work requirements were legislated for certain employable groups and administrative changes placed emphasis on placement rather than training.

WIN has never lived up to the expectations that it would significantly reduce the welfare caseload. By mid-1972, 354,000 had participated in WIN and about 137,000 had been placed in jobs. However, WIN apparently provided little upgrading of enrollees, and even those who were placed in jobs left the program with the same meager skills with which they started. WIN has provided, therefore, no sure exit from poverty. According to Department of Labor estimates, no more than one-third of WIN participants will remain employed and be able to leave the welfare rolls; another third will continue working and their grants will be reduced.[22]

WIN's limited success in solving problems of dependency is more critical in the case of blacks because blacks are overrepresented on welfare rolls and among WIN participants. Blacks comprised 45 percent of WIN participants in 1973, and 43 percent of family heads on welfare.

Evidently, it will be difficult to reduce welfare caseloads by opening employment alternatives. To create attractive work incentives, the income which can be earned while still receiving benefits must be increased, which widens the range of eligibility for welfare. Work requirements are difficult to enforce and must be supported by job creation and other services such as child care, which may cost more than welfare itself. Reducing or failing to raise the level of welfare benefits in order to force welfare recipients to take jobs may be harmful to those who cannot work.

Another preemployment effort which serves a large black clientele is the Concentrated Employment Program (CEP), initiated in 1967 as a comprehensive and concentrated attack on the manpower problems of central city ghettos. Funds were to be channeled through locally controlled groups which could then purchase or provide a complete range of manpower services to clients. For the most part, community action agencies created under the Economic Opportunity Act were named as prime sponsors for these efforts.

CEP staffs were sometimes highly competitive with, or even antagonistic toward, local employment services. Programs frequently duplicated services already in existence, and administration was sometimes lax. Initially intended to concentrate resources, the resources were spread thinly—CEPs were established in sixty-eight cities and fourteen rural areas. The result was simply another categorical multipurpose program rather than a comprehensive system, with the significant difference that it was largely operated by community groups. A number of blacks were employed within the CEPs, and their focus was on the disadvantaged minorities. Very soon, however, autonomy was curtailed. In 1969 the Labor Department made local employment services the prime sponsors under CEP, so that existing community groups would have to contract from them for the delivery of specific services. Though the causal connection is not clear-cut, the proportion of blacks served by CEPs nationally fell from 81 percent in fiscal 1968 to 58 percent in fiscal 1973.

While most of the manpower programs were federal initiatives, the Opportunities Industrialization Center (OIC) program was a black initiated and black run effort. Founded in Philadelphia by Reverend Leon Sullivan and his Zion Baptist Church, OIC was a self-help skill-training program. Stress was placed on developing and supporting positive work attitudes, with intensive group and individual counseling. The result was to attract the most achievement-oriented of the disadvantaged, who in turn were relatively easy to train and place.

Based on its success, OIC was expanded to over one hundred cities with federal support funneled through a national OIC office in Philadelphia. In early 1972 the Department of Labor estimated that over 50,000 blacks or other minority group members had been placed by OICs at a cost of only $1,000 each, making this perhaps the most cost-effective of all federal manpower programs. It is not known to what extent the low unit cost was achieved by careful selection (and self-selection where no stipends were paid) of the most qualified clients.

Despite these high marks, OICs were threatened by the passage of the Comprehensive Education and Training Act in 1973. Under the new legislation OIC will no longer be funded through a grant to the black run national center; rather, local elected officials will have the option of continuing OIC support out of manpower revenue sharing funds. In some cities OICs are well-established and will not be threatened. In others, however, little leverage has been achieved because they have operated outside the local funding system, and there is a good chance that operations will be curtailed. At any rate, power will be shifted to state and local officials and out of the hands of blacks, and the special attributes of the program with its stress on black identity and pride may be deemphasized.

Earning and Learning on the Job

One of the weaknesses of pre-employment assistance is that jobs may not be available when participants complete their training. A more effective approach in some situations is to provide training and other services on the job, combining earning and learning.

In 1968 President Johnson announced a new partnership program—Job Opportunities in the Business Sector (JOBS)—under which businesses would provide jobs for the disadvantaged with the government subsidizing the extra hiring and training costs. Participants had to be poor and either unemployed or underemployed, under twenty-two or over forty-five years of age, minority group members, less than a high school graduate, or handicapped. Though JOBS was not intended as a black program, it began that way, with blacks accounting for three-fourths of all those hired in the first two years.

Both the quality of training and the extent of new opportunities that were opened under the program have been in doubt. A study by the General Accounting Office revealed that most of the subsidized jobs were low-skilled, dead-end positions, little better than the participants could have gotten on their own without help. The federal subsidies—which averaged around $2,500 per slot—were sometimes unrealistic, with reimbursements for training costing up to $3,600 for janitors and $3,900 for laborers. Overall, the training was usually informal and sometimes nonexistent.[23]

There may have been, however, a substantial spillover effect as employers changed their general hiring requirements as a result of jawboning by the National Alliance of Business which coordinated the program. Though statistics are not very dependable, it is estimated that the number of jobs pledged by employers without federal subsidy exceeded subsidized jobs by a factor of three or four to one, and the characteristics of the persons hired under these two segments were surprisingly similar.[24] With the recession, however, voluntary efforts quickly evaporated and subsidized positions also declined substantially. In October 1970 contract hires peaked at 43,000. By May 1973 the number was down to 13,600. A related program, JOBS-Optional, or JOP, was initiated in October 1971 and offered a smaller subsidy with fewer restrictions on employers; enrollment in this program fell from 13,800 in its first year to 11,200 in May 1973.

There is some indirect evidence that it was the black participants who more frequently suffered the consequences of these cutbacks. Some of the 30,000 decline in JOBS employment was due to participants graduating into full-time jobs, but layoffs and quits were the major factor. The proportion of JOBS participants who were black fell from 74 percent in fiscal 1970 to 41 percent in 1973, suggesting that blacks were more likely to get the pink slips.

Job Creation

In slack labor markets, neither jawboning nor subsidies can produce enough openings to employ all who need work, and government must step in to create jobs in the public sector. To combat high and rising unemployment in the early 1970s, the Emergency Employment Act of 1971 created the Public Employment Program (PEP) providing federal funding at the state and local level for a peak of over 180,000 jobs. These were to be transitional opportunities for the unemployed and underemployed, combining work experience, training, job restructuring, and civil service reform to assure permanent jobs for the majority of participants.

An estimated 75,000 blacks were hired under the program from its inception, 94 percent of whom were unemployed. Though their wages were comparable to those of whites, blacks more frequently had jobs in public works and social service. Of blacks who left the program, 27 percent moved into permanent jobs in the public sector and another 10 percent were placed in the private sector. Overall, blacks tended to find permanent employment as frequently as whites and to experience about the same wage changes.

In 1973 the administration recommended the termination of PEP on the grounds that the program's high cost was not justified during a period of declining unemployment and strong inflationary pressures. The phase-out decision may have been premature in light of the program's popularity and effectiveness. PEP demonstrated that productive rather than make-work jobs could be created at the state and local level to deliver useful services and to employ those who would otherwise be out of work. Blacks were employed as successfully as whites. If a 4.5 percent unemployment rate is considered the cut-off point when job creation is no longer required, there is a long way to go before blacks reach this level.

A Smaller Share of a Smaller Pie

In general, manpower programs were a boon to blacks in the late 1960s, with clear short-run and possible long-run benefits. While these programs continued to expand through fiscal 1973, several changes occurred which threatened to reduce the impact for blacks.

1. The growth of manpower outlays apparently ended in 1973. The fiscal 1974 budget represented a 3 percent cutback of $144 million from the previous year. When the impact of inflation is considered this equaled a decline of 11 percent in real terms.[25]

2. The black share in most manpower programs declined noticeably in the 1970s, as priority was placed on employing other minorities and veterans, and as more whites were put out of work by the recession (figure 12-1). It is doubtful that blacks will ever regain their previous share.

3. Manpower revenue sharing under CETA threatened many of

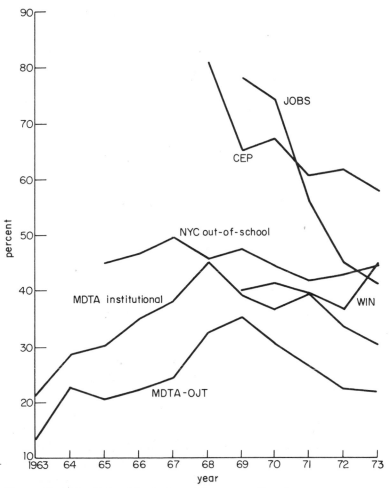

Figure 12-1. Declining black share of new enrollees in manpower programs, fiscal 1963–1973.

Source: *Manpower Report of the President* (Washington: Government Printing Office, 1967–1973), annual issues 1967–1974.

the programs of special interest to blacks. The two major programs in which the black share continued to rise in the 1970s were the Job Corps and the Neighborhood Youth Corps summer program. Under CETA, NYC would be placed at the mercies of state and local governments and the Job Corps would be curtailed.

Have Human Resource Investments Helped?

Neither compensatory education nor training were explicitly designed to compensate for racial inequalities. But since blacks accounted for a large share of the nation's underdeveloped human resources they benefited disproportionately. Some of the compensatory programs such as aid to higher education, the Job Corps, and the Concentrated Employment Programs have served mostly black clienteles. Others, though not serving blacks primarily, have been important simply because black needs were greatest and the programs were of substantial size. In 1972 Title I of the Elementary and Secondary Education Act delivered half a billion dollars to schools educating more than 2 million black children, and in black schools in some cities ESEA funds amounted to a third of the school budget. Though these expenditures did not come close to equalizing the resources available for educating the disadvantaged, they were steps toward that goal.

The critical issue is not the extent of the investment, but the level of payoff. In the schools it is clear that the level of aid so far expended has wrought some small but not inconsequential improvements in the educational status of blacks. They are more able and more likely to enroll in the once largely white educational preserves at the two ends of the public school system—preschool and college. In the years between, a start has been made toward equalizing the quality of the educational experience available to blacks and whites. These changes have worked no miracles in terms of achievement results, but they have, in combination with federal efforts to insure equal representation and full integration of all types of schools, been instrumental in black educational gains.

The fundamental difficulty with federal aid to education is that the federal government is not and cannot be the primary agent of change. The control of education remains in the hands of private institutions and state or local governments, and the federal government has only the rather blunt tool of dollars with which to affect the system. In a few cases, such as Head Start and Follow Through, federal programs sought to create new independent educational vehicles. Not surprisingly, these innovative efforts have had some success. On the other hand, successful federal efforts at the college level have been modest efforts to help limited numbers of poor and minority students by exerting leverage in their favor in the selection process. But where the government has sought to help all the educationally deprived and has been forced to depend on the efforts of the established public and private school systems, its efforts have had less effect. The federal government has had some impact by encouraging greater enrollment and integration of blacks and in funding innovative improvements, but local or individual initiatives still hold the key to the greatest progress for educationally disadvantaged blacks.

Manpower programs have been created almost exclusively by the federal government and for this reason, perhaps, their impacts on blacks have been more substantial. Whatever the success and shortcomings of the individual manpower programs, there is no doubt that blacks benefited greatly by their rapid expansion. The weight of evidence is that they have improved wages and reduced unemployment somewhat, providing significant gains for at least a minority of participants. There have also been indirect benefits. The stipends paid under most of these programs have been as important in supporting individuals as an equal amount of dollars provided through welfare or unemployment compensation. Additionally, some of the programs such as Opportunities Industrialization Centers and the Concentrated Employment Program placed administrative control in the hands of blacks and thus gave them some power over institutions. Manpower programs have been and still are a major prop for community based organizations.

There is no doubt that the rapid expansion of the manpower programs and the large share of services going to blacks made a significant contribution to their welfare. By the same token, the proposed budget cutbacks or at least slowing growth in the manpower programs in the mid-1970s, as well as the reorganization which is likely to reduce further the already declining black share of resources, will have negative consequences.

Clearly, neither compensatory education, nor vocational training has even begun to develop much of the untapped human resources of blacks. Yet the programs cannot be declared failures because they have not redressed the imbalances between the education and employability of blacks and whites. Many programs have succeeded, and others have had their greatest impacts on blacks, even if they have achieved less than had been hoped. If national evaluations reveal that the problems have not been solved, they reflect more the enormity of the task of equalizing human resource development than failures of design or implementation of federal programs.

13

CHANGING THE RULES OF THE GAME

Income maintenance, in-kind aid, and human resource development all directly compensate for the unequal status of blacks. More of them are poor, so they receive more money; more are ill-housed, so they get a disproportionate share of federal housing subsidies; and more are educationally disadvantaged, so they more often participate in compensatory education and remedial manpower programs. This is not just a matter of treating the symptoms. Deficiencies in different dimensions of life are causes as well as effects. Inadequate education limits job opportunities; inadequate earnings affect housing and health; poor nutrition may make education impossible. Improvements on any front should lead to improvements elsewhere. But in each case there is a significant segment of the problem which is not explained by these factors. For instance, adjusting for education, central city residence, lack of training, and other variables still leaves substantial differences in employment and earnings between whites and blacks.

Blacks are worse off because the cards have been, and remain, stacked against them. Their dollars of income will not buy them equal housing. Their years of schooling will not open up equal jobs. And their best efforts will not produce an equal income. Discrimination exists in every dimension, setting limits to progress. Cash, in-kind, and human resource development programs can only equalize black status to the threshold of discrimination, which is still far below whites.

Eliminating discrimination is not like building homes, providing medical services, creating jobs, or supplementing income. The prob-

lem is seldom obvious or well-defined. Most institutional arrangements or individual decisions are subtly discriminatory rather than
obviously racist; the rules of the game are usually unstated and
frequently flexible. Moreover, to change the rules often involves overcoming long-standing practices, deeply ingrained beliefs, and cher-
ished privileges and priorities of whites. If intransigence is widespread,
and the conflicts-of-interest are great, changes in laws, or incentives to
encourage changes in behavior, may have little effect.

It should not be surprising, then, that discrimination in employment, education, housing, and other areas has proved difficult to
overcome. Yet significant efforts were made in the 1960s to try to get
at these causes of black problems.

Equalizing Employment Opportunities

Title VII of the 1964 Civil Rights Act outlawed discrimination on
the basis of race, color, religion, sex, or national origin in hiring,
compensation, and promotion. The law applied to all private employers, employment agencies, and labor organizations employing or
serving twenty-five or more persons, and an Equal Employment
Opportunity Commission was created to enforce its provisions. Initially, this commission's role was limited to information-gathering,
mediation to encourage voluntary compliance, and "friend of the
court" legal support in antidiscrimination suits brought by others.
Amendments in 1972 extended coverage to smaller organizations
(fifteen or more people) and to state and local governments, government organizations, and educational institutions. More significantly,
the EEOC was empowered to act as a plaintiff bringing civil actions in
federal court seeking remedies on behalf of those who had suffered
from discrimination.

The number of charges of discrimination flowing into the EEOC
has nearly tripled since 1970, reaching over 47,000 during fiscal
1972. Approximately six of every ten allege racial discrimination.
Over 85 percent of the complaints are against employers, with the rest
against unions, employment agencies, and, in a few cases, against other
parties. Complaints of racial discrimination usually involved a refusal

of employment, a discharge, or an inferior job classification. Charges of exclusion from unions on the basis of race were relatively rare, accounting for 4 percent of the racial discrimination charges against unions; complaints about unequal referral practices were more common.

Despite this rising caseload, the EEOC did not have a major impact in its first six years. Unable to actively use the courts, it relied on the conciliation process, seeking written voluntary agreements complying with the legal standards of Title VII; formal decisions were less frequently rendered. The procedures were time-consuming and the results were meager. In fiscal 1972 the Commission completed action on over 2,800 cases without a formal decision, and in only 412 of them was a written agreement achieved; of the 970 cases closed after a decision was issued, 314 ended with agreements.

Even when conciliation agreements were reached, they had no legal force and thus often produced meager changes in the market place. A typical example involved the complaint of two black women who were twice refused sales jobs in a small southern general merchandise store in 1966. After an initial investigation established "reasonable cause" to suspect discrimination, the EEOC negotiated an agreement with the home office of the parent company, which offered the two women jobs and $1,300 in back pay. In addition, the company agreed to treat the job applications of blacks and whites equally and to develop policies to recruit and promote blacks. By 1971, however, no substantial changes had occurred. The women had ultimately refused the jobs they were offered, blacks had not filled the two positions, and only one black had been promoted. The EEOC had not checked back to monitor the terms of the agreement. Instead, the home office of the store had issued several policy statements on equal employment opportunities. The overall impact of the conciliation was to benefit the two complaining parties without any continuing influence on black employment or any specific change in company policy.

Such ineffectiveness was not uncommon. Conciliations often dealt with less severe discrimination problems. A study comparing firms charged with discrimination by the EEOC with others not involved in such actions found that one in four of the respondents had better minority employment records than other similar firms. The overall effects of the EEOC activities were usually not discernible. In Memphis, Tennessee, where sixteen successful conciliations were negotiated in 1967 and 1968, minority employment among employers subject to the law increased only from 29.1 to 29.7 percent for men between 1966 and 1969. In Atlanta, Georgia, where eight conciliations were successful during 1967 and 1968, minority employment among males dropped from 16.5 to 16.0 percent.[1] Apparently, there were too few successful conciliations to have a direct impact on total employment in the community, and few uninvolved employers felt threatened enough to reduce discrimination.

The basic compliance procedure remained unchanged throughout the period prior to March 1972 when the expanded powers became law. However, as court decisions broadened the definition of discrimination and the employers' liability for such acts, the EEOC gained leverage. In 1971 the Supreme Court ruled (*Griggs* v. *Duke Power Co.*) that Title VII "proscribes not only overt discrimination but also practices that are fair in form, but discriminatory in operation." Pre-employment tests that were not job-related were ruled illegal since arbitrary achievement tests were more likely to exclude blacks and other minorities. The precedent was expanded to other job requirements that were not business necessities. The Court ruled (*Gregory* v. *Litton Systems, Inc.*) that a company's policy of refusing to employ people with a number of arrests, but no convictions, was discriminatory because blacks are statistically more likely to be arrested than are whites. Perhaps most significantly, a landmark case in 1971 (*Robinson* v. *Lorillard Co.*) established the principle of monetary relief in class action cases and raised the specter of substantial settlement costs.[2]

The commission's new potential for filing civil court class actions with large settlements caused considerable concern among employers. Many who feared conciliation activities might be abandoned in favor of litigation became much more amenable to conciliation. In 1973 the American Telephone and Telegraph Company signed a consent decree providing $15 million in restitution and back pay for several classes of female employees and a $23 million promotion package for women and minorities.[3] This agreement was the first shot in a stepped up campaign, and during 1974 a number of other large restitutions were won from employers. The EEOC's staff of lawyers was increased more than fivefold in the first six months of 1973 and the goal was to file 600 suits during the succeeding year. Priority was placed on cases involving major companies and unions with large numbers of outstanding charges against them, with the aim of benefiting the maximum number of people with each settlment. In all likelihood, then, the impact of the EEOC will increase in the 1970s, forcing large employers to respond out of fear of reprisal.

Exerting Leverage in the Marketplace

Another way to pursue equal employment opportunity is to use the market leverage of the government. The Office of Federal Contract Compliance (OFCC) in the Department of Labor is responsible for administering equal employment regulations affecting government contractors. The OFCC was created in 1965 by Executive Order 11246 which forbade discrimination by government contractors on the basis of race, creed, color, sex, or national origin. In February 1970 OFCC issued orders requiring contractors to examine their utilization of minority workers, to establish "affirmative action" goals and timetables for filling the goals, and to collect data to demonstrate their progress.

Unlike the EEOC, the OFCC from its beginning has had specific enforcement powers. It could cancel, terminate, or suspend current contracts, and it could blacklist offenders from future participation in government contracts. These enforcement powers applied to companies employing an estimated one-third of the labor force.[4] But the OFCC did not fully utilize these powers, limiting its enforcement thrust to delaying contract negotiations while establishing affirmative action plans with contractors and unions. In only a few cases were contractors blacklisted and in only one case, that of Edgeley Air Products, Inc., in 1971, was a contractor barred.[5]

Even without strict enforcement actions, OFCC exerted strong pressure on many contractors, particularly those in aerospace and construction. In 1969 the Department of Labor issued the Philadelphia Plan for affirmative action by federal construction contractors in that city which required them to increase their hiring of minority craftsmen from the current 2 percent up to goals of 4 to 9 percent in the first year and 19 to 26 percent by the fourth. If they failed to meet these goals, the employers had to be able to demonstrate that they had made every possible effort to do so. After congressional attempts to ban these types of plans and several trips to the courts by unions and contractors, the Supreme Court in October 1971 refused to review a lower court decision allowing the Philadelphia Plan, and affirmative action plans became an integral part of civil rights law.[6]

Despite this power, the OFCC has not had great success in significantly altering extreme or long-standing practices of employment discrimination. The major reason is that the problems involve an interrelated system of institutions and interests which support discrimination. As an example, in 1967 the OFCC found that at the Sparrows Point, Maryland plant of the Bethlehem Steel Company eight of every ten black employees were working in fourteen of the plant's dirtiest and hottest departments, storing coal and manning the furnaces. Each of the company's departments had its own "lines of progression," and within the "black" departments there were few highly skilled jobs. To transfer to a department with better job progression, blacks were required to start at the bottom, frequently losing pay as well as seniority.

In 1968 the Department of Labor ordered the company to give the plant's 5,400 black employees the opportunity to transfer to better jobs without loss of seniority. But this settlement violated the terms of the union agreement and threatened the cornerstone of union organization—the seniority system. Whites in other departments felt their advancement opportunities were being threatened and they complained bitterly. Five years after the original decision the Department of Labor reviewed the case, reversed itself, and no transfers were affected. The case illustrates the inherent difficulties of ignoring existing institutional arrangements and the dangers of failing to consider the potential damages to the interests of the whites involved.[7]

Even where plans are clearly articulated and enforced, changes may not be sweeping. As a result of a Justice Department suit decided in 1971, 1,600 black employees in Bethlehem's Lackawanna plant were granted the right to transfer. Given four months to sign up, only

430 did and only 70 actually changed jobs. Some were unqualified for the new positions; others with lengthy service saw no advantage in moving as they drew close to retirement; some preferred to stay in departments where they were familiar with the job and with co-workers. Clearly, a long-standing status quo of institutional discrimination cannot be easily erased, even by judicial decree.

This was especially well illustrated by the meager success of OFCC efforts to overcome discrimination in the construction trades in Washington, D.C. In 1971, central city blacks were overrepresented among the 70,000 construction workers in the metropolitan area, but grossly underrepresented in the skilled trade segments paying the highest wages. They made up over 90 percent of union laborers, 85 percent of roofers, 87 percent of teamsters, and 71 percent of cement workers, but less than 1 percent of electricians and less than 5 percent of glaziers, iron workers, pipefitters, plumbers, and painters—occupations paying above average wages.[8]

To combat this discrimination, the Labor Department in 1971 initiated the Washington Plan which, like its predecessor in Philadelphia, established goals and timetables for the hiring of minority workers with the aim of getting the black employment share of skilled workers up to their proportion in the metropolitan population (26 percent).

By May 1972 aggregate data revealed that hiring was already lagging behind the targets for asbestos workers, elevator constructors, glaziers, lathers, painters, and sheet metal workers. Some contractors were shifting minority employees from nonfederal to federal sites and from one federal site to another to satisfy inspectors. Unskilled minority workers had been hired at the last minute and had been given titles and wages as skilled craftsmen, although in fact they were doing other work. A large proportion were neither apprentices nor union journeymen; rather they were trainees or workers who had been given temporary work permits by the unions. Between June 1968 and May 1971 a hundred extra minority apprenticeships, at most, could be attributed to the Washington Plan, and less than half of those entering could be expected to become journeymen if the usual dropout rate occurred. At best, the impacts of the Washington Plan were marginal.[9]

This modest success was typical of that experienced in other areas.

Some attempts were made to meet quotas and lip service was paid to the regulations, but there was little institutional change. A few blacks were hired in better paying jobs, certainly justifying the effort, but as the record of the struggles in the building trades suggested, conditions could quickly return to the old status quo when enforcement pressures were eased. Institutional discrimination will not evaporate in the face of government pressure unless it is more consistent and more forceful than in the past.

The Employment Impacts

Statistics on actions, successful settlements, and policies of the EEOC and OFCC provide only some of the clues to their real impact. There may be, for instance, important spillover effects as employers change their practices in fear of government sanctions. Voluntary affirmative action efforts may also result from appeals to corporate conscience. If even small marginal changes are widespread, the impacts can be very beneficial for blacks. In 1972 there were over 3 million nonagricultural business establishments with payrolls, and if only one in six hired another black, the unemployment rates of whites and blacks could have been equalized. On the other hand, there may be many institutional impediments which remain obdurate. Court orders and government mandates may receive only nominal support from employers.

One way to estimate the net impact of OFCC, EEOC, and federal court actions is to compare the experience of firms that have government contracts with those that do not. The assumption is that the former would be more responsive to governmental affirmative action policies. Data for a sample of over 40,000 establishments filing EEOC reports on minority employment in both 1966 and 1970 showed that after controlling for firm size and region, firms with government contracts increased their employment of black men by 3.3 percent more than those not doing business with the federal government. In firms with no black employees in 1966, those with government contracts were 10 percent more likely to have hired at least one black male than those without. The employment effect was largest in firms with more than 500 employees. But the occupational upgrading of blacks was only slightly greater in government contracting firms. Overall, the wage share of black workers in the average firm with government contracts increased by 28 percent between 1966 and 1970, compared with 25 percent in other firms.[10]

While such gains are modest in terms of changing discriminatory practices, it may be that none would have occurred either in contracting or noncontracting firms if no governmental efforts had been exerted on behalf of blacks. In general, the marginal changes in the behavior of a number of firms may have ended up having a substantial impact for blacks. Evidence suggests, however, that progress has been meager in overcoming more serious impediments to equal opportunity.

Integrating the Schools

When the Supreme Court ruled in 1954 that racially segregated schools were inherently unequal, the great majority of all children in both the North and the South were attending all white or all black schools. Though many instances of segregation still exist, complete racial isolation has declined sharply and there has been some progress toward full integration. The courts have played a fundamental role.

The Battle in the Courts

The history of Supreme Court rulings concerning school desegregation is one of initial unwillingness to dictate solutions, followed by growing impatience with the speed of integration in many jurisdictions, culminating in detailed and sometimes drastic orders for complete and immediate desegregation, and finally some backing off in the 1970s from hard-line solutions.

1. *Brown* v. *The Board of Education of Topeka, Kansas, 1954*— In two successive decisions the court held dual school systems to be denials of constitutional rights and directed "a prompt and reasonable start toward full compliance."

2. *Cooper* v. *Aaron, 1958*—The court repeated that no law or policy of state or local governments (whether it involved the school boards or not) could directly or indirectly have the effect of promoting racial segregation.

3. *Griffin* v. *Prince Edward County, Virginia, School System, 1964* —The court declared that there had been "entirely too much deliberation and not enough speed" in implementing its 1954 decision, and held the closing of Prince Edward County schools while other schools in the state remained open to be an infringement of the equal rights of blacks.

4. *Bell* v. *School City of Gary, Indiana, 1964*—In a decision which attracted much attention, the court refused to review a lower court decision which upheld de facto segregation on the grounds that policies of government were not involved.

5. *Wallace* v. *Bibb County, Alabama, Board of Education* v. *United States, 1967*—The court for the first time ordered an entire state, Alabama, to desegregate its schools.

6. *Green* v. *County School Board of New Kent County, Virginia, 1968*—The court found a "freedom of choice" plan to be inadequate because it failed to achieve desegregated schools and because it placed the burden of eliminating segregation on parents and children rather than on the government which had fostered it.

7. *United States* v. *Montgomery County, Alabama, School System, 1969*—Moving toward its position in the 1970s requiring schools to be racially indistinguishable, the court held that school faculties could not be segregated.

8. *Swann* v. *Charlotte-Mecklenberg County, North Carolina, Board of Education, 1971*—The court upheld the use of busing, numerical ratios, and gerrymandered districts as temporary measures to achieve integration if the school system had failed to end segregation by other methods. The court ruling applied only to school districts which had previously enforced racial segregation.

9. *School Board of Richmond, Virginia* v. *Virginia State Board, 1973*—In a 4–4 split decision, the court upheld the reversal of a widely heralded lower court decision which would have forced the consolidation of the predominantly black Richmond school district with two white suburban districts.

10. *Keyes* v. *School District No. 1, Denver, Colorado, 1973*—In the first decision in a case in which school segregation had not been imposed by law, the court held that school board policies had helped establish segregated schools and that the school board thus bore the responsibility for desegregation.

11. *San Antonio, Texas, School District* v. *Rodriguez, 1973*—The court refused to strike down the property tax as a method for financing schools, holding that education was not a constitutional right, and that variations in expenditures could not be proven to be "invidiously discriminating" against a specific class of persons.

The gradual expansion of the Supreme Court's role in equalizing education is clear. Not only students, but teachers and administrators have come under court review; not only southern laws, but the policies and practices of northern school districts have been cited to justify judicially decreed desegregation. Most important, the court has ordered not just an end to the policies which encourage segregation, but also an active effort by formerly discriminatory school systems to insure fully integrated schools.

Some of the recent dissenting opinions have gone even farther to urge that the distinction between de facto and de jure segregation should be abandoned, claiming that any type of segregation is a denial of equal protection. But the court has retained its original rationale for ordering desegregation: if agencies of government have by policy or law fostered segregated schools, then they have the responsibility to right this injustice by whatever means are necessary. If there is no proof of state or local discriminatory practices, then integration may not be mandated.

Compliance Efforts

At first the job of enforcing the Supreme Court's decisions fell entirely to plaintiffs in lower courts. The federal government intervened occasionally during the Kennedy administration as a "friend of the court" or (using the authority of the Civil Rights Acts of 1957 and 1960) by threatening to take away aid to school districts impacted by federal installations. But these efforts achieved very slow progress.

The Southern Education Reporting Service estimated that in 1964, 89 percent of all black children in southern and border states still attended all black schools.[11]

In that year the responsibility for enforcement shifted more directly to federal shoulders with the passage of the Civil Rights Act. Titles IV and VI of the act authorized the government to intervene to insure that desegregation was progressing. Title IV provided for assistance to help school districts to desegregate and authorized the attorney general to sue to obtain compliance. Title VI authorized a cut-off of federal funds to any program guilty of racial discrimination.

Though it was originally envisioned that Title IV would be the chief mechanism of enforcement, the passage of the Elementary and Secondary Education Act in 1965 increased the leverage of Title VI. With approximately $1 billion annually being distributed to schools with disadvantaged children, the threat to take away federal funds grew suddenly from a weak reed to a powerful club.

Enforcement by court action was a time-consuming, scatter-shot method, and the degree of integration obtained by court order seldom matched that which could be achieved by negotiation coupled with the threat of fund withdrawals. Thus, initial efforts to enforce desegregation relied on actions by the Department of Health, Education, and Welfare under Title VI. The United States Office of Education and later the United States Office for Civil Rights issued guidelines to be met in order to obtain federal education money. Initially, only paper compliance was required, and school districts were free to adopt freedom of choice plans allowing parents to decide where they wished to send their children. When these methods proved ineffective, the rules were gradually tightened to force school systems to show clear progress measured by percentages of students desegregated.

By June 30, 1969, the funds of 129 school districts had been cut off, of which 60 had later decided to comply in order to retain the lost federal dollars. Most of these early efforts were directed at southern states. Since the Civil Rights Act specifically forbade attempts to correct racial imbalance caused by housing patterns, action in the North was limited.

The Justice Department was also active prior to 1968, filing 207 suits (of which five were outside the South). In 1969 the new administration elected to shift its enforcement efforts entirely to court action by the Department of Justice under Title IV. Already scheduled fund cutoffs were allowed to go into effect, but no new actions were initiated. A stepped up Justice Department effort was begun in both the South and the North. At the same time, the administration unsuccessfully sought the passage of a $1.5 billion bill to aid school systems in their desegregation efforts.

This change in policy was defended on the grounds that the disadvantaged were the ones hurt most by the withdrawal of federal funds, while legal actions affected the perpetrators rather than the victims. But there may have been other reasons for these actions. Southern congressmen opposed the federal tightening of education grant guidelines as unjustifiable interference in their school systems. An administration with a more sympathetic ear may have elected to substitute a carrot in the form of grants to integrating districts, and a gentler prod in the form of court action against the worst offenders, for the stick of threatened fund cutoffs.

Considerable controversy followed this change in policy. A number of officials in the Department of Health, Education, and Welfare resigned, claiming the administration had given up the effort to integrate the schools. In 1970 the NAACP Legal Defense Fund sued the Department to force a return to its practice of terminating funds for noncomplying schools. The courts ruled in favor of this suit in 1973, and cutoff proceedings were again initiated.

Progress Toward Integration

Despite the changes in policy, progress in achieving desegregation continued during the late 1960s and early 1970s. According to surveys conducted by the Office of Education, the percentage of blacks in majority black schools dropped from 77 percent in 1968 to 63 percent in 1972. Blacks in all black schools declined from 40 to 11 percent (table 13-1).

Progress was most marked in the South. From 1968 to 1972 the proportion of blacks in desegregated schools in seventeen southern states and the District of Columbia rose from 39 to 88 percent. By

Table 13-1. Racial segregation of blacks in public schools, 1968–1972

Status of black students	Total			South and border states			North and West		
	1968	1970	1972	1968	1970	1972	1968	1970	1972
Total black students (thousands)	6,282	6,707	6,641	3,579	3,818	3,810	2,703	2,890	2,831
Percent in schools with a majority of blacks	76.6	66.9	63.2	79.8	62.5	57.4	72.4	72.5	70.9
Percent in schools 80 percent or more black	68.0	49.4	44.5	76.1	43.1	36.0	57.4	57.6	55.9
Percent in all black schools	39.7	14.0	10.9	61.4	15.6	11.5	12.3	11.9	10.0

Source: Department of Health, Education, and Welfare, Press Release, Office of the Secretary, April 12, 1972; and *Digest of Educational Statistics, 1971*, National Center for Educational Statistics, p. 136.

1972, except for a few remaining totally segregated schools, blacks in the South were less racially isolated than those in the North.

This evidence of sharp improvement in the South but little change in the North and West reflects the hands off federal policy where segregation is caused by housing patterns. The large, and in some cases increasing, percentages of racially isolated northern black school children are primarily the result of the influx of blacks to central cities and the exodus of whites, developments over which neither the executive, legislative, nor judicial branches of government have had much influence. In 1971, in thirteen of the fourteen cities with the largest number of black people, 90 percent or more of black children were in majority black schools. In eight of the nine northern or western cities with the largest black populations, racial segregation was at an all time high in 1971 (table 13-2).

Yet housing segregation is not the only cause of racial isolation. Within the cities, and especially the central cities, white flight has occurred not only to the suburbs, but also to the private schools. In 1970, 23 percent of white elementary children in the central cities went to private schools compared to 6 percent of blacks. In secondary schools, 17 percent of whites but 3 percent of blacks were in non-public schools. Though blacks made up 27.4 percent of the central city school-age population in 1970, they accounted for 32.4 percent of children in public schools. Moreover, these aggregates disguise the extent to which whites may abandon public schools in areas with the largest black populations. In fifteen central cities of large metropolitan areas surveyed by the Commission on Civil Rights in 1965, 39 percent of whites had placed their children in private schools. In some cities the percentages were even higher. In Washington, D.C., 48 percent of whites sent their children to private school, and the school system was 95 percent black. In Philadelphia more than 60 percent of white students were privately enrolled, while 61 percent of all public school children were black.

Thus, the results of integration efforts have been mixed, with progress against de jure segregation but stagnation or regression in the cities where de facto segregation prevails. Even in school districts which have been desegregated, segregation frequently begins again at the schoolhouse door. In some southern school districts, students in

Table 13-2. Segregation in public schools in the 25 cities with the largest black populations, 1950–1971

Cities in order of black population	Percent of school system black 1971	Percent in schools with black majority			Percent in schools with 90% or more black enrollment		
		1950	1965	1971	1950	1965	1970
New York	34.2	N.A.	55.5	83.9	N.A.	20.7	57.9
Chicago	55.8	N.A.	96.8	97.8	N.A.	89.2	89.7
Detroit	65.0	91.1[a]	91.5	93.7	69.9[a]	72.3	73.9
Philadelphia	60.5	84.8	90.2	92.6	63.2	72.0	70.0
Washington, D.C.	95.2	N.A.	99.3	99.7	N.A.	90.4	95.0
Los Angeles	24.9	N.A.	87.4	93.2	N.A.	39.5	83.3
Baltimore	68.2	N.A.	92.3	90.8	N.A.	84.2	79.2
Houston	37.8	N.A.	97.6	91.3	N.A.	93.0	73.3
Cleveland	57.3	84.4	94.6	95.4	51.4	82.3	89.2
New Orleans	71.4	N.A.	96.7	93.4	N.A.	95.9	78.6
Atlanta	72.1	N.A.	98.8	92.0	N.A.	97.4	77.9
St. Louis	67.7	N.A.	93.7	97.9	N.A.	90.9	82.7
Memphis	53.7	N.A.	98.8	92.9	N.A.	95.1	89.5
Dallas	36.3	N.A.	90.3	85.0	N.A.	82.6	91.4
Newark	72.0	N.A.	90.3	97.4	N.A.	51.3	86.4
Indianapolis	37.7	88.2	84.2	76.5	83.2	70.5	55.6
Birmingham	56.4	N.A.	92.8	86.1	N.A.	91.6	69.7
Cincinnati	46.1	70.7	88.0	86.3	43.7	49.4	39.5
Oakland	58.1	71.1[a]	83.2	93.7	7.7[a]	48.7	58.6
Jacksonville	31.3	N.A.	87.4	64.0	N.A.	87.4	54.9
Kansas City	52.2	N.A.	85.5	90.3	N.A.	69.1	74.8
Milwaukee	28.0	66.8	86.8	85.2	51.2	72.4	60.4
Pittsburgh	41.4	51.0	82.8	76.6	30.4	49.5	56.5
Richmond	69.1	N.A.	98.5	93.3	N.A.	98.5	44.7
Boston	31.7	N.A.	79.5	85.1	N.A.	35.4	52.0

Sources: U.S. Commission on Civil Rights, *Racial Isolation in the Public Schools,* 1967, pp. 4–9; and U.S. Congress, Senate, Select Committee on Equal Educational Opportunity, *Toward Equal Educational Opportunity,* 92nd Cong., 2d Sess., Report 92-000, pp. 116–117.
   [a] 1960.

desegregated schools have been placed in all black or all white class-rooms. At others, black teachers and administrators lost jobs when schools were consolidated.[12] Sometimes black students in desegregated schools were excluded from participation in the extracurricular activities of their new schools.[13] In the early 1970s a new stage may have been reached in the struggle to achieve integrated schools, with progress in the South beginning to encounter more subtle obstacles and with the drastic measures required to eliminate de facto segregation elsewhere proving too unpopular to implement.

The Controversy Over Busing and
Property Tax Financing

The uncertain nature of the American commitment to equal educational opportunity and the formidable obstacles to further progress are illustrated by the current controversies over busing and property tax financing of the schools. State-aided student transportation for convenience and efficiency has been practiced since 1869, and by 1969, 43 percent of all students were bused to school. But the suggestion that busing should be used to equalize racial imbalances caused by housing patterns set off a backlash which threatened to halt progress on integration.

Busing was initially required to end de jure segregation in the South. But during the late 1960s and early 1970s court decisions extended the busing mandate to northern districts, and in some cases to entire metropolitan areas. These legal decisions antagonized a majority of the public.

By 1971 a Gallup Poll found 77 percent of the nation opposed to busing, and this national consensus transmitted itself to Congress. Although busing foes were not able to command majorities in 1968, the balance shifted during 1970 and 1971 until an antibusing amendment was passed as part of the 1972 Higher Education Act. The compromise measure prohibited the implementation of court-ordered busing to achieve racial balance until all judicial appeals had been exhausted. Significantly, many of the supporters of this legislation were former busing advocates from northern states, who had switched sides after their districts had been required to initiate busing plans.

Though the Supreme Court refused to honor the "no implementation" antibusing amendment, congressional and public sentiment was still strongly behind tighter antibusing laws. In both 1972 and 1973 hearings on the antibusing constitutional amendment were undertaken, and the House voted more than 2 to 1 to outlaw busing in all grades and to restore the status quo in school systems which had already been forced to bus. Apparently, as desegregation began to cross neighborhood lines and to upset the racial, economic, and social isolation of white suburbs, the public began to waiver in its commitment to equal education through integration.

Another related issue is the method of school finance. Property taxes are the primary source of local funds to support the public schools, and for this reason resources available to the schools vary widely (see Chapter 4). By the beginning of 1973 courts in eight states had ruled that these disparities in educational resources (and the presumed inequality of the educational services delivered) denied the poor equal protection under the Fourteenth Amendment. In the most noted case, *Serrano* v. *Priest,* the California supreme court struck down the use of local property taxes to finance schools, ruling that the state's efforts to equalize resources were insufficient to prevent discrimination. Acting on a similar case arising in Texas, however, the Supreme Court voted 5 to 4 to uphold the use of property taxes to finance schools. Though this decision has slowed the judicial effort to reform school financing, other court challenges have been mounted against unequal school outlays and a number of legislated reforms have been proposed. The suggested alternatives include: redrawing school district lines to equalize the tax base; greater compensatory use of state funds, for example, a system of vouchers distributed to parents redeemable by schools for state money; and federal tax relief or increased federal educational expenditures for poorer districts.

Though the issue of unequal school resources had not truly come of age by 1973, it promised to be more important in the future. The burden which school expenditures have placed on homeowners stirred sentiment for abolishing or reforming property taxes. Tax reforms, however, may come to be perceived—like busing—as federal infringement on the rights of parents to educate their children as they wish; in this case, bitter protests against reform may ensue.

The greatest stumbling block to school finance reforms may be the difficulty of establishing new formulas which are fair and acceptable to all parties. Plans which draw on state or federal revenue sources inevitably bring state and federal controls, anathemas to advocates of community schools; formulas which seek to equalize local tax resources encounter the thorny problem of what should be equalized. Some central city districts have large tax revenues from industrial and commercial taxpayers but low average family income. If property tax bases were equalized, they would lose money, while if income formulas were used, they would gain. Some variations in school expenditures result from differences in tax effort. Equalizing tax rates would conflict with the wishes of some parents to spend more on their children's educations. Moreover, the rationale for equalizing school finances may conflict with efforts to provide compensatory education to disadvantaged children. Finally, the disputed effectiveness of additional expenditures in improving the quality of education has raised doubts whether school finance reform will actually have the hoped for benefits to school children. These reservations suggest that equalizing school finances may be neither palatable to the electorate nor an effective solution to the problems of unequal educational opportunities.

How Much Have the Rules Been Changed?

Certainly, social reform brought one fundamental educational change during the 1960s. In the South total racial isolation established by law was largely eliminated. Moreover, throughout the nation, the rights of blacks and especially poor blacks to equal education opportunities were recognized, if not always realized.

But the national consensus which dictated these reforms and the national sense of the injustice of segregated schools were dissipated as the efforts to obtain equality expanded. At first, national policy dismissed southern indignation over forced integration as the outcry of diehard reactionaries. But the consensus of northern liberals crumbled as enforcement spread to northern suburbs and began to blur the lines between de jure and de facto segregation. As the courts began to dictate percentages of blacks and whites, to require busing, and to force redrawing of district lines, former advocates of integration reneged on their commitments. And though the debate over school resource equalization had not been perceived in racial terms, this issue threatened to further slow the impetus toward desegregation if identified as a threat to the rights of white, middle class parents.

Despite the slogans of the 1960s, the country was clearly not yet willing to take the necessary steps to eliminate racial and economic isolation in the public schools. Changes which could be made without infringing on the rights of the majority were easily accepted, but those affecting the majority were bitterly opposed. The first steps to equality in education were accomplished easily because a national consensus supported them. With that consensus eroded or reversed, the next steps proved to be much harder.

Not-So-Fair Housing Efforts

In Title VIII of the 1968 Civil Rights Act Congress outlawed discrimination on the basis of race, color, sex, religion, or national origin in the sale or rental of housing. The fair housing law applied to all units insured or assisted by the federal government with coverage extended to conventionally financed apartment units in 1969 and to most single family homes in 1970. In 1973 the law applied to an estimated four-fifths of all housing.

Congress passed this law in the face of widespread opposition. A national survey in June 1967 revealed that 63 percent of whites were opposed to any law forbidding discrimination in housing.[14] A fifteen-city survey a year later revealed 51 percent against fair housing laws compared with only 23 percent who opposed laws enforcing equal employment opportunities.

This less liberal stance on housing compared to other civil rights reflected both deeply ingrained social values and pragmatic fears. Most Americans apparently feel that the ownership of private property is an inalienable right, and that an owner should be able to sell or rent his home to whomever he pleases. Most believe that they should have the right to congregate in areas with compatible neighbors and that exclusive neighborhoods based on income differentials are legitimate. There is also the apprehension, based on bitter experiences in many areas where racial balances shifted rapidly, that the increased concentration of blacks would undermine property values. Equal opportunity laws are thus viewed as a threat to the major form of wealth which most people own.

Yet, when the questions are phrased in terms of abstract principles rather than specific laws, support for open housing is greater. The majority of whites tend to believe that blacks should be able to live wherever they can afford. In the cited fifteen-city survey where 51 percent of whites opposed fair housing laws, 65 percent agreed that blacks should have equal housing opportunities. In a national sample in 1970 only 21 percent of all whites claimed it would make any difference if a black with the same income and education moved next door.[15]

In principle, then, most whites are in favor of fair housing. Their opposition is to fair housing laws which they believe violate their own rights. But in any particular case where the general principle of equal rights for blacks directly challenges the specific interests of whites, self-interest will usually prevail. These conflicting attitudes toward fair housing are important in understanding congressional and administrative acts. Where principle could be sustained on a general basis or remedial measures were limited to particular cases of severe abuse, actions could be taken. But where administrative or legislative decisions required broad changes and aroused the ire of vested interest groups, inaction was more frequent.

The courts took the major initiative in the implementation of the fair housing law, greatly expanding the definition of what was unfair as well as the required remedies.

1. *Kennedy Park Home Associates* v. *City of Lackawanna, New York, 1971*—This decision ordered the elimination of barriers to subsidized housing in Lackawanna, New York, claiming that city officials had opposed some low-income housing projects for reasons of racial discrimination.

2. *Gautreaux* v. *Chicago Housing Authority and HUD, 1971*—The City of Chicago was ordered to begin building half of all subsidized units in white areas.

3. *Shannon* v. *Philadelphia Housing Authority and HUD, 1971*—
Further construction of subsidized units in segregated central city areas
was banned in Philadelphia.

4. *Crow* v. *Fulton County, Georgia, Commissioners, 1971*—
Fulton County, Georgia, was ordered to develop an acceptable metropolitan-wide plan of housing dispersal.

State courts were also actively involved, especially in cases dealing
with restrictive zoning. In a number of cases they limited the authority
of zoning boards to exclude nonresidents. Acreage restrictions which
ruled out subsidized construction were overturned in several cases.

Administrative fair housing actions were much less aggressive than
the courts. The Department of Housing and Urban Development
established machinery to handle fair housing complaints. Most complaints were dealt with outside the courts in conciliation proceedings
seeking to place blacks in homes or apartments where they had been
discriminated against, to get compensation where this was appropriate, or to get the broker, builder, or manager to agree to an affirmative action plan. Efforts were also made to publicize that "unfair
housing is not only unfair—it is illegal." Fair housing posters were
required in all real estate and rental offices and in model homes. The
aim was to help the victims of discrimination, or at least to acquaint
them with the procedures for obtaining help.

Properties financed with government loans or guarantees were also
required to meet affirmative marketing regulations insuring that sales
and rentals would be advertised in the minority community. In addition, in 1971 HUD began considering the degree of racial integration
as a criterion for approval of federal subsidized housing projects.
Areas practicing discrimination were not liable for fund cutoffs but
their share of new grants could be reduced.

These actions fell far short of utilizing the full governmental
leverage. In 1970 and 1971 the Secretary of Housing and Urban
Development spoke boldly of achieving integration by threatening
discriminatory localities with partial loss of their housing monies and
possibly also their water, sewer, and Model Cities grants unless they
cooperated in affirmative action. But in a June 1971 address the
President backed away from this aggressive policy, declaring: "We
will not seek to impose economic integration upon an existing local

jurisdiction . . . This administration will not attempt to impose federally assisted housing upon the community."[16] This decision not to use the threat of fund cutoffs was couched in terms of not "imposing" economic integration, but there were obvious implications for efforts to eliminate racial segregation.

Yet an increasing number of court decisions required the Department of Housing and Urban Development and city and county governments to do what the President would not—to break down the barriers of economic segregation which effectively segregated along racial lines. The dilemma was sidestepped when an eighteen month moratorium on all new assisted housing construction was announced in late 1972. This action was defended on budgetary grounds and because of alleged program ineffectiveness, but it also short-circuited court efforts to force housing integration. The federal government could exert little leverage outside of federal housing grants. Also, revenue sharing proposals to lump together Model Cities, urban renewal, water and sewer, and housing grants threatened to eliminate any remaining federal leverage. With block grants, there would be no project-by-project approval in the light of detailed guidelines and program formats, that is, no way to police fair housing efforts separately. Neither would there be any way to compare or judge areas' aggregate performances since most allocations would be made to cities and counties separately, and metropolitan-wide plans to achieve a suburbanization of low-income and black families would be unlikely. Finally, areas could choose to use all their funds for urban renewal or sewers if there was a threat that housing programs would result in enforced integration.

Federal fair housing efforts must be measured against the difficulty of the task. Housing discrimination is harder to attack than either employment or educational discrimination because the decision-making units are smaller. Entire school systems can be sued or threatened by the loss of grants, and large employers are vulnerable to class action suits with expensive settlements. But in the housing market, only a small proportion of all homes are sold or rented by large corporations. Discrimination occurs in the sale and rental of individual units and must usually be combated on a case-by-case basis.

Housing discrimination is also more difficult to pin down than other forms. Where a real estate broker may work aggressively for a white customer, he may move more slowly for a black buyer in a white neighborhood. The seller may have two or three contract offers and choose a white client even when there is no economic justification for his choice. Bank lenders may be more demanding in judging the financial dependability of black buyers and there is really no way to prove such discrimination. Blacks themselves may be discouraged by the difficulties of acquiring the home of their choice and may register no complaint. There may be a number of parties involved, each of whom may play only a small role in producing discrimination, but the result may be to establish insurmountable racial barriers. Finally, it is difficult to enforce any law or to change any practice where the majority of the population does not agree with it and where some people's rights have to be sacrificed. Most Americans probably do not support the right of the government to tell them to whom they must sell or rent their house or how they must go about it.

Of course, some gains have been made. Blacks' rights to get into almost any neighborhood they choose are now protected by law, and institutional arrangements have been created to deal with grievances if their rights are violated. As income and education rise, it is likely that more blacks will move among whites of equal income and education.

Yet the fact remains that housing segregation continues. The white propensity to flee from an increasingly black neighborhood appears stronger than the black's desire to endure the difficulties of moving into a white community. As a result, black neighborhoods continue to become blacker and white ones whiter. Against this current, it is difficult to view present efforts as even modestly successful, and it is problematical that more effective approaches will be designed.

The Rules of Rule Changing

The effort exerted and the progress achieved in the fight against discrimination has not been equal in the areas of employment, education, and housing. The problems and institutions are different in each case. Yet there are some common threads running through the separate experiences which suggest the constraints and potentials of rule changing.

1. Progress depends on the level of support. Public opinion favored equal employment opportunity and the integration of southern schools but opposed busing and fair housing laws. Predictably, the most progress has been achieved in the labor market and in the southern schools and the least in achieving integrated communities.

2. Enforcement is easiest in isolated cases of flagrant violation. For instance, in education there was quick progress in eliminating completely segregated schools, but efforts to overcome less obvious degrees of racial imbalance proved more difficult to achieve.

3. The courts have been the vital mechanism for the implementation of broad principles. Legislatures have been reluctant to define the law and executive agencies have been equally slow in applying it because threats to the status quo were usually met with vigorous opposition from the affected groups and the political losses usually outweighed the gains. It is argued that the courts have overstepped their authority in many cases by interpreting legislation broadly, but in fact, most of the decisions were consistent with the broad principles endorsed in the 1964 and 1968 Civil Rights Acts and the Constitution. Politicians agreeing with these principles have been more than happy to let an "impartial" institution take the first actions and bear the brunt of public ire.

4. The most effective leverage in applying court decisions is money. Institutions can be threatened with legal action and cajoled with appeals to their consciences, but they are most likely to react when there is a financial penalty for violating the law. Employers tended to ignore EEOC conciliation efforts until threatened by class action suits with stiff settlements for past discrimination. School systems reacted more to the possible loss of federal funds than to the threat of legal actions. The cutoff of water, sewer, Model Cities, and other grants was perceived as a potent weapon by communities which practiced discrimination in their subsidized housing.

5. Most of the black gains were the product of broad but marginal changes rather than intensive restructuring of institutions. Where the latter course was tried, there was frequently foot-dragging and only nominal compliance despite active enforcement efforts. On the other

hand, the more drastic examples may have helped to encourage compliance by the majority, and it would be unfair to judge the impact of antidiscrimination efforts on the basis of their limited effect in difficult cases.

6. Finally, despite the promulgation of equal rights doctrines during the 1960s there was no massive effort to apply these principles and to significantly restructure institutions. Given a choice between "compensatory" or "handicapping" approaches which provided blacks with extra income, special education or subsidized housing, as opposed to adjustments in the system which supported racial inequality, society chose the former. No one was really hurt by a few more dollars in taxes going into social welfare programs, but many people were challenged by rule changes which undermined their perceived status or privileges.

14

BUILDING INSTITUTIONS

Black controlled institutions are a vital ingredient in the achievement of black economic and social power. They can provide political
and administrative leverage to affect government policies, countervail-
ing power against the machinations of other interest groups, and
support for individuals in need. The government's efforts to build and
sustain such institutions have not been impressive in scale or impact
and must be assessed more as demonstrations than action programs.
Essentially, they have consisted of encouraging the poor and minorities to participate in the design and implementation of government
programs and of creating the means for self-help.

Community Action

A fundamental concept of the War on Poverty was community
participation in decisions concerning the coordination and delivery of
public services. In the words of the Economic Opportunity Act of
1964, projects were to be "developed, conducted, and administered
with the maximum feasible participation of the residents of the areas
and the members of groups served." Some interpreted this to mean
merely that community groups would be racially integrated, while
others viewed it as a totally new strategy of decision-making. The
broader interpretation was manifested in the initial design of the
antipoverty programs. Unlike other federal grants-in-aid which dealt

primarily, if not exclusively, with state and local governments, the Office of Economic Opportunity was given the authority to contract directly with nongovernmental community-based groups to be supported with federal funds—the community action agencies (CAAs). More than 1,000 CAAs were formed and the residents of the areas affected, including clients of the poverty programs, were represented on their boards. They were given decision-making authority for the development and implementation of federally subsidized but locally designed efforts as well as administrative authority over national anti-poverty programs.

Community action agencies quickly gained an image of being black run. In the South many were identified with civil rights organizations, challenging the establishment; elsewhere black militants either gained control over the antipoverty agencies or used them as a base of support. The goal of improving the delivery of services to the poor brought the CAAs into inevitable conflict with old line agencies, and many projects were highly controversial.

Soon Congress redefined "maximum feasible participation," sharply curtailing the options of CAAs to develop their own projects. First, programs initiated at the national level—Head Start, Upward Bound, Legal Services, and so forth—cut into the funds left for locally designed efforts. It is debatable whether local groups could have done better on their own, but the very limited resources clearly restricted their initiatives. By 1969 it was estimated that only a third of the more than $900 million distributed to the community agencies went for locally designed projects.[1]

A second constraint on the freedom of community agencies was a 1967 amendment to the Economic Opportunity Act which gave mayors and county officials oversight authority. In a few cases the newly-granted powers led to the reorganization of controversial CAAs. More often, however, the amendment served notice that "community action" did not mean "black power," and that the anti-poverty agencies would have to toe the mark.

A third constraint was the policy of "spinning off" national programs from the Office of Economic Opportunity to other departments, mainly Health, Education, and Welfare and Labor. OEO had tended to leave much flexibility for local decision-making. Local antipoverty agencies provided placement and manpower services in competition with employment service offices; neighborhood health centers were created which cut into the turf of the local medical establishment; and legal services competed with traditional legal aid societies. By transferring power back to the federal bureaucracies, the competition was controlled if not eliminated.

More fundamentally, the idea of community participation was never pursued vigorously. The Economic Opportunity Act required that area residents represent at least one-third of board membership, but this did not insure effective impact upon operations. In the early days newly emerging community leaders became self-appointed spokesmen for local constituencies, but among the controlling two-thirds of "outside" CAA board members in 1968, four-fifths were white, nine-tenths professionals or managers, and 85 percent college graduates. Even among target area representatives, two-fifths were white, three-tenths professionals or managers, and over a fifth college graduates.[2] And while these boards showed some interest and ability in coping with specific problems of local concern, their input diminished as nationally designed programs predominated and local initiative funds were cut back.

It is unclear whether or not the community agencies could have developed into more effective program planners and operators with more time, money, and flexibility, but in any case, the issue is moot. After five years of operation, obligations leveled off and then declined.

	(millions)		
1965	$115.2	1970	$371.2
1966	274.6	1971	410.2
1967	275.5	1972	351.0
1968	323.3	1973	285.3
1969	380.1		

In 1973 and 1974 the administration gradually dismantled the Office of Economic Opportunity, with the transfer of its programs to other agencies. The new administration policy was to have local antipoverty agencies supported out of revenue sharing funds, effectively placing them under state and local control.

Though the lofty goal of community—and in many areas black—

control over a comprehensive range of social welfare services was never fully tested, the community action approach had favorable impacts.

1. Delivery of services with at least nominal participation of recipients increased the payoff for them. Community action agencies were more willing than other agents to use paraprofessionals and to take a chance on employing the more disadvantaged. In 1968 there were an estimated 83,000 full-time and summer nonprofessionals employed by the CAAs in such jobs as social workers, counselors, day care aides, and outreach workers. According to an earlier study, as many as three-fourths of these were blacks.[3] Blacks were also the beneficiaries of CAA services—60 percent in the Concentrated Employment Program, 55 percent in the Neighborhood Youth Corps, and half under Head Start. If the same programs had been run by other agencies from the outset, it is doubtful that these high black shares would have been achieved.

2. The community action agencies improved the delivery of government services. The major innovation was the neighborhood service center, a multipurpose unit located in poverty areas to provide comprehensive services or referrals. Roughly 2,500 of these had been created with community action funding through 1970.[4] Dispersed in many locations, the centers were able to hire neighborhood residents for the paraprofessional jobs and to draw inputs from local citizens' associations for center policies. The poverty area residents were apparently impressed with the neighborhood centers and a majority received some assistance.[5]

3. The community action agencies frequently proved effective in solving specific problems with their flexible funds. There are any number of success stories—farm cooperatives funded in rural Mississippi, school buses provided for ghetto children in Flint, Michigan, or special education classes for retarded students in Omaha, Nebraska. Action was most meaningful when the problems identified were a cause of widespread community concern and where continuity of action or close coordination with outside agencies was not required.

4. There was some success in mobilizing outside resources. One survey of 591 agencies found that between 1966 and 1972 they had received $1.3 billion in funds other than OEO or national program

grants, with more than half of this representing nonfederal monies.[6] Organized institutions operating with sustained federal funding can exert more leverage to obtain grants from the private sector than ad hoc groups which experience difficulties in maintaining their identity.

5. Finally, community action established the principle that the recipients of services should have their say (even if their counsel may subsequently prove impractical). While contacts with target populations may remain at arm's length, at least some participation arrangement is now pro forma under most social welfare programs.

Model Cities

The Model Cities program, begun on a demonstration basis in 1966 and expanded into a full-scale program in 1968, shared the community action goals of concentrating and coordinating disparate federal efforts in areas with severe needs and of stimulating widespread citizen participation. Model Cities and community action agencies overlapped both geographically and functionally. Initially, Model Cities jurisdictions were well-defined, but gradually they were expanded to include areas with CAAs. Both programs funded an assortment of social and welfare activities, including education and day care, health, urban renewal and development, housing, and manpower projects, though the Model Cities agencies did not have to accept prepackaged national programs.

In its design and implementation, however, Model Cities was much less oriented toward institution building. The community demonstration agencies created by Model Cities to administer local efforts were established as an arm of the mayors' offices with the aim of avoiding the conflicts which had accompanied the antipoverty agencies. And in contrast to the rapid proliferation of CAAs, Model Cities demonstration projects were more tightly controlled. The initial 63 cities were chosen from nearly 200 applicants in 1966 and the total number was restricted to 150. Where an effort was made to get an immediate payoff from antipoverty programs, planning was an integral part of the Model Cities strategy with full funding intended only after several years of organization and experimentation. Residents were to be involved in this process, but the mayor was to administer the program. In several cities citizens gained a veto power over proposals and enough control to hire their own planners, but the more common practice was to have an unfunded neighborhood advisory committee and a minority of blacks and other target area residents on the policy board of the community demonstration agencies.[7]

While the residents of Model Cities areas tended to be black, they rarely had a major voice in running the projects. One study found that within the black community there was a lack of awareness about the program, that involvement was slight, and that expectations were limited. Neighborhood residents were apparently more responsive to a crisis-solving approach rather than to long-range planning.[8]

The payoff is uncertain since the program was intended as a planning effort with most funds promised for later. Expenditures were $86 million in 1970, mounting to $328 million in 1971 and $500 million in 1972. The big money to fund Model Cities operations was to start flowing in fiscal 1974 and thereafter. However, proposed revenue sharing proposals for community development called for a melding of the program into a block grant. During 1971 and 1972 twenty test cities were selected to experiment with "planned variations" in funding under which they would seek to coordinate grants-in-aid for the entire city. The idea was to test the feasibility of a block grant system which would replace the urban renewal, open space land, neighborhood facilities, public facilities, rehabilitation, Model Cities, and water and sewer programs with a single appropriation.

Planned variation and revenue sharing involved more than a reorganization of the flow of dollars. The base was changed from Model Cities target areas to entire cities, diluting the share of funds for the areas of greatest need. The role of poverty area residents was consequently reduced. In other words, in hopes of achieving increased administrative efficiency the Model Cities approach was to be abandoned.

Aiding Small Businesses

Control over the allocation of federal funds is ultimately constrained by the reluctance of governmental decision-makers to turn loose the pursestrings. Self-determination for blacks can only come when resources are generated internally—when the purse is in the hands of blacks. This requires the ownership of wealth and especially the ownership of businesses.

There are three conceptually different approaches to expanding minority ownership: helping individual minority businessmen; providing incentives for larger corporations to develop joint ventures and minority enterprises; and supporting broader community ownership.

The major governmental agency providing assistance to the black entrepreneur is the Small Business Administration (SBA). Prior to 1968 aid was limited largely to economic opportunity loans established under the 1964 antipoverty act and a related program which offered small amounts at low interest rates. Under Project Own in 1968 these small loan programs were expanded and emphasis placed on aiding minorities under the other regular programs. By mid-1973 the SBA made loans and guarantees totaling $334 million to minority businessmen, a tenfold increase in four years. Other agencies, particularly the Departments of Agriculture and Housing and Urban Development, doubled their loans between fiscal 1970 and 1972 to $55 million.[9]

While this growth rate was impressive, some reservations are in order. Because of an even faster growth in nonminority loans, the minority share of the SBA portfolio declined from 23 percent in fiscal 1970 to 16 percent in 1972 in terms of loan dollars, and from 41 to 32 percent in terms of the number of loans. The black share declined even more. In fiscal 1970 they got 65 percent of minority loans, or 67 percent by dollar value. By fiscal 1972 the proportions had fallen to 51 and 58 percent, respectively.[10] The black share of SBA dollars was thus less than the black share of the population—hardly living up to the rhetoric of compensating for the ownership gap between blacks and whites.

Moreover, even by Small Business Administration standards minority loans are small. Three of every five in fiscal 1972 were of the economic opportunity type, with $50,000 limit. The average minority loan was less than two-fifths the average for whites.

Another problem was that in order to reach ambitious targets, standards were drastically reduced, but supportive services were not adequate for the increased activity. By 1972 a fourth of minority loans were in liquidation, delinquent sixty days or more, or charged off, as business conditions drove many new firms into the red. This loss rate was about four times higher than under the regular business loan program.

Loans are not the only way the Small Business Administration provides support. The agency is authorized to let government contracts on a noncompetitive basis, giving mostly new minority firms up to three years of sheltered markets while they get on their feet. From fiscal 1969 to fiscal 1972 the dollar value of such contracts increased from $9 to $152 million, mostly representing purchases by the Department of Defense and the General Services Administration. Competitive purchases from minority entrepreneurs rose even faster over this period from less than $4 million to more than $240 million.[11]

Mobilizing Private Sector Resources

In the late 1960s a number of large corporations established branch plants or subsidiaries in ghetto areas to employ low-skilled minority workers. Most of these firms were major defense contractors: AVCO Corporation opened a printing plant on Boston's Roxbury ghetto; Fairchild-Hiller established a subsidiary in Washington, D.C., to manufacture wood pallets; EG&G opened a metal fabrication plant, also in Roxbury; Aerojet-General created the Watts Manufacturing Company, initially producing tents and other products for the government; Martin-Marietta opened a light manufacturing firm in the Washington ghetto; Warner-Swazey established the Hough Manufacturing Company, a small machine shop in Cleveland; Xerox joined with a community group in sponsoring FIGHTON to produce electrical transformers and metal stampings in Rochester. In all of the above cases, the intent was to sell some or all of the stock to minorities including the employees.

Most of these operations floundered. EG&G Roxbury lost $75,000 in 1968, $250,000 in 1969, and an unreported amount in 1971. The Watts Manufacturing Company was eventually spun off, but has yet to prove profitable and has been supported almost entirely by government contracts. Fairchild-Hiller's Washington, D.C., subsidiary closed down, as did the Hough Manufacturing Company. The lessons were discouraging.

1. Sophisticated technology could not easily be applied to unskilled labor intensive ventures.

2. Problems of operating in the ghetto were more intractable than expected.

3. Corporate commitment was shallow, with many firms preferring charity to losses which would show up in the corporate balance sheets.

4. Low-income workers were not enthusiastic about buying stock in ventures of questionable profitability.

One way to overcome such problems would be to provide tax and other incentives making it profitable to operate in the ghetto. A large-scale experiment with this approach—the Opportunity Funding Corporation—proved only that if difficult obstacles were to be overcome, sizable incentives and subsidies would be needed. Rather than offering such inducements on a large scale, an attempt was made to find something less costly.

The selected mechanism was the Minority Enterprise Small Business Investment Company (MESBIC), a vehicle for packaging private sector expertise and attracting private and public resources to help minority owned businesses. The MESBICs were given $2 of Small Business Administration loans for each $1 from corporations or other private sector groups; the sum, in turn, could be used to secure private financing, hopefully $5 for each $1 for a total leverage of ten to one. With these funds risk capital and/or long-term subordinated loans could be made available to minority businesses.

MESBICs had not had much success through 1972. Only fifty-one MESBICs were formed because most banks and large firms considered the risks too great and the potential gains too small. The MESBICS tended to be undercapitalized and burdened with too much overhead. They provided a total of $36 million worth of aid for 442 projects through 1972, but the leverage factor was roughly five to one rather than the anticipated ten to one, and much of this came only as a result of Small Business Administration loan guarantees in addition to its loans. Few MESBICs provided technical assistance to borrowers. Finally, most of them proved to be unprofitable.[12]

In late 1972 new incentives were added to increase MESBIC

profitability and attractiveness. The ratio of government to private funds was increased, with the SBA loans provided at below market interest rates. With such aids, more MESBICs may move out of the red.

Another approach to mobilizing private sector resources was the creation of Business Resource Centers and Local Business Development Organizations financed by the Commerce Department's Office of Minority Business Enterprise. These groups, initiated in some fifty cities through fiscal 1973, were to coordinate private sector resources with small business needs. This new bureaucracy duplicated similar efforts by a number of private and nonprofit agencies, many of which were minority controlled, raising the already high overhead in venture funding for minorities.

Community Development Corporations

A by-product of community action efforts was the development of community-based organizations to initiate and own businesses in poverty areas and to perform a number of welfare and service functions. These "community development corporations," or CDCs, were to be controlled and/or owned by residents. The hope was that they would eventually become self-supporting and would promote community self-determination through control over resources. In 1967 antipoverty funds were used to support a large CDC in Bedford-Stuyvesant, New York, and Congress expanded these efforts in fiscal 1969 when fifteen CDCs were funded. But legislation proposed in 1968, which would have provided capital and federal borrowing power and various tax incentives to community development groups, failed passage as support for the self-determination concept waned. Funding by the Office of Economic Opportunity rose from $12 million in fiscal 1969 to $37 million in 1970, remaining at this level through fiscal 1973.

CDCs varied widely in their organization and activities. Some were profitmaking enterprises, though most were nonprofit; some sold stock, while others had a voting membership; those in rural areas tended to concentrate on manufacturing and agricultural activities, while those in urban areas put more emphasis on property development.

While no one CDC was typical, the Bedford-Stuyvesant Restoration Corporation and its "establishment" auxiliary, the Development Services Corporation, was the largest and probably best known community development effort. Created with the strong support of Senators Robert Kennedy and Jacob Javits and a galaxy of business leaders, the Restoration Corporation had received commitments of $31 million from the Office of Economic Opportunity through fiscal 1972, roughly a fifth of all funds going to support community development groups. Additionally, the Restoration Corporation received $11 million in loans, grants, and technical assistance from foundations and corporations, plus $3 million in Small Business Administration loans and guarantees and $65 million in Housing and Urban Development funds for its projects.[13] These resources exceeded manyfold those received by other CDCs. The Restoration Corporation experience, then, suggests what can be accomplished with the most generous support.

1. The CDC's primary goal was business development. Using its own loan funds and SBA guarantees, Restoration had funded thirteen manufacturing firms, fifteen service ventures, seventeen retail establishments, and four construction firms by the end of 1972. The forty-nine firms employed 458 persons, or an average of less than 10 each. Restoration owned two of the companies; it had a minority interest in two more; the rest were owned by private entrepreneurs receiving loans and guarantees to open or expand businesses.

A financial analysis of eighteen enterprises revealed that seven were profitable, two were breaking even, eight were operating at a loss, and two were closed down at the end of 1972. Of the profitable firms, three were construction-related efforts which were assured a profit by CDC construction projects. Total losses for the businesses far outweighed total profits, though most were less than two years old and still in the start-up period.

2. The employment impact of Restoration was limited. In addition to the 458 working in funded ventures, the CDC had 232 employees in 1972 and had generated at some time an estimated 3,700 jobs by its other activities, including 400 full-time jobs in an

IBM plant, as well as a number of temporary laboring jobs in neighborhood clean-up operations. Employees of the business ventures and Restoration were earning less than half a million dollars more annually than in their previous jobs.

3. The Restoration Corporation did well in getting corporate and foundation financial support for itself, but it was not very successful in tapping financing institutions for its projects, especially without Small Business Administration guarantees. Perhaps the single most important development was the establishment of the IBM plant, but this came about largely as a result of the membership of the president of IBM on the Development Service Corporation board of directors.

4. Property acquisition and development were a major focus. One of the first projects was a face lifting for neighborhood housing and the rehabilitation of a community center. The Restoration Corporation arranged for the construction of a 53-unit apartment building, and rehabilitated 151 family units through 1972. Further subsidized housing construction was planned.

In assessing the costs and benefits of these activities, the need to establish a new organization and to experiment with alternatives must be considered, as well as the intangible products—such as community pride and a sense of control. Some questions must, nevertheless, be raised about Restoration's ability to meet its primary goal—self-sufficiency. Given known and projected losses of the funded ventures, there will be little turnover of funds to reinvest or profits to plow into social and welfare activities. It is difficult to envision how the corporation can operate without continued outside help. This being the case, it must be viewed as another delivery mechanism for outside aid—much the same as other social efforts—rather than a self-supporting, self-determining institution. The Restoration Corporation has had more flexibility in planning and applying its funds, and has also had more support and resources from the government and the private sector, but has not been able to outgrow its dependent status.

Most other community development corporations have not done even as well as Restoration. A study of thirty groups which received the bulk of OEO money found that only 117 ventures had been funded through 1972 (including the 49 in Bedford-Stuyvesant); these ventures employed only 1,427 and CDCs themselves 639. It is estimated that 5,455 secondary jobs were generated in related activities, mostly in construction (and mostly in Bedford-Stuyvesant). The estimated annual wage gain over previous jobs totaled $630,000. A careful examination of sixty-one funded ventures, only half of which were established with CDC help, revealed that at the end of fiscal 1972, only thirteen were in the black, with total profits of $165,000. The remaining unprofitable ones lost a total of $4.4 million in the previous year. Optimistic projections suggested that less than half of the firms would be out of the red by the end of fiscal 1973.

Despite this poor record in business development, there were other benefits. Some of the persons hired were able to get off relief. One of every two employees received some on-the-job or formal training. Three-fourths claimed they stayed in the target area at least in part because of their CDC jobs. And there was evidence that the community development corporations achieved a fair degree of participation, as well as making a mark on the community with visible real property development ($31 million in projects had been undertaken through the end of fiscal 1972).

However, the various achievements of the thirty sampled CDCs carried a substantial price tag. Through fiscal 1972 the Office of Economic Opportunity had obligated $56 million, banks had loaned $18 million, corporations had supplied $2 million in loans and $9 million in grants or investment, and foundations contributed $1.4 million in loans and $2.5 million in grants. When investments from other government programs are considered, it is possible that CDCs cost more than $100 million to realize wage and profit gains of less than $1 million annually.

Most of these community development corporations were not self-supporting in 1972 and were not likely to become so. A good deal of overhead proved necessary to develop businesses to carry on other activities which could not be supported on the profit base of the funded businesses. This being the case, CDCs must be judged on the basis of whether they are more effective than other approaches in getting dollars into the hands of those in need. Whatever their drawbacks, the fact remains that these groups are employing local residents and trying to make decisions which will be best for their communities. The same cannot be said for the alternate methods of business development—MESBICs and direct government assistance. The dollar costs of various tax incentives to MESBICs are very large, and there is no proof (and a lot of reason to doubt) that this approach is less costly than aiding community development groups, or that it will be more effective. Nevertheless, the evidence to date does not support the hope that a significant measure of self-determination can be achieved among low-income, minority groups.

Cooperatives

Cooperatives are more limited in scope and are concentrated in rural areas. Machinery cooperatives pool resources to acquire expensive equipment. Purchasing cooperatives are used to buy materials wholesale at reduced prices. Marketing cooperatives use market leverage to get higher prices, frequently by packaging and processing the products or delivering them to buyers.

The achievement of economies of scale is especially vital for rural blacks, who are overwhelmingly small farmers—undercapitalized, unable to take advantage of government subsidies, and often poorly serviced if not exploited by local institutions. More than three of every four blacks in rural areas live in poverty, and underemployment is widespread, so that meager supplements to income generated through cooperative action can substantially improve welfare.

Under the Economic Opportunity Act, the Farmers Home Administration and the Office of Economic Opportunity were authorized to fund cooperatives. The Farmers Home Administration concentrated on small loans for product-related investment. During the first six years of operations, its loans averaged only $16,000, but their impact was positive. Members of machinery cooperatives reportedly increased their net farm income 11 percent annually, while those in marketing cooperatives increased income 15 percent (though much of this came from wages in off-farm work).[14]

The Office of Economic Opportunity cooperatives were multipurpose and aimed at a lower income clientele than those funded by the Farmers Home Administration. The OEO viewed cooperatives as a means of organizing, as well as increasing the income of the rural

poor, especially minorities. Between 100 and 150 cooperatives received support from local community action agencies and 10 cooperatives were funded with OEO's research and development funds. The
membership of these cooperatives was predominantly black and several coops challenged or were challenged by local white interests
(which in several cases eventually led to the demise of the funded
cooperatives).

Despite these problems OEO cooperatives raised income even more
than did more selectively focused efforts.[15] The economic gains from
the larger scale cooperatives were apparently greater than those of the
more limited ones, though, of course, the costs were also greater. The
OEO-funded cooperatives also had other payoffs, giving blacks and
other low-income individuals the leverage not only to compete on
somewhat better terms with agri-business institutions, but also to
pursue their aims politically. As judged by participation in community
meetings, voter registration, and community campaigns, 40 percent of
the members of business-social cooperatives increased participation in
community affairs.

The several hundred dollar average income gains and the services
and other contributions provided by cooperatives may not seem
extensive. But the total cost of supporting the seventy-six cooperatives
included in one study was only $1.8 million, and the per capita
income of members' households was only $932, so that a few hundred
dollars of extra income was very significant. The members of these
rural cooperatives were persons with limited options: two-thirds were
forty-five and over, 70 percent had less than a high school education,
and two-thirds were nonwhite. Financial analysis suggested that at
least a third of the cooperatives would never be profitable, but the
income gains of members more than justified the outlay of government funds as an alternative to income maintenance.

A Tight Grip on the Reins of Power

Relative to the money and effort which went into income maintenance, in-kind aid, and human resources development efforts, institution-building received a very low priority. The experiment with client

participation and control in the antipoverty programs was short-lived. Model Cities, despite its rhetoric, rarely fostered community participation and was always under the wing of the local power structure. Programs to aid minority owned small business expanded, but the impact was marginal. The private sector was given an increasing role in business development, with a variety of financial carrots, but this approach had limited success and had the effect of excluding blacks and community groups from the decision-making process. Community development corporations have an uncertain future because of the imminent demise of OEO and are not likely to become self-supporting. Cooperatives for low-income, rural blacks have proved very effective in raising income, but the government has been reluctant to work toward large-scale organizations which could compete on equal terms with agri-business.

There are practical reasons for this limited effort. Institution-building has little immediate payoff, and the achievements are difficult to measure over the long run. A dollar of welfare, medical care, or vocational training can be justified by tangible impacts, but the benefits of community control are much more indirect. In allocating funds, efforts that can claim no quantifiable benefits tend to lose out. For instance, action programs designed and implemented at the national level under the War on Poverty took precedence over locally planned efforts which took longer to design and implement and whose benefits could not easily be documented.

Policymakers are also noticeably fickle in their support of institution-building programs. Community action agencies were the answer to problems in 1964, community demonstration agencies were in vogue in 1966, community development corporations were ballyhooed in 1968, and revenue sharing had the spotlight in the 1970s. Lasting institutions cannot be built by panacea hopping and organizational rearrangements are no substitute for certain and substantial funding.

A major function of power is the ability to change things, but the government has supported institutions of black control only so long as they have accepted the status quo. Several rural cooperatives that challenged local establishments were terminated, as were a number of unmanageable community action agencies. The initial activism of the

War on Poverty led to quick reprisals. The powers of community-based organizations were constrained and the control by local establishments increased. The private sector and the government bureaucracy assumed an ever-increasing role in minority entrepreneurship efforts, swallowing the black community's meager "piece of the action." There must be some question, then, whether new institutions which require sustained support can be built with federal social welfare dollars that tend to focus on instant solutions rather than long-term efforts.

These facts do not mean that institution-building should be abandoned. Even if only a few viable institutions result, the *process* can be beneficial. The community action agencies, for instance, changed the way programs were administered resulting in more consideration being given to minority interests. A few successful businesses were created by community development corporations, and income was generated at least in the short term. And as long as black controlled institutions exist, even if they change from year to year, dollars are being channeled through the hands of those in need rather than skimmed off long before they reach the target population. Institution-building programs may therefore be useful and worthwhile as a means of improving welfare, even if they do not create viable and lasting institutions.

15

CONSIDERING BLACK INTERESTS
IN FEDERAL POLICYMAKING

Blacks, like all citizens, are vitally affected by government policies. In addition to the social welfare, equal opportunity, and institution-building efforts already discussed, several other federal activities have significant impacts. Aggregate economic policies, minimum wage laws, and military and correctional policies all have disproportionate impacts for blacks.

Aggregate Economic Policies

The federal government is charged by law with maintaining high employment, stable prices, and economic growth; but there is a forced tradeoff among these goals. Lower unemployment can only be attained at the cost of more rapidly rising inflation, with varied impacts on different groups. A judgment is implicit in selecting the beneficiaries and victims of economic policy. Blacks are overrepresented among the unemployed, and their status is vitally affected by the rate of economic growth. When income is rising and employment expanding, blacks tend to gain more than proportionately; when economic conditions sour, they are more frequently the victims.

1. The rate of growth of income tends to fluctuate more widely for blacks than whites (figure 15-1).

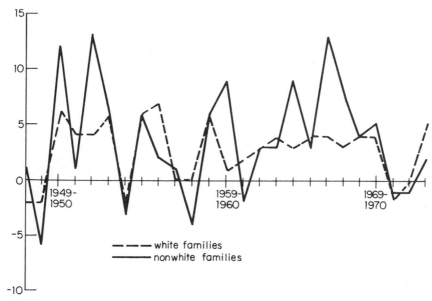

Figure 15-1. Year-to-year percentage change in median family income, 1947–1972.

Source: Table 2-1.

2. The changes in nonwhite employment tend to be greater than for total employment (figure 15-2).

3. The penetration of blacks into better paying jobs is affected by the rate of expansion or contraction of such jobs; this is especially apparent in the craft occupations (figure 15-3).

4. Blacks tend to make up more ground relative to whites when the economy is healthy. Relative black income gains (see Chapter 2) were most rapid between 1948 and 1955 and from 1963 to 1968 (years of low unemployment), and improvements relative to whites were meager in the 1956 to 1962 and 1969 to 1972 periods (years of higher unemployment).

One of the keys to helping blacks is to maintain rapid income and employment growth and a low rate of unemployment. But this has its tradeoff in increased pressure on prices and inflation. The Phillips Curve, which plots annual rates of unemployment and price change, is one method of visualizing the policy alternatives; the slope of the

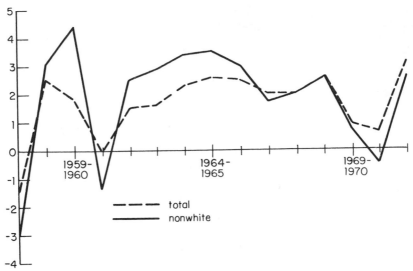

Figure 15-2. Year-to-year percentage change in employment, 1957–1972.

Source: *Manpower Report of the President, 1972* (Washington: Government Printing Office, March 1973), table A-5.

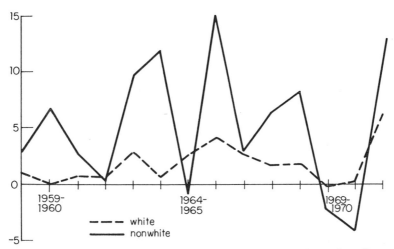

Figure 15-3. Year-to-year percentage change in number of craftsmen, 1958–1972.

Source: *Manpower Report of the President, 1972* (Washington: Government Printing Office, March 1973), table A-12.

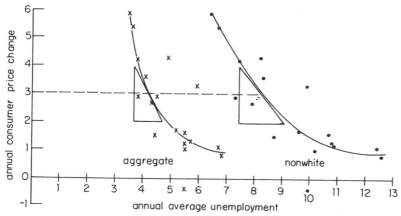

Figure 15-4. Inflation-unemployment tradeoff, 1954–1971.

Source: *Manpower Report of the President, 1973* (Washington: Government Printing Office, March 1973), tables A-5, G-5.

curve at any point suggests how much inflation has been associated with a given change in the level of unemployment (figure 15-4). The data suggest that for blacks a low rate of unemployment can be achieved only with a very rapid increase in prices.

The Phillips Curve is not what it is often described—a menu of policy choices. The record of trying to reach specific equilibrium points through combinations of monetary and fiscal and, more recently, price control policies has not been impressive in the 1970s. But the curve does illustrate that the goals which are optimal for whites are not optimal for nonwhites: blacks are better off when labor markets are tighter. When high levels of average unemployment are tolerated by policymakers as a means to combat inflation, blacks suffer.

Minimum Wages

A controversial macroeconomic policy affecting the working poor and, therefore, many blacks is the minimum wage. Since its establishment in 1938, with a minimum of 25 cents per hour in firms producing goods for interstate sale, the minimum's level and coverage have been increased periodically. From 1968 through 1973 the minimum for most workers was $1.60 per hour. In 1974 new legislation authorized the minimum to rise to $2.30 per hour by 1976, and extended protection to many previously uncovered workers. In this as in every case where changes in the minimum have been considered, there was a wide difference of opinion about the likely consequences. Advocates of a higher wage and broader coverage viewed the minimum as a means of pushing up earnings and income for those at the bottom of the economic ladder. In 1970, for instance, there were 3.1 million jobs (1.3 million full-time and 1.8 million part-time) paying less than $1.60 per hour, and 11.1 million (5.8 million full-time and 5.3 million part-time) paying less than $2.00.[1]

Opponents of a broader or higher minimum wage rate stressed the negative unemployment effects. Forced to pay higher wages, marginal firms might go out of business; employers might substitute capital for labor or hire fewer high wage laborers rather than more low earners; operations might also be transferred overseas to areas with lower labor costs. All of these would reduce the number of jobs available for the less skilled. Workers dropping out of the labor force or joining the ranks of the unemployed would suffer.

There is strong evidence that the aggregate wage gains from minimum increases in the past have exceeded the wage losses from foreclosed jobs. It is not clear, however, whether equity is being served and whether the wage gains of some can be balanced against the losses of others.

In determining minimum wage policies, the interests of blacks have been largely ignored, possibly because it is unclear where their best interests lie. One fact is clear, however: blacks are overrepresented in the most recently covered industries and in the lowest paying jobs, so that they are relatively more affected for good and for bad than whites. In 1970 one of every eight full-time black wage and salary workers in the central city poverty areas earned less than the then current hourly minimum and nearly a fourth (397,000) were earning less than $2.00.[2] In three rural poverty areas in Arkansas, Alabama, and North Carolina, 44 percent of blacks working full-time, full-year earned less than $1.60 and two-thirds were earning less than $2.00.[3]

While data from urban and rural poverty areas undoubtedly overstate the incidence of low wages among blacks generally, there is probably a higher percentage of blacks than whites in low-wage jobs. For example, a national survey conducted in 1969 by the United States Department of Labor found that 60 percent of employed nonwhite youths age sixteen to twenty-one (including part-time workers) earned less than $2.00 per hour compared to 53 percent of whites.[4] These differentials undoubtedly widen among those in older age groups.

The minimum wage has greater impact on blacks and especially on black youths, not only because they are in lower wage jobs, but also because they are disproportionately affected by any changes in employment. The rising minimum wage has accordingly been cited as the culprit contributing to the secular increase in black teenage unemployment. The postwar changes in the minimum rates were frequently associated with a jump in the ratio of nonwhite teenage to general unemployment, especially after the 1965 increases. After adjustments for declining black teenage participation rates, the ratio of nonwhite to white unemployment rose in five of the six years following an increase in the minimum wage.[5] Several other studies have also found a relationship between changes in the minimum and increases in teenage unemployment, and in these cases the effects on black teenagers are stronger than for whites. In other cases, however, the results have been less clear-cut, leaving some uncertainty about the correlations between changes in the minimum and subsequent increases in black teenage unemployment.[6]

But even if there are no clearly visible effects immediately after changes in the minimum, they could have contributed to the steady rise in black teenage unemployment to a rate of 33.5 percent in 1972. It is tenuous to argue that the losses of those displaced by the minimum have been balanced by wage gains to other black teenagers who did find employment. One youth losing a $1.60 per hour job balances out four who increase their wages from $1.60 to $2.00, even if no consideration is given to the claim that for youths it is better to spread wages among more workers.

The number of employed blacks aged sixteen to twenty-one in central city urban areas in 1970 earning more than the minimum wage was only seven-tenths the number employed part-time involuntarily for economic reasons, employed at less than the minimum wage, unemployed, or outside the labor force because of discouragement (table 15-1). It is unknown how many of these black youths were

Table 15-1. Central city blacks age 16 to 21 years potentially affected by minimum wage boosts (thousands)

Status	Total	Potential gainers	Potential losers
Total	713	170	239
Employed	242		
Part-time involuntarily for economic reasons			21
Others earning less than $1.60 per hour[a]			50
Others earning $1.60 to $1.99 per hour[a]		39	
Others earning $2.00 and over[a]		131	
Unemployed	109		109
Not in the labor force	362		
Want job but feel none available or lack skills			59

Source: U.S. Bureau of the Census, *Employment Profiles of Selected Low-Income Areas: United States Summary—Urban Areas,* Series PHC(3)-1, January 1972, tables 1a, 3a, 9a, and 15a.
[a] Estimated from wage distribution of full-time workers, therefore overstating possible gainers and understating possible losers.

pushed out of work by the minimum wage or ended up with higher wages as a result. But only a fourth of employed sixteen- to twenty-one-year-olds earning more than the minimum earned between $1.60 and $1.99—the range where the legislation most likely affected wages. It is doubtful that the wage gains outweigh the losses for ghetto teenagers.

Teenagers account for less than 9 percent of the black labor force, and the evidence suggests that the minimum has helped raise wages of older blacks without any noticeable impact on unemployment. Regression analyses of the unemployment impacts of the minimum have failed to reveal any statistically significant relationships between the increases and extensions in the minimum and changes in adult non-white male or female unemployment rates. The circumstantial evidence which suggests a deleterious balance for black youths suggests the opposite for black adults, since the male unemployment rate has declined in both absolute and relative terms, remaining relatively stable for females, while the number of black workers earning low wages has fallen precipitously, as noted previously. While the minimum wage has had negative consequences for teenage blacks, it has probably been beneficial for black adults.

Further boosts in minimum wages are therefore likely to continue the gains of black adults while intensifying teenage unemployment difficulties. One possible means of avoiding this undesirable tradeoff is a dual minimum wage achieved by increasing the rate for adults while leaving it at $1.60 per hour for teenagers. This might make it relatively more attractive to hire teenagers, allowing more to find $1.60 an hour jobs rather than a lucky few earning $2.00. On the other hand, the differential could reduce employment opportunities for adults to the degree employers favored teenagers over heads of families. While the interests of black teenagers would undoubtedly be best served by such a dual system, older blacks would likely be the victims of any increased job competition. Given the seriousness of the job crisis for black youths, the dual minimum must at least be considered as an option to supplement expanded youth employment programs, but careful experimentation is required.

The Military

In 1972 the armed forces contained 168,000 nonwhite males age eighteen to twenty-four and 77,000 age twenty-five to thirty-four, representing 10 and 5 percent, respectively, of the noninstitutional male populations. These proportions compared with 11 and 4 percent, respectively, among white males. At the peak of the Vietnam war in 1969 there were 304,000 black males age eighteen to thirty-four in the service, or 11 percent of the male population of these ages, including 17 percent of those age twenty to twenty-four.[7] Even larger proportions have spent some time in the service. In 1972 a fourth of all nonwhite males age twenty to twenty-nine in the civilian population were veterans, as were a third of white males.[8]

The record of the military in equalizing opportunities for blacks has been only slightly better than that of society as a whole. Until 1948 blacks were segregated in their own units, usually commanded by white officers. In 1949 there were only 1,600 black officers, less than 1 percent of the total, while blacks comprised 7.5 percent of enlisted men.

Progress was slow in increasing representation because blacks had trouble getting into the armed forces and were often among the less qualified enlistees. Between 1950 and 1971 only four of every ten potential black draftees qualified compared with over six of ten whites. Only half as many blacks were medically disqualified, but four times as many failed the mental examination.[9] Moreover, black enlistees have been more likely than whites to be educationally and mentally disadvantaged. Only 7.3 percent of black enlistees in early 1972 scored above average on the armed forces qualifying examination, and less than 10 percent had any college education[10] (table 15-2).

To qualify more of the disadvantaged, mental and physical requirements were lowered beginning in 1967. The men entering under these new standards comprised about 11 percent of the enlisted force, and approximately four in ten were black. However, many problems were encountered, with higher discharge rates, less success in training, slower advancement, and disciplinary problems.[11] The program was ended in December 1971.

Even among regular enlistees, lower education and aptitude have made blacks more likely to be assigned to the less skilled occupations. Over four of ten are in combat or service and supply handling specialties compared with only a fourth of whites. Only 26 percent of blacks are in the electronic and mechanical equipment repair, communications, and intelligence specialties compared with 44 percent of whites. Discrimination may exist in the assignment of positions, but certainly the lesser education of blacks is a major factor.[12]

Table 15-2. Characteristics of enlistees, 1971

Category	White	Black
	(percent)	
Years of education		
4 or more years college	2.2	0.7
1 to 3 years college	9.3	6.6
High school graduate	63.8	66.1
Less than high school graduate	24.7	26.6
Mental category		
Top fourth	5.4	0.2
Second fourth	36.0	7.1
Third fourth	46.4	49.3
Lowest fourth	12.2	43.4

Source: U.S. Office of the Assistant Secretary of Defense, *En-listees: Percent Distribution by Mental Group, Educational Attainment, Race and Military Service, January 1972–March 1972* (M&RA), July 1972.

Another consequence of lesser education is slower advancement. Promotions above the rank of E-3 for enlisted men are on the merit basis. Each service sets its own standards, with the army giving priority to the appraisal of a promotion board, while the navy and the air force rely to a greater extent on written examination. Not surprisingly, blacks with less educational achievement have a harder time advancing in the latter two services. Only 6 percent of blacks separating from the air force after a four-year tour of duty during fiscal year 1969 had reached the E-5 level, compared with 14 percent of whites; in the navy, the rates were 18 and 32 percent, respectively. After a two-year duty in the army, 24 percent of blacks and 39 percent of whites had reached E-5. Because black enlisted men were more likely than whites to make the military a career, however, they were slightly overrepresented among noncommissioned officers, making up 11.4 percent of those with rank of E-5 or higher in 1970, though they were 11.0 percent of all enlistees. But they were still a small fraction of commissioned officers, only 2.2 percent in 1970, a scant improvement from two decades earlier.[13]

It is important to note that when aptitude and education are controlled, the black/white promotion differential narrows only slightly. In the army only 54 percent of college educated blacks, compared to almost 68 percent of college educated whites, had risen to at least E-5 rank after a two-year tour of duty. Fifty-seven percent of white compared with 48 percent of black first-term army enlistees in the top ten aptitude percentiles reached the E-5 or above levels.

While discrimination is an obvious explanation, another important factor is the effect of disciplinary actions. Almost twice the proportion of blacks in the navy and air force and one-third again as many marine and army blacks are subjected to nonjudicial punishment and court martials as whites.[14] When the offenders are subtracted from a sample of 1969 army enlistees with two years experience, the variations in the pay grade distributions disappear.[15]

While the armed forces may discriminate against blacks, there is some evidence that there is less discrimination than in civilian life. Roughly one in every four blacks who enters the military without a diploma leaves with one as a result of the army education (though this compared unfavorably with four of every ten whites). Training can be acquired, especially by career enlisted personnel. Blacks apparently value these opportunities and military pay more than whites, since their reenlistment rate, despite declining precipitously in the late 1960s, has remained almost double that of whites. In 1969 a fourth of army enlisted personnel with five to ten years of service were black.

Blacks have also demonstrated their judgment that the military is a good deal, at least compared to their status in the civilian labor market, by enlisting in record numbers for the all-volunteer army. In 1970 nonwhites accounted for 12.8 percent of inductions and initial enlistments. By 1973 they averaged 17.6 percent of the total and the trend was upward.[16]

Black participation in the military may also be beneficial for those who remain at home by removing potential job competitors and opening opportunities for others. In the 1967 to 1972 period the unemployment rate for young black males was inversely related to the armed forces levels (table 15-3). The number of males age eighteen to twenty-four in the service fell by 50,000 between 1969 and 1972, and the number of unemployed rose by 28,000. Aggregate economic

Table 15-3. The interaction of the military and the civilian labor market for nonwhite men, 1967–1972 (numbers in thousands)

Employment status and age	1967	1968	1969	1970	1971	1972
In armed forces						
18 to 19 years	42	42	45	35	34	40
20 to 24 years	135	156	173	160	149	128
25 to 34 years	83	92	86	80	77	77
Total noninstitutional population						
18 to 19 years	439	456	474	480	496	528
20 to 24 years	855	908	993	1,028	1,096	1,115
25 to 34 years	1,241	1,285	1,355	1,385	1,437	1,444
Armed forces as percent of total noninstitutional population						
18 to 19 years	9.6	9.2	9.5	7.3	6.9	7.6
20 to 24 years	15.8	17.2	17.4	15.6	13.6	11.5
25 to 34 years	6.7	7.2	6.3	5.8	5.4	5.3
Unemployed						
18 to 19 years	50	50	43	64	71	71
20 to 24 years	50	53	49	91	125	118
25 to 34 years	49	44	36	74	94	86
Unemployment rate						
18 to19 years	20.1	19.0	16.7	23.1	26.0	26.2
20 to 24 years	8.0	8.3	7.3	12.6	16.2	14.7
25 to 34 years	4.4	3.8	3.1	6.1	7.4	6.8

Source: Derived from *Employment and Earnings*, annual issues, table 1.

changes were a more important factor, but certainly the return of thousands of black veterans during the recession did not help matters.

In summary, then, the military has probably helped blacks at least as much as other government institutions. During the past decade blacks achieved a much stronger foothold in the armed services, and though there may have been some negative consequences in terms of the suffering of blacks who lost life or limb, the net impact was probably favorable. The challenge for the 1970s will be to prevent the greater opportunities for blacks in the military from establishing a predominantly black armed forces.

The Correctional System

Like the military, the correctional system also affects vast numbers of black males. In 1970 there were 135,000 blacks in federal and state prisons and local jails and workhouses. Nearly 2 percent of the black male population, and 4 percent of those aged eighteen to thirty-four, were incarcerated (table 15-4). White males were only one-sixth as likely to be institutionalized and blacks accounted for two of every five prisoners. Moreover, the institutional population has become

Table 15-4. Individuals in correctional institutions, 1970

Age	White male	Black male	White female	Black female	Per-cent white males	Per-cent black males
Total	182,096	128,673	7,960	6,419	0.3	1.8
14 to 17 years	4,550	5,029	428	129	0.1	0.5
18 to 24 years	59,920	47,918	2,480	2,480	0.6	3.9
25 to 34 years	56,184	40,974	2,312	2,004	0.5	3.3
35 to 44 years	32,699	21,569	1,058	1,012	0.3	2.0
45 to 64 years	25,760	13,193	929	778	0.1	0.8
65 and over	2,983	890	387	16	—	0.1

Source: U.S. Bureau of the Census, *Persons by Family Characteristics,* Series PC(2)-4B, January 1972, table 2.

increasingly black. Between 1960 and 1970, while the correctional population fell from 349,000 to 332,000, the nonwhite proportion increased from 38 to 43 percent.[17]

Many more persons on probation and parole are also under the jurisdiction of the correctional system. While no exact numbers are available, there were 4.6 juveniles and 1.6 adults on parole or probation for each one institutionalized in 1966. If this same ratio held true in 1970, it would mean that approximately 232,000 black males were on probation or parole, and the true figures may be higher because of the increasing use of these noninstitutional treatments.[18] At a minimum, then, 5 percent of the black male population was under the supervision of the correctional system in 1970, and roughly one of ten aged eighteen to thirty-four.

While there is no way to estimate the exact number of blacks with arrest, conviction, or prison records, they undoubtedly represent a sizeable segment of the male population. The turnover each year in federal and state prisons is 100 percent, and it is higher in jails. Even allowing for the fact that between three-fourths and four-fifths of new inmates are recidivists, there is a good chance that a black will have an arrest record. Studies variously estimate that between a half and three-fourths of ghetto youths have serious encounters with the law before reaching age twenty-five. Whatever the exact numbers, it is obvious that the correctional system has a far-reaching impact.

While few analysts can agree on the causes or solutions of the problems of the courts, parole, probation, prison, and jail systems, there is widespread consensus that they all have serious shortcomings. Their multiple purposes are to protect society from lawbreakers and to punish and reform offenders. As social attitudes have changed, treatment and reform of prisoners has received increasing emphasis. But a six-year follow-up of arrests by the FBI found that two-thirds had been rearrested at least once; or in other words, the system successfully reformed or deterred only one in three offenders, a record which might have prevailed even if there had been no first arrests (figure 15-5). The failures were in all segments of the system. Nine out of ten arrestees whose cases were dismissed or acquitted were rearrested, as were two of five individuals receiving a fine or probation; three-fifths of those eventually paroled after serving time were

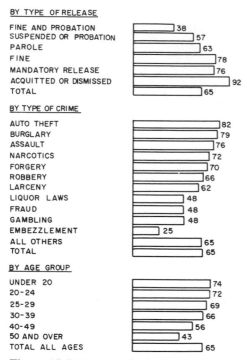

BY TYPE OF RELEASE

FINE AND PROBATION	38
SUSPENDED OR PROBATION	57
PAROLE	63
FINE	78
MANDATORY RELEASE	76
ACQUITTED OR DISMISSED	92
TOTAL	65

BY TYPE OF CRIME

AUTO THEFT	82
BURGLARY	79
ASSAULT	76
NARCOTICS	72
FORGERY	70
ROBBERY	66
LARCENY	62
LIQUOR LAWS	48
FRAUD	48
GAMBLING	48
EMBEZZLEMENT	25
ALL OTHERS	65
TOTAL	65

BY AGE GROUP

UNDER 20	74
20-24	72
25-29	69
30-39	66
40-49	56
50 AND OVER	43
TOTAL ALL AGES	65

Figure 15-5. Percent of persons rearrested within six years.

Source: Federal Bureau of Investigation, *Uniform Crime Reports for the United States, 1969* (Washington: Government Printing Office, 1970), pp. 38–39.

also rearrested. The system was less successful rehabilitating blacks: 71 percent of black arrestees in the FBI study recidivated, compared with 61 percent of whites.[19]

The reason for this poor record may simply be the nature of the correctional system. By removing offenders from society and the labor force, and by concentrating them in a milieu with other offenders, problems and criminal tendencies may be exacerbated. But much of the problem is a question of resources: it is costly to maintain the police, court, and correction systems. Operating without adequate funding, they can often do little more than catch, sentence, and incarcerate offenders rather than try to alter their behavior or improve their potential. For instance, there is some connection between low education, low earning capacity, and the probabilities of committing first and multiple offenses. Yet in 1966 only one in ten jails and workhouses, which contained roughly two-fifths of the institutionalized population, had educational facilities and only one in seven provided for recreation. Less than one in eight state prisons offered vocational training to more than a fifth of inmates, and three-fifths offered educational courses to less than a fifth. The situation in federal prisons (containing a tenth of prisoners) is better, but a survey of 1964 releasees found that only 35 percent had participated in any training or education.

Recognizing these shortcomings, the courts have relied increasingly on noninstitutional treatment. In 1966 it was estimated that the number of probationers equaled the number of prisoners; by 1975 it was projected that the ratio would be three to two. There has also been a trend toward earlier parole, partial release for work, or release to community institutions. Yet the treatment received during parole and probation is also dubious. As of 1965, an average adult probation officer had a caseload of over a hundred, permitting little but the most cursory counseling and services. Since then, the situation has not improved much, if any.

The failures of the correctional system also lie in society as a whole. Private employers often refuse to hire anyone with a police record. Licensing and bonding are also difficult to obtain. The record of the public sector is no better; more than half the state and county governments and three-fourths of those in large cities require disclosure of past brushes with the law. Ideally, the offender who has paid society's penalties should begin again with a clean slate. Rarely is this the case, and sometimes the obstacles placed in the way of readjustment may contribute to recidivism.

A variety of efforts have been mounted to improve the performance of the correctional system, but they have met with mixed success, reaching only a small proportion of offenders. Vocational training and education have been offered in prisons under the Manpower Development and Training Act, serving approximately 5,000 inmate trainees in 1970. But a follow-up of participants found that their post-release employment success was no higher than among controls and that recidivism in the year following release declined, at most, by 5 percent. Education, prison employment, and work release programs, as well as those offering a complete package of services to prisoners also achieved very limited results.

Pretrial intervention efforts, that is, working with first or second offenders to keep them out of the institutional system, have proved more successful. For instance, an experimental project in Washington, serving a younger, mostly black, clientele was able to find jobs for these offenders, improving their wages and reducing the rate of recidivism by 30 percent in the two months after participation. Similar efforts in New York and other cities have also proven worthwhile.

Some steps have been taken to help ex-offenders. Bonding is now widely available under government subsidy. Parole staffs have been beefed up in the same areas. A variety of groups have been funded to provide half-way house treatment and placement services to releasees. Again, there is little evidence of any dramatic success.

Improvement in the correctional system is vital. While riots at Attica and other prisons have highlighted the worst conditions, the treatment of offenders is neither humane nor effective from arrest to parole and after. Since blacks make up a disproportionate segment of the population receiving "correctional treatment," they are the ones who suffer most from its deficiencies.

Doing the Best for Blacks

To recapitulate, the interests of blacks are clear-cut in the case of aggregate economic policymaking. A low rate of unemployment and a rapid rate of income and employment growth are the keys to black gains. It is easier to get a larger share of an expanding pie, and many of the achievements of the 1960s would not have been possible if the higher average rates of unemployment in the early 1960s had prevailed throughout the decade.

There is also no doubt that blacks would benefit from improvements in the correctional system. Arrest is too frequently a one-way street, and an arrest may lead many black youths to a life of crime or one of stunted opportunities. Justice needs to be more swift and fair, correctional institutions more corrective, and treatment of those with past records more considerate. Prisons and jails may well prove to be one of the critical problem areas of the 1970s, and it is a problem borne disproportionately by blacks. Anything to improve the situation will be a boon.

Discrimination exists in the armed forces, but the decision of an increasing number of blacks to volunteer apparently represents their collective judgment that it offers better opportunities than civilian life. Though most policymakers wish to avoid a predominantly black armed forces, to ration these opportunities by actively recruiting whites in order to maintain a "balanced force" is not in the best interests of those with no other alternatives.

Finally, the best minimum wage policy from the black viewpoint is unclear. The minimum wage has apparently contributed to the secular rise of black teenage unemployment. But it has also helped to raise the wages of many black adult breadwinners. A dual minimum wage system might be able to help the former without unduly hurting the latter, but this remains to be tested. At any rate, black views must be solicited and carefully considered since blacks stand to both benefit and lose most from minimum wage changes.

PART 3

POLICY AND CHANGE

16

CAN THE DREAM BE REALIZED?

On August 28, 1963, 200,000 white and black Americans standing in the shadow of the Lincoln Memorial were stirred by the words of Dr. Martin Luther King:

I have a dream that my own little children will one day live in a nation where they will not be judged by the color of their skin, but by the content of their character.

The ten years following this historic event were tumultuous. The Civil Rights Acts of 1964 and 1968 and the Voting Rights Act of 1965 reiterated the constitutional rights of blacks, mandating equal voting privileges and access to public accommodations, jobs, and housing. The Economic Opportunity Act of 1964 was the opening round of the War on Poverty which sought to equalize opportunities for the disadvantaged, necessarily concentrating on the problems of blacks. Court decisions and administrative actions gave teeth to these laws. Programs proliferated and funds for social welfare purposes increased several times over.

These efforts may not deserve the label of a "Second Reconstruction," but they certainly had a massive impact. Blacks now freely utilize public facilities. They vote without harassment or restriction. Though they are still denied equal opportunities in housing and employment, they have more effective mechanisms for the redress of these grievances.

As a result of these expanded rights and compensatory efforts, blacks have made substantial gains. Attending and completing high school and college in ever-increasing numbers, they have substantially narrowed the educational gap relative to whites. They have moved into better paying and higher status jobs. With increased income, they have been able to afford more and better quality food, housing, and health care, as well as some of society's luxuries.

Yet the ten years since the articulation of the "dream" also had their darker side. Dr. King's assassination, the Jackson State killings, the treatment of the Black Panthers, and the massive urban riots in Harlem, Watts, Detroit, Newark, and other large cities demonstrated that both blacks and whites could be guilty of intolerance and violence, and that sustained protest and even force was necessary to move the "establishment" to correct past wrongs. For each of these major events, there were thousands of acts of repression, injustice, and callousness. Many blacks did not share in the general gains, and many were justifiably discontented with the painfully slow progress toward the realization of a society in which "all men are created equal."

Ten years after the Washington march neither the engineers nor the analysts of change are able to reach a consensus about what has been accomplished. There is recognition of general progress, but from differing perspectives analysts disagree concerning the direction and degree of change. Others may reach different judgments from the same information, yet several conclusions seem inescapable.

The Spectrum of Progress

To allocate resources where needs are greatest it is necessary to assess relative rates of improvement in the various socioeconomic dimensions. The most clear-cut advances during the past decade were in employment and education. Significant gains were also made in income, health, and what has been labeled "black power," but on these fronts there are more caveats concerning the rates and impacts of progress. There were some improvements in housing and family status, but these were offset by other less desirable developments. The following order is therefore suggestive of the balance of gains and losses.

1. *Employment and earnings.* In the labor market, blacks have probably made more progress than in any other socioeconomic dimension, though their status is still far from equal. Blacks generally still earn less and fill lower status jobs, yet they have registered significant occupational gains during the past decade. Black women have made the greatest relative advances and their earnings have almost reached equality with those of white women. The increased earnings of working wives have had a major impact on black family income and may also have contributed to greater independence on the part of black women. But the gains made by males over the last decade were not insignificant. Their penetration into the white-collar occupations was not as great as for women, but they got increasing proportions of better jobs in all sectors, frequently as a result of unionization.

Labor market problems remain severe but some progress has been made. The relative unemployment rate of adult black males has declined. Black teenage unemployment rates have climbed to crisis levels accounting for over a third of total black unemployment in 1972, but in the overall picture the gains of adult black breadwinners must be weighed more heavily than the losses of youths with part-time and intermittent work goals. The labor force participation rate of black males fell, in part because discouragement rose over the late 1960s, but more importantly because nonwork income alternatives became more available. Blacks who quit work to receive disability benefits, welfare, and other income maintenance usually did so because they were thereby better off. More and higher paying jobs are certainly needed, but the facile explanation that blacks were forced out of the labor market in large numbers gives a false impression of the changes which occurred.

Looking to the future, the major problem on the employment front will be to solidify the gains made over the last decade. Blacks have achieved more equal entry into better jobs, but the issue is whether they will continue to advance in these jobs and move up into responsible higher paying positions. Though it is much harder for public policy to deal with questions of upgrading and mobility than entry, more emphasis will be needed in these areas.

2. *Education*. Black gains have been dramatic at all levels of education. A larger proportion of black than white children are enrolled in preschool programs. The proportion of nonwhites aged twenty to twenty-four with a high school diploma rose from 42 percent in 1960 to 68 percent in 1972, or from three-fifths to four-fifths the rate for whites. The proportion of nonwhites aged twenty-five to twenty-nine with college degrees doubled from 6 to 12 percent between 1960 and 1972, increasing from 47 to 58 percent of the comparable proportions for whites.

These educational improvements are closely related to employment gains. The better educated are less likely to be unemployed, more likely to be in white-collar jobs, and tend to earn more. Among black males in 1970, nearly nine out of ten with a college degree worked in professional, technical, and managerial occupations compared to one in four high school graduates. The average earnings of college graduates were a fourth higher than those of high school graduates.

More education is not synonymous with a better education. An assessment of educational gains must also consider qualitative improvements. The only comprehensive survey of achievement in 1965 found black students in the twelfth grade lagging more than three years behind their white counterparts in reading ability and arithmetic comprehension. In a number of school systems with higher concentrations of blacks, these achievement gaps have not improved. Blacks are also concentrated in smaller and less prestigious colleges and universities. Their newly-won educational credentials may have been undermined, therefore, to some degree.

Improving the quality of black educational credentials is more difficult than increasing years of school. There is no convincing proof that integration, increased per pupil outlays, more relevant curricula, or any other changes have had or will have a rapid and significant impact. There is only the hope that all of these things working together will contribute to gradual progress. Mixed schools and metropolitan-wide funding may improve the quality of education, and there will be a continuing shakedown of new methodologies and approaches. Hopefully, there is a learning curve in the learning business. But as more blacks attend college and more complete high school, job competition may become quality, rather than credential, oriented. It is vital, therefore, that efforts be mounted to improve black educational achievement.

3. *Income.* In the areas of employment and education, blacks gained both in absolute and relative terms. The income picture is less favorable because the absolute gains, while substantial, did not markedly improve the relative position of blacks. On the positive side, real median income of the average black family roughly doubled in the 1960s. The number of blacks in poverty declined from 9.9 million in 1959 to 7.7 million in 1972, while the proportion of blacks living in poverty fell from more than half to less than a third. At the other end of the income spectrum, the gains were also significant. In 1960 only 13 percent of nonwhite families had an income over $10,000 (in 1972 dollars); by 1972 this proportion had increased to 34 percent.

Despite these absolute gains, per capita black income was still only three-fifths that of whites by 1972. The absolute dollar gap between blacks and whites actually widened between 1960 and 1972. Though median black family income rose from 55 percent that of whites in 1960 to 62 percent in 1972, there are reasons to question the reliability of these measured gains. Cost of living increases due to migration, underreporting of capital gains, the growth of nonwage compensation, and changes in the structure of black families may have inflated the comparative gains of blacks. Adding the value of in-kind assistance to black income would improve their relative gains significantly. But in-kind aid is not the same as dollars in the pocket, and improvements resulting from increased government subsidy cannot be considered as encouraging as those accomplished through increased self-sufficiency.

Black income gains leveled off after 1969 and this could herald a slower rate of improvement during the 1970s. In the 1960s black family income rose as a result of massive advances in employment and education, increased numbers of wives entering the labor force, and added billions of federal welfare dollars directed to the poor. It is unlikely that the rates of improvement of any of these factors can be sustained through the 1970s.

4. *Health*. Higher income and expanded assistance for the medically indigent have improved the quality and availability of health care. Maternal deaths per 100,000 live births declined among nonwhites from 98 in 1960 to 64 in 1968, a rate of improvement equivalent to whites. Infant deaths declined from 43 per 1,000 births in 1960 to 30 in 1971. The death rate from tuberculosis, pneumonia, and influenza also fell precipitously.

Gains in medical care were balanced by other factors. The virtues and rewards of rural living may be more myth than reality and reflect a nostalgia for the past, but the urbanization of blacks may not have been beneficial to their health. Blacks were victimized more than whites by health problems related to urban social pathologies. Venereal disease, alcoholism, drug addiction, and the concomitants such as cirrhosis of the liver and hepatitis all rose among blacks. Ironically, gains in income and status may have also had negative consequences as blacks more frequently experienced the illnesses of an affluent nation such as diabetes, heart disease, and ulcers.

Whether, on the balance, the status of black health has improved relative to whites is uncertain. One crude measure is life expectancy, which fell slightly for black men but rose for black women between 1960 and 1969. Other proxies of health may not be very accurate. For instance, bed days and reported disabilities may have increased as more blacks were covered by sick leave provisions or became eligible for disability benefits. Since many black health problems are the cumulative result of years of neglect, the benefits of greater preventative care may not show up for years.

Though medical subsidies have undoubtedly reduced outlays by low-income families and improved the quality of services, the fact remains that black health deteriorates much faster than that of whites, whether measured in terms of incidence of disease, limitation of activity, or higher rates of mortality. The medical delivery system does not provide the same services for low-income families as for the more affluent, and on the average, blacks are treated by physicians and dentists less often than whites.

5. *Power and responsibility*. Black power in its most positive sense increased over the last decade. A few blacks moved into higher paying jobs with decision-making and supervisory responsibility, and they

have gained positions of leadership in some union locals and isolated positions of influence at the national level. A few black businesses are penetrating the broader marketplace rather than merely serving black clientele, and many more black politicians occupy city halls and seats in Congress and state legislatures.

Yet these advances have hardly made a dent in the gaps between blacks and whites. Much has been made of what are in truth very meager changes in the balance of power. In politics, where the most widely publicized gains have occurred, blacks still hold less than 1 percent of all elected public positions, and these are almost exclusively in areas where they constitute a majority or at least a substantial block of the voters. As long as black victories require black majorities, political representation will remain less than proportional. Though blacks may gain control of some city halls or county courthouses, they are unlikely to obtain equal representation in state houses or at the federal level because of the dilution of their votes. Moreover, to the extent that political influence is still a function of wealth rather than votes alone, blacks have little pocketbook power.

The unions' sustained record of supporting black interests does not alter the fact that blacks are grossly underrepresented in union decision-making positions. The white majority has usually resisted quota systems, rump locals, and other means used to realize black goals where these have diverged from their own interests.

Most of black upward mobility into higher paying jobs is in staff rather than line positions which normally involve limited decision-making or supervisory responsibility. If all civil rights, equal opportunity, community affairs, and marketing staffs were excluded, the increase of black managers and professionals would be slim indeed.

Finally, there has been little improvement in business ownership and control of wealth. There are probably fewer black businessmen today than a decade ago, and it is doubtful that the total value of black businesses has increased. Few fortunes are made from wages or salaries, and the modest relative gains of the last decade have probably done little to close the wealth gap.

6. *Housing*. In each of the preceding socioeconomic dimensions, there can be no doubt that, despite reservations, blacks were better off as a result of the changes of the last decade. In housing, however, the

balance of gains and losses is less certain. There was a substantial reduction in the number and proportion of ill-housed blacks measured by inadequate roofing and plumbing. Some of this was due to urbanization, since homes in the city usually have plumbing, whatever their other drawbacks. Yet there is no doubt that low-income blacks improved their housing in both urban and rural areas. Gains were also made by middle and upper class blacks, with more purchasing homes and moving into units with more amenities and living space.

There were, however, few relative gains. The proportionate reduction in substandard units was greater among whites than blacks. The average white home improved more in terms of size, bathrooms, and appliances. Blacks largely excluded from the suburbs, where their efforts to move into better mixed neighborhoods led time after time to the flight of whites. When black middle and upper class families moved away from the problems of the ghettos, they found that they were pursued and that there was often no escape from ghetto problems.

Despite the integration of public facilities, schools, and the labor market, residential segregation has increased dramatically. In the insular black community, problems become magnified, while whites in distant suburbs close the door on blacks and their needs. Residential segregation complicates job and school integration and creates severe financial strains on central cities as they are increasingly cut off from the resources of the affluent suburbs.

There is no welfare calculus to compare the gains of individual blacks who have moved into more solid and attractive homes with the less tangible but certainly unhealthy consequences of segregation. In the short-run, and from the perspective of each black, there may have been improvement, while from a long-term perspective for all blacks, the developments may have been undesirable.

7. *Marital and family changes*. Marital and family patterns are the only social dimension in which the balance of change was clearly for the worse. The extent of deterioration is sometimes exaggerated, but the directions of change are unmistakable: blacks are now less likely to marry; their marriages more frequently end in separation or divorce; and their children more often grow up in split homes. Birth

rates have declined among blacks as among whites, but the drop has been greater among married than unmarried women. More than a third of black births each year are illegitimate, and the incidence of illegitimacy among black women in their young teens has not declined.

Despite some debate over the adequacy of the data, it is clear that blacks are increasingly less likely to maintain stable families with the father fulfilling primary breadwinning responsibilities. The issue is less the existence of this trend than its implications. In the short-run, the decisions underlying marital break-up are frequently rational and the changes beneficial. Where potentially unhappy marriages are delayed or forestalled, the end result may be greater happiness.

From society's viewpoint, however, the consequences are inimical. Family deterioration can become epidemic, as both black men and women come to accept the postponement or dissolution of marriage. Once these patterns become the dominant ethic, their effects may become pervasive and difficult to change. Despite debates over the efficiency of the nuclear family and predictions that childrearing in the future will be communal or institutional, there is obvious value in having both father and mother present during the upbringing of children—not only for the children's psychological development, but also on purely economic grounds. Split homes more often than not mean poverty. Two-fifths of black children are growing up poor, of whom two-thirds are in female-headed households. The attitudes and values of these youths toward marriage and childbearing will be influenced by their childhood experience.

While the deterioration in marital and family patterns has not been a major detriment to progress on other fronts—and may be a reaction to change—the impacts may loom larger in the future. The assertion that the "whole fabric of black society has deteriorated" is overblown, but the problems in this dimension are serious.

The Process of Change

No single measure can sum up all the changes which have occurred or integrate them into a composite socioeconomic index. Suffice it to say that blacks made very substantial absolute gains in most dimensions while relative improvements were less striking and only in a few cases went far toward eliminating white/black gaps.

Summaries of change on the separate socioeconomic dimensions leave crucial questions unanswered: Are the changes reversible or is the developmental process ratchet-like? Do they have momentum or delayed impacts? What individual adjustments are needed to adapt to change? Are the gains and losses of change evenly distributed? Some tentative answers are suggested by the previous analyses.

1. *The momentum of change.* In the early 1970s there was concern that black gains might be eroded by adverse shifts in public policy. The number of black poor rose in 1972, as did the black/white unemployment ratio. The Office of Economic Opportunity, which had been a symbol of aid to disadvantaged minorities, was effectvely eliminated, and housing and other social programs of special interest to blacks were being cut back or reorganized offering potentially less help to blacks. There was fear that for blacks the 1970s might mean a step backward after the two forward during the 1960s.

While some social programs may be eliminated or curtailed, it is not likely that the gains won by blacks during the last decade will be significantly reversed. Radical ideas become commonplace after a few years, as food stamps, Medicare, birth control services, and many other examples would suggest. The expectations of the public and of those who benefit from federal aid seem to rise irresistibly as services increase. Client groups, delivery agents, and those who provide the goods and services can unite to protect their turfs. For example, despite five years of calls for its elimination, the Job Corps was still in existence in 1974. Apparently, old social programs seldom die, and resist even fading away.

The critical issue is not whether progress will be reversed, but whether it will slow appreciably due to current socioeconomic and policy changes. There is definitely a lag effect, with many of the favorable developments of the late 1960s and early 1970s the result of momentum generated earlier. The expansion in welfare which accelerated in 1969 to 1971 was caused by the legal decisions, benefit increases, and administrative arrangements adopted during the mid-1960s. Manpower programs kept expanding as new initiatives were added to older programs without changes in the law. In housing, the enabling legislation was passed in 1968 and subsidized construction reached its highest point ever in 1971. The Nixon administration began cutting and retrenching the social programs in 1973, and the Great Society momentum was checked.

While it is easier to turn the federal spigots on than to turn them off, the lack of governmental social initiatives in recent years may slow progress in the 1970s. There are apparently cycles not only to socioeconomic change but also to the evolution of public social policy, and the early 1970s were a leveling off period.

Yet there is a longer run momentum of progress which is independent of government effort. Black workers who have gotten better jobs will gain seniority and authority. They will increasingly qualify for pensions, social security, and other perquisites. Black politicians will also gain stature as they build political machines and age into positions of authority. The success of blacks graduating from college will serve as a model for others and higher goals will be set for their children. There is a definite momentum for continuing improvements, although this may be inadequate to accomplish desired goals in a short period of time.

2. *Adjustment problems.* Even if it is for the good, change can be an ordeal which generates tensions and adjustment problems. The urban riots of 1965 and 1968 were certainly such manifestations. Profiles of rioters found that they were not exclusively the hard-core who had been left behind by progress, but also those who were stable workers holding good jobs. Apparently, the gains which were being made generated more rapidly rising expectations, and the "black psyche" was undoubtedly strained by the simultaneous emphasis on the pride of blackness and the pressure to succeed in white society.

White blacklash was also part of the adjustment process. Despite the publicity given to blue-collar antipathies, opinion surveys indicated no significant shifts in their racial attitudes. Union members thought conditions were changing too fast, but did not retreat from support for basic civil rights.

Some of the family deterioration in the 1960s may also have been an adjustment phenomenon. The uprooting resulting from migration to the cities and the availability of welfare had massive impacts on many black families. If the pace of change slows, greater stability may be achieved in the black family.

Though it is difficult to prove, it is possible that lagging adjustment to change impeded the full realization of opportunities. Blacks probably experienced the nouveau-riche phenomenon as they found more money in their pockets. In trying to build institutions, blacks sometimes settled for immediate payoffs rather than investing for long-term returns.

The disenchantment with social programs which emerged in the early 1970s might also be a transient adjustment phenomenon. Failures and inconclusive results were to be expected with large-scale social experimentation, but the judgment that government was altogether ineffective in altering economic conditions inflated these failures and ignored the successes.

3. *The benefits and burdens of change.* The process of socioeconomic change is frequently spearheaded by an elite, while others are left behind. But the benefits and burdens of black progress over the past decade were widely distributed. Blacks at the upper end of the spectrum advanced because of their improved credentials and the greater willingness of employers to treat them equally. There were gains in the middle level related to unionization, equal employment opportunity efforts, and the increased earnings of black wives. At the bottom, government social welfare programs were largely responsible for improving conditions.

The burdens of change were cushioned during the 1960s by economic expansion. But when the pie could not be expanded and had to be redistributed, the interests of some claimants had to be sacrificed. Hiring or college scholarship quotas helped blacks, but they hurt others who lost out on jobs or scholarships. Continued black gains will require increasing tradeoffs in the future, and it is vital that some attempt be made to cushion adverse impacts on those who are directly affected.

Varying Policy Impacts

Governmental intervention has had important impacts on the status of blacks. Welfare and other income maintenance programs had direct effects, putting dollars in black pockets and reducing poverty. Combined with in-kind assistance, they probably made the most difference for blacks in the short-run. Equal opportunity and human resource development efforts with a long-run focus had mixed results. Institution-building programs were not vigorously implemented and consequently had the least impact resulting in the establishment of few viable organizations. Finally, general federal policies were formulated with little consideration given to black needs and interests.

1. *Income maintenance programs.* In 1971 blacks received nearly $7 billion in income supplements from social security, welfare, unemployment and workmen's compensation, government pensions, and veterans' programs. Although the share of total black income from these sources did not increase much during the 1960s, the dollar amount more than quadrupled in real terms, rising most rapidly between 1967 and 1971. For low income blacks, the impacts were very great. The income deficit of all nonwhite poor declined (in 1972 dollars) from $5.6 billion in 1959 to $3.6 billion in 1972.

The purpose of these programs is not just to reduce poverty, but also to insure against loss of income as a result of disability, unemployment, forced retirement, or the death of a provider. Though black poor are more likely than whites to receive public assistance and welfare benefits, there are some indications that the social insurance system does not serve them as well as whites. The black unemployed are less likely to be insured, the disabled are less likely to be in jobs covered by workmen's compensation, and elderly blacks frequently qualify for only minimum social security pensions. Expanding coverage, more liberal eligibility criteria, and changes in black employment patterns may be expected to improve black benefits under the nonwelfare social insurance programs.

2. *In-kind aid.* In addition to the billions distributed to blacks under income transfer programs, they received an estimated $5 billion worth of goods and services from in-kind programs in 1972, more than a tenfold increase since 1960. Health care accounted for $3.7 billion (two-thirds under Medicaid), food programs $1.2 billion, and housing programs $0.5 billion. As much as a third of the real total income of poor blacks may be in the form of such goods and services, and in the

case of medical care for the nonwhite poor, it appears that government dollars provide nearly twice as much treatment per person as is privately purchased.

The issue with in-kind aid is whether the dollars could be more efficiently distributed by direct cash stipends. The benefits of targeting assistance to the most severe problems must be balanced against the inefficiencies of creating large administrative agencies to deliver benefits. Some argue that food and housing programs do little more than replace private with public dollars and that raised welfare benefits coupled with housing allowances could provide as much service with less administrative overhead. Though such reforms deserve study in the establishment of more comprehensive policies in the future, they present problems. For one thing, it would be politically unfeasible to lump all funding for the support of the poor under one appropriation for cash payments. More important for blacks, alternative delivery methods for services may reach individuals in the ghetto who would not otherwise be helped. Community health services, birth control clinics, and improved housing would not have been available had the money been simply distributed as cash rather than as in-kind aid.

3. *Equalizing opportunities.* The landmark legislation and court decisions of the last decade have outlawed discrimination in the labor and housing markets and in the schools. There is no doubt that court and government action has forced educational changes. Initially, federal guidelines backed by the threat to cut off funds were the chief tools used to encourage desegregation. But even after this policy was downplayed in 1969 in favor of judicial enforcement, integration continued to make headway. By 1972, 91 percent of blacks in the South attended desegregated schools compared with 32 percent in 1968.

The federal government may be approaching the limits of its intervention in the conduct of the schools. Though federal courts have upheld busing to desegregate school systems, public opposition has led to the passage of an antibusing bill by Congress and has aroused support for an antibusing amendment to the Constitution. Similarly, though state courts have sought to overturn apparently discriminatory property tax financing of the schools, the Supreme Court has declared such financing legal.

Progress in changing discriminatory labor market practices has been less noteworthy. Until 1972, when it was given the power to bring civil actions in federal courts, the Equal Employment Opportunity Commission had little power and its voluntary compliance efforts had limited impacts. The Office of Federal Contract Compliance had potentially more leverage, with its power to withhold federal contracts from discriminatory contractors, but it generally failed to use it. The Philadelphia and other construction industry hiring plans were highly publicized but while they resulted in more blacks being hired on specific projects, they did not effect overall changes in union and employer practices. There may have been spillover from jawboning and threats of action but the evidence suggests that corporate concern was more rhetoric than substance. Only 6 percent of the wage gain of black males in firms contracting with the federal government could be correlated with their dependence on federal funds. The new powers of the Equal Employment Opportunity Commission and the beefing up of its staff may make it a more effective mechanism in the years ahead. For example, the consent decree signed by AT&T in 1973 compensating for racial and sex discrimination sent shock waves through the private sector, with many companies scrambling to improve their performance relative to blacks and women.

Efforts to integrate housing have been the least effective. The point of greatest federal leverage is the publicly assisted housing program, since legal action against discriminatory zoning laws is a fragmentary and time-consuming process. The freeze in housing programs in 1972 temporarily eliminated this source of federal control. In most other cases discrimination is too easily masked and so fractionated that meaningful enforcement is difficult.

4. *Education and manpower programs.* There is no doubt that blacks are handicapped by deficient education and training, but the evidence is inconclusive that expenditures for compensatory education improve achievement or employability. There are those who argue that the scale of funding was too small to result in nationwide change; others claim that money was a necessary but not sufficient condition for improvement; some view the billions expended on disadvantaged students as a massive boondogle. It is clear that funds to educate the

disadvantaged have sometimes been misused and wasted on super-fluous equipment and educational frills. Despite the constraints and the limited evidence that increased educational expenditures nation-wide have had a substantial payoff, few would claim that the resource-starved central city school systems would be just as well off without this aid. It is unrealistic to expect federal dollars for compensatory education to work miracles beyond the normal capabilities of the public schools. If aid to education is to be expanded, however, it must be on good faith rather than proven performance.

The evidence is more convincing for manpower training. A variety of studies have shown that institutional training raises the earnings of blacks, mostly by reducing subsequent unemployment. On-the-job training and placement have an immediate employment payoff and public job creation provides earnings as well as some level of public services. If the secondary payoffs of the manpower programs are considered—especially their income maintenance aspects and the opportunities they provide for minorities in their administration—there is no doubt that the expenditures have been worthwhile even if the cost/benefit ratios comparing individual employment gains with program costs are only mildly favorable. There is certainly no ground for assuming, as has become fashionable in some quarters, that the programs do not work because success cannot be unequivocally demonstrated on the balance sheet.

5. *Institution-building.* Over the long run, the progress of blacks can only become self-sustaining when black institutions exist to pursue and defend their interests and when blacks control sufficient resources to help themselves. But public policy is rarely focused on the more distant future, and the meagerly funded and cautiously administered government efforts proved to be too short-lived to plant many lasting seeds. By 1973 the dismantling of the poverty and Model Cities pro-grams, the emphasis on revenue sharing, and the gradual erosion of the administrative authority of community groups had reduced most poverty and minority organizations to powerlessness. "Maximum fea-sible participation" became "minimum, nominal participation," and the promised "piece of the action" proved to be little more than table scraps.

Community Action was not sustained long enough or with enough flexibility to determine whether it could work. The Office of Economic Opportunity accounted for a large share of community action budgets, and the 1967 amendment requiring local government approval of antipoverty projects further constrained the flexibility in using federal funds. The flurry of action in the first years of the poverty programs gave way to plodding delivery with a gradually eroding jurisdiction. Under Model Cities, the poor were not given much voice in the first place and subsequent actions altered the initial goal of concentrating aid in low income and minority target areas.

Attempts to create minority controlled institutions to undertake large-scale development of businesses and jobs never moved from the experimental stage. Emphasis was placed instead on the formation of small black businesses and an extensive federal bureaucracy was created to provide assistance. Proposed tax incentives and financial leveraging were never made available to community development corporations, with the result that most became simply minor delivery mechanisms for entrepreneurship assistance.

In all these cases, there were unrealistic expectations of success. Support and flexibility were cut back whenever the establishment was challenged, and resources were always limited. The result is that there are few self-sustaining black institutions created with federal aid, and there must be some doubt whether government support can ever develop black institutions on a significant scale.

6. *Considering black interests in broader policies.* Blacks have minimal political clout, occupy few positions of authority, and thus have little voice in general policymaking, even when the decisions substantially affect them. Blacks are more frequently the wage gainers and the job losers from minimum wage increases and coverage extensions. The proposed lower minimum wage for youths is a crucial issue for blacks, considering the staggering unemployment rate of black sixteen- and seventeen-year-old youths, yet the judgments of spokesmen for blacks have been given little consideration in the debate over these issues.

Similarly, black interests clearly lie with any measure which will expedite the judicial process and reform the correctional system. It is only a slight exaggeration to argue that the corrections system is for many urban blacks what college is for most suburban whites—a key institution shaping values and attitudes during the process of maturation. There is no doubt that blacks would be better off if the billions of dollars which have been expended to punish criminals had gone instead to crime prevention and to rehabilitating offenders.

Military policies are another area where black interests have been given inadequate consideration. Although the military has been a leader in equalizing civil rights, recruitment practices have ignored black needs. When there was front-line fighting to be done, rules were changed to give more blacks the opportunity to join the ranks. On the other hand, in peacetime, under a volunteer system, there is a full-scale effort to find white recruits if not to discourage blacks in order to keep a balanced force.

The crucial issue is the lack of a black voice in general economic policymaking. To the extent there is a tradeoff between unemployment and inflation, blacks are better off with less unemployment and more inflation. If whites suffered as much forced idleness as blacks there is no doubt that the goals of macroeconomic policy would be different. In the longer run, tight labor markets are a must if black economic and social progress is to continue.

Blacks have a major interest in other policies. They would stand to benefit disproportionately from child care, mass transit, income and job guarantees, health insurance, and housing programs. During periods of social and economic progress, when mass transit systems are being built which provide jobs and transportation for blacks, when health insurance is being expanded, when houses are being subsidized and constructed, there is less need to stress black interests. But when blacks must settle for a declining share of a shrinking or slowly growing social welfare pie, policymakers at all levels need to give closer attention to their needs.

The Sputtering Engine

Whatever criticisms can be made of the vigor and effectiveness of governmental efforts, they have clearly served as the primary catalyst

and engine for change over the past decade. From the initial confrontations—a governor standing on the steps of a southern university
to block the entrance of blacks—to the most recent victories—the
nation's largest employer agreeing to massive reparations for its past
discrimination—the federal government has been the initiator of
action to enforce equal rights. And these cases which made headlines
were only the most visible manifestations of widespread pressure on
employers, unions, local governments, and private and public institutions to assure blacks a measure of equality.

The social welfare carrot was as important as the enforcement
stick. The dramatic expansion of public programs of all types provided the wherewithal and the incentive for public and private decision-makers to hire, train, educate, and serve more blacks. Cash
transfers and in-kind services directly reached those in need, and these
measures had a massive impact on the welfare of blacks. In 1970, 21
percent of all employed blacks were government workers, an additional 9 percent were employed in nongovernmental jobs directly
linked to government expenditures. A fifth of all black families
received public assistance payments and another fifth received social
security or other government payments. While there is some duplica-
tion in these categories, their sum is a rough proxy for the direct
impact of the government, suggesting that a majority of blacks depend
very directly on the government as an employer or source of other
income.

A variety of circumstances fired this engine of change and encouraged governmental action to focus on the problems of blacks.

1. Most important was the magnitude of the injustices to blacks
and the sudden realization that little had been done to right these
wrongs. In the 1960s the issues were forcibly presented by the protests
of blacks in the South and the violence which followed. More educated, more liberal, and more affluent than in the past, the nation was
shocked into action by the exposure of completely unjustifiable inequities.

2. Underlying this change in public attitudes was a change in
economic realities. Blacks had increasingly moved from the farm to
the cities, and out of the South to the North and West, to compete for
jobs. Exploitation continued in the urban labor markets, but it was

less prevalent than in the rural South because it was frequently in the best interests of unions and employers to move toward greater labor market equality. Not only could discrimination in an open market be costly to employers, but unions were more likely to organize blacks to protect their working standards.

3. Another critical factor was the community of interest between the problems of blacks and those of the white majority. The trial balloons of the War On Poverty were launched against Appalachian rather than ghetto poverty. Though poverty programs were sometimes "taken over" by blacks because of their disproportionate representation among the disadvantaged, they were not initiated with this in mind. Housing subsidies, food assistance, Medicaid, and other in-kind efforts were intended for a mixed clientele, since many more whites than blacks were in need despite the greater incidence among the blacks. The programs which came to mean so much to blacks were expanded or initiated to help both whites and blacks in need.

4. The urban riots which occurred in many large cities between 1965 and 1968 undoubtedly helped to loosen federal purse strings, especially for "fire-fighting" programs such as the Neighborhood Youth Corps, the Concentrated Employment Program, and Model Cities. In the late 1960s, there was hardly a book, article, or speech on black problems which failed to allude to the smoke rising from the central cities.

If these factors encouraged federal efforts and contributed to widespread support, other circumstances maximized their impacts and eased the friction attendant to the changes.

1. The first steps toward achieving equality did not threaten any vested interest groups, although they may have challenged traditional notions of white status and privilege. Broad principles on equal rights could be acclaimed and the worst cases handled without personal cost to most individuals or institutions. Income maintenance programs could be expanded with only a slight additional burden on the majority. In-kind efforts were supported by farm and construction lobbies which stood to benefit. Few persons were really hurt or challenged by the efforts in the 1960s. Where such frictions occurred, changes were quickly made in response to criticism, or else increased federal funds compensated for any difficulties and bought off the opposition.

2. A major factor was the newness of the programs and the deceiving clarity of the problems. While it may seem naive in retrospect, the rhetoric of the New Frontier and the Great Society was that socioeconomic conditions could be substantially and quickly altered by government intervention. The public was willing to support and expand a variety of programs in the faith that they would bear fruit.

3. A last and very vital factor was the centralization of governmental authority and expenditure at the federal level. Between 1960 and 1972 federal outlays more than doubled, and the share of rising state and local expenditures financed by the federal grants-in-aid rose from 14 to 22 percent. Because the federal government was more often doing the pushing in racial matters, blacks benefited by the increased federal presence.

The Clouded Outlook

To the extent these factors were important determinants of public policy and its effectiveness, the outlook for the future is not particularly sanguine. There has been a leveling off of governmental efforts in a number of cases, and a reversal in some. The slowing of black economic and social gains in the early 1970s was partially a cyclical phenomenon—a breather after the tumultuous changes generated by the Great Society. The critical issue is how far the policy pendulum will swing back in the direction of activism and what effect this will have. The evidence indicates that the favorable circumstances of the 1960s will not be duplicated in the years ahead, and that the rate of progress will probably slow to the degree that it is dependent on public policy.

The moral issues are far more clouded than in the previous decade. There are fewer bigots with axe-handles blocking progress; instead a pervasive and elusive system of discrimination has survived, in which fragmented decisions by individuals or institutions represent often unclear and unprovable prejudice. To change this system will adversely affect a number of individuals and the "wrong" done to them must be balanced against the "right" done to blacks. In 1974 the issue reached the Supreme Court in a case in which a white was denied entrance to law school in favor of less qualified minority students. The

Court refused to make a definitive ruling in the case, indicating the degree to which even civil libertarians are divided on such issues. If quotas are used to advance blacks, whites will suffer from reverse discrimination. If middle class white children are bused to less adequate schools, their educational progress may suffer. In these and other tradeoffs, the justice of black interests is not as clear-cut as in the 1960s: compensatory treatment is not as inalienable a right as equal treatment.

The economic setting of the years ahead may also be less conducive to improvement for blacks than the recent past. As the labor market grows closer to equality, employers and unions are being asked to make compensatory efforts which are not always in their interests. For those out of the work force, rising welfare benefits may also collide with economic realities, for welfare levels will always be kept below the wages of those who must pay the costs.

It is probably also true that shifting social priorities and a declining unity of interest between blacks and whites will slow change. Social welfare programs have alleviated the most immediate needs of the disadvantaged and greater priority is being given to issues affecting the total population—the environment, energy shortages, and inflation. The most likely additions to social welfare programs are measures such as national health insurance and expanded child care which will affect many blacks but which will serve broad clienteles. Housing allowances or some form of guaranteed income may be implemented, but the likely thrust of welfare reform is to consolidate and reorganize rather than to expand.

In broader terms, the community of interest may be further eroded by increasing housing segregation. As the white financial and personal involvement with the central cities decreases, the biracial constituency which supported redevelopment and city welfare programs may dissipate. Suburbanites may be more willing to support the abstract ideals of equality, but when their interests collide or do not coincide with those of blacks, their support for social programs is likely to diminish.

The urban riots, which encouraged federal action several years ago, are becoming a memory whose urgency is fading. Moreover, it is doubtful that renewed rioting would have the same motivating force as in the past decade. Fewer whites are immediately threatened by increasingly black central cities. Businesses and populations have suburbanized and further riots would accelerate this process. In the present climate, the reactions of police and politicians would no doubt be less sympathetic so that future confrontations would either be less effective or more violent.

Even if the federal government were to more actively pursue the interests of blacks, opposition may become more widespread to governmental measures. If the gains of blacks must be purchased at the expense of whites, and if the number of blacks who stand to gain is smaller than the number of whites who feel threatened, government policies can only push individual, corporate, and institutional decision-makers so far. The more interests conflict, the more the laws will be violated and opposed.

Government efforts will also be less effective to the degree that people believe them to have failed. In the early 1970s there was a widespread disenchantment with social programs shared by policy-makers and the general public. Though these beliefs may be as ill-founded as the inflated expectations of the 1960s, the impact of the doubts may be long-standing. If employers, unions, and private and public institutions believe that federal efforts are fruitless tinkering, they will be reluctant to support them in either the voting booth or in their individual decisions.

A final factor which may undermine efforts in aid of blacks is revenue sharing. The basic concept is to decentralize decision-making authority to the state and local level in order to improve program efficiency and give the people more control over their government. Whether such a system will be implemented or whether it will change the present balance of power is uncertain, but the implications for blacks are not favorable. Repeatedly, the federal government has had to step in to eliminate discriminatory practices by state and local governments or to enforce equal opportunity laws. Moreover, local decision-makers are more vulnerable to the demands of vested interest groups and entrenched power blocks, while federal decision-makers are more able to look at the broader issues and to give more weight to social justice and black needs. In the allocation of funds, formulas will be used which spread the money to many localities (including affluent communities) rather than concentrating it on specific target areas and groups. The likely result of any revenue sharing is, thus, to reduce the currently large share of funds going to central cities and to cut back the size of programs serving predominantly black clienteles.

Realism demands the recognition of these present and future constraints on government efforts for blacks. Even if the plateau of the early 1970s is not permanent, the pace of improvement is unlikely to attain the momentum of the 1960s unless there is a significant change in public priorities rather than a mere shift in political parties. To recognize that this is a likely scenario does not mean that the outcome is desirable or inevitable. The tasks of achieving racial equality are difficult, but this does not mean that they should be abandoned or that they can never be accomplished.

No careful reading of the evidence could leave the impression that further efforts are unnecessary. There is meager evidence to support the contention that the system has reached the limits of its capacity to change; in any case, the nation has already enjoyed a period of breath-catching during which the pace of change has strained nothing except the hopes of blacks.

If there are any simple lessons to be learned from the information and analysis which has been presented, they might be:

1. Substantial progress has been made by blacks, in large part as a result of governmental efforts. These have been especially important in helping to improve the status of the most disadvantaged who lack other options.

2. Because of the size of the initial gaps, the often inadequate commitment of resources and energies, and the problems inherent in new approaches to deep-rooted problems, there is still a long way to go before conditions are equalized.

3. Unless federal efforts on behalf of blacks are renewed, the rate of progress will slow as the obstacles become more formidable and as the momentum of the 1960s dissipates.

4. Programs for blacks can continue to have high payoffs. Millions are still poor, ill-housed, and ill-fed; there can be absolutely no doubt that money or in-kind aid will improve their status. Under the conditions in which many blacks are still forced to live, the question of diminishing returns is moot. Rates of gain in employment and education may slow, but progress can continue and can have a substantial impact.

The future, then, is a matter of choice. The progress of the 1960s has demonstrated that Martin Luther King's vision is a realizable but still distant possibility. The decisions and actions of national, state, and local policymakers, and the response of institutions and individuals will determine how quickly it will become a reality, if ever. Though policy issues become more complex and the decisions more difficult, the underlying moral question remains: Are we committed to a just society which offers equal opportunity to all?

A Dream Deferred

What happens to a dream deferred?
Does it dry up like a raisin in the sun?
Or fester like a sore—and then run?
Does it stink like rotten meat?
Or crust and sugar over—like a syrupy sweet?
Maybe it just sags like a heavy load.
Or does it explode?

NOTES

INDEX

NOTES

1. THE BLACK POPULATION

1. *Manpower Report of the President, 1973* (Washington: Government Printing Office, March 1973), tables A1 and A5.

2. U.S. Bureau of the Census, *Characteristics of the Low-Income Population, 1972,* Series P-60, no. 88, 1973, table 8.

3. U.S. Bureau of the Census, *The Social and Economic Status of the Black Population in the United States, 1972,* Series P-23, no. 46, July 1973, table 2.

4. U.S. Bureau of the Census, *Negro Population,* Series PC(2)-1B, 1973, table 3.

5. Andrew F. Brimmer, "Regional Growth, Migration and Economic Progress in the Black Community," *Congressional Record* (daily edition), September 23, 1971, p. 9867.

6. Larry H. Long and Lynne R. Heltman, "Income Differences Between Blacks and Whites Controlling for Education and Region of Birth," paper presented to the Population Association of America, New York City, April 1974.

7. Derived from U.S. Bureau of the Census, *The Social and Economic Status of the Black Population in the United States, 1972,* p. 14.

2. THE COMMON DENOMINATOR: INCOME

1. Murray S. Weitzman, *Measures of Overlap of Income Distribution of White and Negro Families in the United States,* Technical Paper No. 22, U.S. Bureau of the Census (Washington: Government Printing Office, 1972).

2. U.S. Bureau of the Census, *Money Income of Families and Individuals in The United States, 1971,* Series P-60, no. 85, December 1972, table 9.

3. U.S. Bureau of the Census, *The Social and Economic Status of the Black Population in the United States, 1972,* Series P-23, no. 46, July 1973, p. 68.

4. Ibid., pp. 21–23.

5. Herman P. Miller, "Recent Trends in Income Differentials Between Blacks and Whites," Center for Manpower Policy Studies, George Washington University (processed), pp. 84–87.

6. Calculation based on CPI component changes, 1960–1972, using methodology developed in Robinson Hollistor and John Palmer, *The Impact of Inflation on the Poor* (Madison, Wisc.: Institute for Research on Poverty, 1970).

7. Derived from U.S. Bureau of the Labor Statistics, "Autumn 1972 Urban Family Budgets and Comparative Indexes for Selected Urban Areas," 1973, Release 73–253.

8. U.S. Bureau of the Census, *The Social and Economic Status of the Black Population in the United States, 1972*, table 7.

9. U.S. Bureau of the Census, *Sources and Structure of Family Income*, Series PC(2)-4C, 1964, tables 6 and 7; and *Sources and Structure of Family Income*, Series PC(2)-8A, 1973, tables 4 and 5.

10. Herman P. Miller, "A New Look at Inequality in the United States—Without Rose-Colored Glasses," 1971 (mimeographed), p. 2.

11. U.S. Bureau of Labor Statistics, "Employee Compensation Reached $4.54 an Hour in 1970," November 23, 1971, Release 71–612.

12. Walter W. Kolodrubetz, "Private and Public Retirement Pensions: Findings from the 1968 Survey of the Aged," *Social Security Bulletin* (September 1970), p. 20.

13. U.S. Bureau of the Census, *Characteristics of the Low Income Population, 1972*, Series P-60, no. 91, December 1973, table 22.

14. Ibid., table 4.

15. Ibid., tables 5 and 6.

3. EMPLOYMENT AND EARNINGS

1. U.S. Bureau of the Census, *Sources and Structure of Family Income*, Series PC(2)-4C, 1964, table 23; U.S. Bureau of the Census, Consumer Income, *Money Income in 1971 of Families and Persons in the United States*, Series P-60, no. 85, December 1972, table 63.

2. Derived from U.S. Bureau of Labor Statistics, *Black Americans*, Bulletin 1731 (Washington: Government Printing Office, 1972), pp. 6–16.

3. U.S. Bureau of the Census, Subject Reports, *Earnings by Occupation and Education*, Series PC(2)-8B, January 1973, tables 1, 2, 7, and 8.

4. U.S. Bureau of the Census, *Vocational Training*, PC(2)-5C, May 1973, tables 1–3.

5. Derived from U.S. Bureau of the Census, Subject Reports, *Earnings by Occupation and Education*, table 1.

6. Derived from U.S. Bureau of the Census, *Occupation by Earnings and Education*, Series PC(2)-7B, 1963, table 1.

7. Derived from U.S. Bureau of the Census, *Earnings by Occupation and Education*, tables 1 and 2.

8. Ibid., tables 7 and 8.

9. Anne M. Young, "Work Experience of the Population in 1972," U.S. Bureau of Labor Statistics, *Special Labor Force Report 162*, 1974, table A-8.

10. U.S. Bureau of the Census, *Earnings by Occupation and Education*, tables 1 and 2.

11. Derived from data in *Manpower Report of the President, 1973* (Washington: Government Printing Office, 1973), tables A-12 and 17.

12. *Manpower Report of the President, 1974* (Washington: Government Printing Office, 1974), table A-4.

13. Ibid., tables A-3 and A-4.

14. *Employment and Earnings,* January 1968, table A-1; and January 1973, table 1.

15. *Employment and Earnings,* January 1973, table 31.

16. Sar A. Levitan and Robert Taggart, *Employment and Earnings Inadequacy: A New Social Indicator* (Baltimore: Johns Hopkins University Press, 1974), Appendix p. 110.

17. The following discussion and data are drawn from Sar A. Levitan and Robert Taggart, "Employment and Earnings Inadequacy: A Measure of Worker Welfare," *Monthly Labor Review* (October 1973), pp. 19–27.

4. EDUCATION: QUANTITY AND QUALITY

1. U.S. Bureau of the Census, *The Social and Economic Status of the Black Population in the United States, 1972,* Series P-23, no. 46, July 1973.

2. U.S. Bureau of the Census, 1970 Census of the Population, *General Social and Economic Characteristics of the Population, U.S. Summary,* PC(1)-C1, table 131.

3. U.S. Bureau of the Census, *Social and Economic Characteristics of Students: October 1971,* Series P-20, no. 241, October 1972, table 2.

4. U.S. Bureau of the Census, *Educational Enrollment,* Series P-20, annual data.

5. James S. Coleman and others, *Equality of Educational Opportunity* (Washington: Government Printing Office, 1966), p. 273.

6. Michael J. Wargo, *ESEA Title I, A Reanalysis and Synthesis of the Data from 1965 through 1970* (Palo Alto, Calif.: American Institutes for Research, 1972), p. 103; Finis Welch, "Education and Racial Discrimination," in Orley Ashenfelter and Albert Rees, eds., *Discrimination in Labor Markets* (Princeton: University Press, 1973), p. 73.

7. Samuel Bowles and Henry M. Levin, "The Determinants of Scholastic Achievement—An Appraisal of Some Recent Evidence," *Journal of Human Resources* (Winter 1968), pp. 3–24; Eric A. Hanushek and John F. Cain, "On the Value of Equality of Educational Opportunity as a Guide to Public Policy," in Frederick Mosteller and Daniel P. Moynihan, eds., *On Equality of Educational Opportunity* (New York: Vintage Books, 1972), pp. 116–145.

8. Frederick Mosteller and Daniel P. Moynihan, eds., *On Equality of Educational Opportunity* (New York: Vintage Books, 1972).

9. Coleman and others, *Equality of Educational Opportunity,* p. 299.

10. Dennis J. Dugan, "The Impact of Parental and Educational Investment Upon Student Achievement," in *Inequality: Studies in Elementary and Secondary Education,* U.S. Office of Education, Planning Paper 62-2, June 1969, p. 10.

11. Robert L. Crain, "School Integration and the Academic Achievement of Negroes," *Sociology of Education* (Winter 1971), pp. 1–26.

12. U.S. Congress, Senate, Select Committee on Equal Educational Opportunity, *Toward Equal Educational Opportunity,* 92d Cong., 2d Sess. (Washington: Government Printing Office, 1972).

13. Thomas E. Pettigrew and others, "Busing: A Review of 'The Evidence,' " *The Public Interest* (Winter 1973), pp. 98–99.

14. David J. Armor, "The Evidence on Busing," *The Public Interest* (Summer 1972), p. 100.

15. Ibid., pp. 90–126.

16. Pettigrew and others, "Busing," pp. 88–114.

17. Christopher Jencks and others, *Inequality: A Reassessment of the Effect of Family and Schooling in America* (New York: Basic Books, 1972), p. 106.

18. U.S. Department of Health, Education, and Welfare, *The Digest of Educational Statistics, 1973* (Washington: Government Printing Office, 1974), p. 65.

19. Senate Select Committee on Equal Educational Opportunity, p. 146.

20. Ibid., p. 147.

21. James W. Guthrie and others, *Schools and Inequality* (Cambridge, Mass.: MIT Press, 1971), pp. 79–90.

22. Coleman and others, *Equality of Educational Opportunity,* p. 112.

23. Jencks and others, *Inequality,* p. 108.

24. Arthur R. Jensen, "How Much Can We Boost I.Q. and Scholastic Achievement?" *Harvard Education Review,* 39 (Winter 1969), 111.

25. Robert Rosenthal and Lenore Jacobsen, *Pygmalion and the Classroom* (New York: Holt, Rinehart and Winston, 1968).

26. Hobson v. Hansen, 269 F. Supp. 401 (D.C. 1967).

27. U.S. Bureau of the Census, *Characteristics of Students and Their Colleges, 1966,* Series P-20, no. 183, table 3.

28. U.S. Bureau of the Census, *Social and Economic Characteristics of Students: October 1972,* Series P-20, no. 260, February 1974, tables 3 and 18.

29. U.S. Bureau of the Census, *Characteristics of Students and Their Colleges, 1966,* Series P-20, no. 183, table 6.

30. U.S. Department of Health, Education, and Welfare, *Racial and Ethnic Enrollment Data from Institutions of Higher Education, Fall 1970,* Part I (Washington: Government Printing Office, 1972).

31. U.S. Bureau of the Census, *Population Characteristics,* "Social and Economic Characteristics of Students: October 1971," Series P-20, no. 241, October 1972, table 16.

32. U.S. Commission on Civil Rights, *The Federal Civil Rights Enforcement Effort: A Reassessment* (Washington: Government Printing Office, 1973), p. 193.

33. U.S. Office of Civil Rights, *Racial and Ethnic Enrollment Data from Institutions of Higher Education, Fall 1970* (Washington: Government Printing Office, 1972), Parts II–V.

34. Christopher Jencks and David Reisman, "The American Negro College," *Harvard Educational Review* (Winter 1967).

35. Thomas Sowell, *Black Education: Myth and Tragedies* (New York: David McKay and Co., 1972), p. 256.

36. Derived from U.S. Bureau of the Census, *School Enrollment,* Series P-20, annual data.

37. U.S. Bureau of the Census, *Social and Economic Characteristics of Students: October 1972,* Series P-20, no. 260, February 1974, table 18.

5. THE BLACK FAMILY

1. U.S. Bureau of the Census, *Statistical Abstract of the United States, 1973* (Washington: Government Printing Office, 1973), table 27.

2. U.S. Bureau of the Census, *Statistical Abstract of the United States, 1972* (Washington: Government Printing Office, 1972), table 73.

3. U.S. Bureau of the Census, *The Social and Economic Status of the Black Population in the United States, 1972*, Series P-23, no. 46, July 1973, p. 74.

4. Derived from U.S. Bureau of the Census, *The Social and Economic Status of Negroes in the United States, 1970*, Series P-23, no. 38, July 1971, table 94.

5. Jane Menken, "The Health and Social Consequences of Teenage Child-bearing," *Family Planning Perspectives* (July 1972), p. 46.

6. Robert B. Hill, *The Strengths of Black Families* (New York: Emerson Hall Publishers, 1972), p. 42.

7. U.S. Bureau of the Census, *Marriage, Divorce and Remarriage by Year of Birth: June 1971*, Series P-20, no. 239, September 1972, table 2.

8. U.S. Bureau of the Census, *Persons by Family Characteristics*, Series PC(2)-4B, January 1973, table 2.

9. Ibid.

10. U.S. Bureau of the Census, *Persons by Family Characteristics*, Series PC(2)-4B, 1973, tables 1 and 2.

11. U.S. Bureau of the Census, *Money Income in 1971 of Families and Persons in the United States*, Series P-60, no. 85, December 1972, table 19.

12. U.S. Bureau of the Census, Department of Commerce, *Differences Between Income of White and Negro Families by Work Experience of Wife and Region: 1970, 1969, and 1959*, Series P-23, no. 39, December 1971, tables 5 and 6.

13. U.S. Bureau of the Census, *Birth Expectations of American Wives: June 1973*, Series P-20, no. 254, October 1973, table 2.

14. Charles F. Westoff, "The Modernization of U.S. Contraceptive Practice," *Family Planning Perspectives* (July 1972), p. 9.

15. John F. Kantner and Melvin Zelnik, "Sexual Experience of Young Unmarried Women in the United States," *Family Planning Perspectives* (October 1972), p. 9.

16. Gerald Lipson and Dianne Wolman, "Polling Americans on Birth Control and Population," *Family Planning Perspectives* (January 1972), p. 39.

17. Kantner and Zelnik, "Sexual Experience of Young Unmarried Women in the United States," pp. 9–11.

18. U.S. Department of Health, Education, and Welfare, Welfare Administration, *Study of Recipients of Aid to families With Dependent Children, November-December 1961: National Cross-Tabulation, 1963*, and U.S. Department of Health, Education, and Welfare, Social and Rehabilitation Service, *Findings of the 1971 AFDC Study*, SRS 73–03759, April 1973.

19. U.S. Bureau of the Census, *The Social and Economic Status of Negroes in the United States, 1972*, Series P-23, no. 38, July 1973, table 87.

20. U.S. Bureau of the Census, Subject Reports, *Persons by Family Characteristics*, Series PC(2)-4B, January 1973, table 2.

21. Jacob S. Seigel, "Estimates of Coverage of the Population by Sex, Race,

and Age in the 1970 Census," paper presented to Population Association of America, April 26, 1973 (mimeographed).

22. U.S. Bureau of the Census, *Negro Population,* Series PC(2)-1B, May 1973, table 5.

23. Daniel P. Moynihan, "The Tangle of Pathology" in Robert Staples, ed., *The Black Family* (Belmont, Calif.: Wadsworth Publishing Co., 1971), pp. 40–41.

24. Theodore Lidz, "The Family: The Source of Human Resources," in Ivar Berg, ed., *Human Resources and Economic Welfare* (New York: Columbia University Press, 1972), p. 196.

6. HEALTH AND ITS IMPACTS

1. 1970 White House Conference on Children, U.S. Department of Health, Education, and Welfare, *Profiles of Children* (Washington: Government Printing Office, 1971), tables 25 and 26.

2. Ibid., table 29, p. 99.

3. Jane Menken, "The Health and Social Consequences of Teenage Childbearing," *Family Planning Perspectives,* 4 (July 1972), 46.

4. U.S. Bureau of the Census, *Statistical Abstract of the United States, 1973,* (Washington: Government Printing Office, 1974), p. 52.

5. *Profiles of Children,* table 12, p. 90.

6. U.S. Department of Health, Education, and Welfare, *Monthly Vital Statistics,* January 30, 1970, p. 3.

7. U.S. Bureau of the Census, *The Social and Economic Status of Blacks in the United States, 1972,* Series P-23, no. 46, July 1973, table 71.

8. Ibid., table 70.

9. National Center for Health Statistics, U.S. Department of Health, Education, and Welfare, *Vital Statistics of the United States, 1968* (Washington: Government Printing Office, 1972), table 8.

10. Ibid.

11. Ibid.

12. Don Cahalan, Ira H. Cisin, and Helen M. Crossley, *American Drinking Practices, A National Study of Drinking Behavior and Attitudes* (New Brunswick, N.J.: Rutgers Center for Alcohol Studies, 1969), p. 180.

13. Melvin Zax, Elmer A. Gardner, and William T. Hart, "A Survey of the Prevalence of Alcoholism in Monroe County, New York," *Quarterly Journal of Studies on Alcohol* (June 1967), p. 320.

14. Daniel P. Moynihan, "The Schism in Black America," *The Public Interest* (Spring 1972), p. 24.

15. U.S. Department of Health, Education, and Welfare, *Limitation of Activity,* Vital and Health Statistics, Series 10, no. 80 (Washington: Government Printing Office, April 1973), tables 4, 6.

16. Ibid.

17. U.S. Bureau of the Census, *Persons with Work Disabilities,* PC(2)-6C, January 1973, table 9.

18. Judith A. Segal, *Food for the Hungry* (Baltimore: Johns Hopkins University Press, 1970), p. 15.

7. LITTLE MORE THAN SHELTER

1. U.S. Bureau of the Census, *The Social and Economic Status of the Black Population in the United States, 1972,* Series P-23, no. 46, July 1973, table 61.

2. President's Committee on Urban Housing, *A Decent Home* (Washington: Government Printing Office, 1968), pp. 42–43.

3. U.S. Bureau of the Census, *Negro Population,* PC(2)-1B, May 1973, table 10.

4. Robert Taggart, *Low-Income Housing: A Critique of Federal Aid* (Baltimore: Johns Hopkins University Press, 1970), p. 50.

5. U.S. Bureau of the Census, *The Social and Economic Status of the Black Population in the United States, 1972,* table 67.

6. Henry J. Aaron, *Shelter and Subsidies* (Washington: Brookings Institution, 1972), p. 59.

7. U.S. Bureau of the Census, *The Social and Economic Status of the Black Population in the United States, 1972,* table 64.

8. Thomas Pettigrew, "Attitudes on Race and Housing: A Social-Psychological View," in Amos Howley and Vincent Rock, eds., *Segregation in Residential Areas* (Washington: National Academy of Sciences, 1973), p. 50.

9. Ibid., p. 65.

10. Sar A. Levitan, Garth Mangum, and Robert Taggart, *Economic Opportunity in the Ghetto: The Partnership of Government and Business* (Baltimore: Johns Hopkins University Press, 1969), pp. 2–4.

11. Bennett Harrison, *Education, Training, and the Urban Ghetto* (Baltimore: Johns Hopkins University Press, 1972), p. 116.

12. Angus Campbell, *White Attitudes Toward Black People* (Ann Arbor: Institute for Social Research, 1971), p. 83.

13. Pettigrew, "Attitudes on Race and Housing," pp. 47–48.

14. Ibid.

15. Ibid.

16. Ibid.

8. BLACK POWER

1. U.S. Bureau of the Census, *Occupational Characteristics,* Series PC(2)-7A, June 1973, table 2.

2. Ibid., table 39.

3. Manpower Administration, U.S. Department of Labor, *A Study of Black Male Professionals in Industry,* Manpower Research Monograph no. 26 (Washington, D.C.: Government Printing Office, 1973).

4. "Room at the Top," *Black Enterprise* (September 1971), p. 13.

5. Lester Carson, "Black Directors," *Black Enterprise* (September 1973), pp. 17–28.

6. Christine and Leroy Clark, "The Black Lawyer," *Black Enterprise* (February 1973), p. 15.

7. "Where Are You Black CPAs?" *Black Enterprise* (July 1973), p. 48.

8. "Room at the Top," p. 14.

9. U.S. Bureau of the Census, *General, Social and Economic Characteristics,*

Series PC(1)-C1, June 1972, table 93, and *Industrial Characteristics,* Series PC(2)-7F, June 1967, p. 135.

10. Ray Marshall, *Negro Employment in the South* vol. 3, *State and Local Governments,* Manpower Research Monograph No. 23, Manpower Administration, U.S. Department of Labor (Washington: Government Printing Office, 1973).

11. Bayard Rustin, "The Blacks and the Unions," *Harper's Magazine* (May 1971), p. 75.

12. U.S. Bureau of Labor Statistics, *Selected Earnings and Demographic Characteristics of Union Members, 1970,* Report 417 (Washington: Government Printing Office, 1972), table 6.

13. "Blacks and Organized Labor," *Black Enterprise* (July 1972), pp. 18–20.

14. U.S. Bureau of the Census, *Money Income in 1972 of Families and Persons in the United States,* Series P-60, no. 90, December 1973, table 65.

15. U.S. Bureau of the Census, *Household Ownership of Cars and Light Trucks: July 1972,* Series P-65, no. 44, February 1973, tables 1-5.

16. U.S. Bureau of the Census, *The Social and Economic Status of the Black Population in the United States, 1972,* Series P-23, no. 46, July 1973, tables 62 and 63.

17. U.S. Bureau of the Census, *Minority-Owned Businesses: 1969,* Series MB-1, 1971, table 1.

18. "The Top 100," *Black Enterprise* (June 1973), p. 20.

19. U.S. Bureau of the Census, *Statistical Abstract of the United States, 1972* (Washington: Government Printing Office, 1972), table 600.

20. U.S. Bureau of the Census, *The Social and Economic Status of the Black Population in the United States, 1972,* table 75.

21. "Highlights of Black Political History," *Congressional Quarterly,* June 24, 1972, p. 1524.

22. Penn Kimball, *The Disconnected* (New York: Columbia University Press, 1972), pp. 90–100.

23. Jeff Nesmith, "Atlanta Elects Black Mayor," *The Washington Post,* October 17, 1973.

24. Steven U. Roberts, "Bradley Beats Yorty in Los Angeles Race," *New York Times,* May 30, 1973.

25. *Congressional Quarterly,* April 3, 1970, p. 921.

26. *Congressional Quarterly,* June 24, 1972, p. 1525.

27. Kimball, *The Disconnected,* pp. 90–100.

28. U.S. Bureau of the Census, *The Social and Economic Status of the Black Population in the United States, 1972,* table 76.

29. "Report from Black America," *Newsweek,* June 30, 1969, p. 22.

30. Kimball, *The Disconnected,* pp. 90–100.

31. Dale Rogers Marshall, "Metropolitan Government: Views of Minorities," *Minority Perspective* (Baltimore: Johns Hopkins University Press, 1972), p. 20.

9. RACE AND SOCIAL CLASS

1. U.S. Bureau of the Census, *Occupation by Earnings and Education,* Series PC(2)-7B, 1963, table 1.

2. Derived from U.S. Bureau of the Census, *Sources and Structure of Family Income, 1960,* Series PC(2)-4C, 1964, table 3; and *Sources and Structure of Family Income, 1970,* Series PC(2)-8A, 1973, table 3.

3. ·Fred P. Graham, "The Lawless Image," *Harper's* (September 1970), p. 68.

4. Ibid., p. 70.

5. Charles E. Silberman, "Progress Report Number Three," The Study of Law and Justice, February 1974 (xerox), p. 45.

6. Leonard Goodwin, *Do the Poor Want to Work?* (Washington: Brookings Institution, 1972).

7. James S. Coleman and others, *Equality of Educational Opportunity* (Washington: Government Printing Office, 1966).

8. Philip B. Springer, *Work Attitudes of Disadvantaged Black Men,* Report 401, U.S. Bureau of Labor Statistics (Washington: Government Printing Office, 1972).

9. Thomas Sowell, *Black Education, Myths and Tragedies* (New York: David McKay, Inc., 1972), p. 119.

10. SUPPLEMENTING INCOME

1. Sar A. Levitan, *Programs in Aid of the Poor for the 1970s,* rev. ed. (Baltimore: Johns Hopkins University Press, 1973), pp. 28–35.

2. Derived from U.S. Social and Rehabilitation Service, Department of Health, Education, and Welfare, *Findings of the 1969 AFDC Study: Data by Census Division and Selected States, Part I. Demographic and Program Characteristics,* December 1970, table 2; and *Findings of the 1971 AFDC Study, Part III, National Cross-Tabulations,* April 1973, table 60.

3. Derived from U.S. Social and Rehabilitation Service, Department of Health, Education, and Welfare, "AFDC Families: Race, by Number of Illegitimate AFDC Children, 1971" (unpublished tabulation).

4. Sar A. Levitan and Robert Taggart, *Employment and Earnings Inadequacy: A New Social Indicator* (Baltimore: Johns Hopkins University Press, 1974), p. 111.

5. U.S. Department of Health, Education, and Welfare, *Trend Report,* October 6, 1972.

6. Idella G. Swisher, "Income of the Disabled: Its Sources and Size," *Social Security Bulletin* (August 1971), pp. 19–20.

7. Philip Booth, *Social Security in America* (Ann Arbor: University of Michigan, 1973), pp. 41–57.

8. *Social Security Bulletin, Annual Statistical Supplement, 1971,* table 68.

9. Ibid., table 67.

10. *Manpower Report of the President, 1973* (Washington: Government Printing Office, 1973), table F-9.

11. U.S. Bureau of the Census, *Employment Profiles of Selected Low-Income Areas: United States Summary—Urban Areas,* Series PHC(3)-1, January 1972, tables 21a and 48a.

12. Derived from *Manpower Report of the President, 1972* (Washington: Government Printing Office, 1972), table F-9.

13. *Manpower Report of the President, 1973* (Washington: Government Printing Office, 1973), table A22.

14. U.S. Bureau of the Census, Department of Commerce, *Employment Profiles of Selected Low-Income Areas: United States Summary—Urban Areas,* table 48a.

15. Sar A. Levitan and Karen Cleary, *Old Wars Remain Unfinished: The Veteran Benefit System* (Baltimore: Johns Hopkins University Press, 1973), pp. 29–66.

16. U.S. Bureau of the Census, *General Population Characteristics,* Series PC(1)-B1, 1972, table 52; and *Veterans,* Series PC(2)-6E, 1973, table 1.

11. PROVIDING GOODS AND SERVICES

1. U.S. Department of Health, Education, and Welfare, *Number of Recipients and Amounts of Payments Under Medicaid and Other Medical Programs Financed from Public Assistance Funds,* Publication No. (SRS) 72–03153, NCSS Report, B-4 (CY 69), March 1, 1972, table 26.

2. U.S. Congress, Senate, Select Committee on Equal Educational Opportunity, *Hearings,* Part 12, July and August 1971 (Washington: Government Printing Office, 1971), p. 5802.

3. U.S. Department of Health, Education, and Welfare, *Medicare: In-Patient Hospital Services by Region, 1967 and 1968,* Publication No. SSA 7311702, May 30, 1973, p. 11.

4. U.S. Department of Health, Education, and Welfare, *Medicare: Public Assistance Recipients in the Supplementary Medical Insurance Program, 1969,* Publication No. SSA 7311702, July 5, 1973, p. 6.

5. Sar A. Levitan and Karen Cleary, *Old Wars Remain Unfinished: The Veteran Benefits System* (Baltimore: Johns Hopkins University Press, 1973), pp. 73–76.

6. Frederick S. Jaffe, "Family Planning Services in the United States," paper prepared for the Commission on Population Growth and the American Future, May 1972, p. 14.

7. Office of Economic Opportunity, "Number of Patients by Patient Characteristics According to Sex and Age in the United States," 1973 (mimeographed).

8. "1970 National Fertility Study," in *Center for Family Planning Program Development, Data and Analyses for 1973,* Revisions of DHEW Five Year Plan for Family Planning Services (New York: Planned Parenthood—World Population, 1973), p. 22.

9. U.S. Department of Health, Education, and Welfare, *Services to AFDC Families,* Third Annual Report, DHEW Publication No. SRS 7323024, 1973, p. 108.

10. U.S. Department of Housing and Urban Development, *Fourth Annual Report on National Housing Goals* (Washington: Government Printing Office, 1972), p. 41.

11. U.S. Department of Housing and Urban Development, unpublished tabulations.

12. Robert Taggart, *Low-Income Housing: A Critique of Federal Aid* (Baltimore: Johns Hopkins University Press, 1971), p. 114.

13. United States Commission on Civil Rights, *Homeownership for Lower Income Families* (Washington: Government Printing Office, 1971).

12. DEVELOPING HUMAN RESOURCES

1. U.S. Department of Health, Education, and Welfare, Office of Child Development, *Project Head Start 1969–1970: A Descriptive Report of Programs and Participants* (Washington: U.S. Department of Health, Education, and Welfare, 1972), p. 243.

2. Westinghouse Learning Corporation—Ohio State University, *The Impact of Head Start,* June 1969, in *The Effectiveness of Compensatory Education: Summary and Review of the Evidence* (U.S. Department of Health, Education, and Welfare, 1972), p. 107.

3. *Selected Outcomes of the Longitudinal Evaluation of Follow-Through* (Menlo Park, Calif.: Stanford Research Institute, 1973), pp. 311–315.

4. American Institutes of Research, *ESEA Title I: A Reanalysis and Synthesis of Evaluation Data from Fiscal Years 1965 through 1970* (The Institute: Palo Alto, Calif., March 1972), p. 121.

5. Southern Center for Studies in Public Policy and the NAACP Legal Defense and Education Fund, "Title I of ESEA, Is It Helping Poor Children?" printed in U.S. Congress, Senate Select Committee on Equal Educational Opportunity of the United States, *Hearings,* Part 17, 92d Cong., 2d Sess., pp. 8826–8887.

6. American Institutes of Research, *ESEA Title I,* p. 158.

7. Ibid., pp. 231–275.

8. Harry Piccariello, "Evaluation of Title I," in Joseph Froomkin and Dennis J. Dugan, eds., *Inequality: Studies in Elementary and Secondary Education,* U.S. Department of Health, Education, and Welfare, June 1969.

9. American Institutes of Research, *ESEA Title I,* pp. 231–275.

10. *The Effectiveness of Compensatory Education: Summary and Review of the Evidence,* p. 22.

11. American Institutes of Research, *ESEA Title I,* pp. 165–169.

12. *Manpower Report of the President, 1972* (Washington: Government Printing Office, March 1972), tables A-14 and B-9; and Sar A. Levitan and Robert Taggart, *Employment and Earnings Inadequacy: A New Social Indicator* (Baltimore: Johns Hopkins University Press, 1974), table 8.

13. Sar A. Levitan and Garth L. Mangum, *Federal Training and Work Programs in the Sixties* (Ann Arbor: Institute of Labor and Industrial Relations, 1969), pp. 211–234.

14. Gerald G. Somers and Ernst Stromsdorfer, *A Cost Effectiveness Analysis of the In-School and Summer Neighborhood Youth Corps* (Washington: Urban Institute, November 1970), Working Paper No. 350–22, table 3.

15. *Employment and Earnings,* September 1972, table A-7.

16. Sar A. Levitan, *The Great Society's Poor Law* (Baltimore: Johns Hopkins University Press, 1969), pp. 300–303.

17. Michael E. Borus and others, "A Benefit-Cost Analysis of the Neighborhood Youth Corps: The Out-of-School Program in Indiana," *Journal of Human Resources* (Spring 1970), p. 146.

18. Herbert Hammerman, "Minorities in Construction Referral Unions—Revisited," *Monthly Labor Review* (May 1973), pp. 43–46.

19. Garth Mangum and John Walsh, *A Decade of Manpower Development and Training* (Salt Lake City, Utah: Olympus Publishing Company, 1973), p. 27.

20. Jon H. Goldstein, *The Effectiveness of Manpower Training Programs: A Review of Research on the Impact on the Poor,* U.S. Congress, Joint Economic Committee, 92d Cong., 2d Sess. (Washington: Government Printing Office, November 1972), p. 35.

21. David J. Farber, "Changes in the Duration of the Post Training Period and in Relative Earning Credits of Trainees," Manpower Administration, U.S. Department of Labor, August 27, 1971, figure 8.

22. Sar A. Levitan, Martin Rein, and David Marwick, *Work and Welfare Go Together,* rev. ed. (Baltimore: Johns Hopkins University Press, 1973), p. 140.

23. Sar A. Levitan, Garth Mangum, and Robert Taggart, *Economic Opportunity in the Ghetto: The Partnership of Government and Business* (Baltimore: Johns Hopkins University Press, 1971), pp. 17–45.

24. Charles A. Myers, *The Role of the Private Sector in Manpower Development* (Baltimore: Johns Hopkins University Press, 1972), pp. 30–34.

25. Sar A. Levitan and Garth L. Mangum, "The 1975 Manpower Budget," *The Conference Record,* May 1974, pp. 16–19.

13 CHANGING THE RULES OF THE GAME

1. Arvil V. Adams, *Toward Fair Employment and the EEOC: A Study of Compliance Procedures Under Title VII of the Civil Rights Act of 1964,* prepared for the U.S. Equal Employment Opportunity Commission, August 31, 1972, pp. 117–122.

2. U.S. Equal Employment Opportunity Commission, *Sixth Annual Report* (Washington: Government Printing Office, March 30, 1972), pp. 23–24.

3. Karen E. DeWitt, "Labor Report/Strengthened EEOC Accelerates Action Against Business, Labor Employee Discrimination," *National Journal,* June 23, 1973, pp. 913–923.

4. Sar A. Levitan, Garth L. Mangum, and Ray Marshall, *Human Resources and Labor Markets* (New York: Harper and Row, 1972), p. 485.

5. Adams, *Toward Fair Employment and the EEOC,* p. 101.

6. Levitan, Mangum, and Marshall, *Human Resources and Labor Markets,* pp. 493–494.

7. Maia Licker, "Bringing Equality to the Nation's Steel Mess Is a Long and Bitter Task," *Wall Street Journal,* August 8, 1973, pp. 1, 21.

8. Robert Taggart, *The Manpower System in the District of Columbia: At a Critical Juncture* (Washington: National League of Cities—U.S. Conference of Mayors, March 1973), pp. 80–87.

9. Ibid.

10. Orley Ashenfelter and James Heckman, "Changes in Minority Employment Patterns, 1966 to 1970," prepared for the Equal Employment Opportunity Commission, January 1973 (mimeographed), pp. ii–vii.

11. Congressional Quarterly Service, *Congress and the Nation, 1945–1964* (Washington: Congressional Quarterly, 1964), p. 1599.

12. Ray Marshall, *Negro Employment in the South,* vol. 3, *State and Local Governments,* Manpower Research Monograph No. 23, Manpower Administration, U.S. Department of Labor (Washington: Government Printing Office, 1973), pp. 35–38.

13. Rims Barber, "Swan Song from the Delta," *Inequality in Education* (August 1971), p. 4.

14. Thomas Pettigrew, "Attitudes on Race and Housing: A Social-Psychological View," in Amos Hawley and Vincent Rock, eds., *Segregation in Residential Areas* (Washington: National Academy of Sciences, 1973), pp. 26–27.

15. Ibid., pp. 25–28.

16. *Congressional Quarterly,* June 18, 1971, p. 1321.

14. BUILDING INSTITUTIONS

1. Sar A. Levitan, *The Great Society's Poor Law* (Baltimore: Johns Hopkins University Press, 1969), pp. 119–126.

2. David M. Austin, "Resident Participation: Political Mobilization of Organizational Co-optation?" *Public Administration Review* (September 1972) (special edition), pp. 410–411.

3. Daniel Yankelovich, Inc., *A Study of the Nonprofessional in the CAP,* prepared for the Office of Economic Opportunity, September 1966, p. 104.

4. Edward J. O'Donnel and Otto M. Reid, "The Multiservice Neighborhood Center: Preliminary Findings from a National Survey," *Welfare in Review* (May-June 1971), p. 2.

5. Moses Newsome, Jr., "Neighborhood Service Centers in the Black Community," *Social Work* (March 1973), p. 51.

6. Office of Economic Opportunity, Office of Operations, "Utilization Test Survey Data for 591 CAAs," January 1972 (mimeographed).

7. Howard W. Hallman, *Community Control* (Washington: Washington Center for Metropolitan Studies, 1969), pp. 155–164.

8. Training Corporation of America, *Final Report and Proposal for Resident Observer Study and Report on Model Cities Program,* prepared for the Department of Housing and Urban Development, March 12, 1970, chaps. 2 and 4.

9. U.S. Department of Commerce, Office of Minority Business Enterprise, *Progress Report on the Minority Business Enterprise Program 1972* (Washington: Government Printing Office, 1972), p. 6; and Jack Elsen, "Failures High Among Firms Aided by SBA," *Washington Post,* November 10, 1973.

10. "The SBA and Black Business," *Black Enterprise* (October 1972), p. 50.

11. U.S. Small Business Administration, *Progress Report: The Minority Business Enterprise Program, 1972* (Washington: Government Printing Office, 1972), p. 17.

12. "MESBICs," *Black Enterprise* (January 1973), pp. 19–22.

13. Abt Associates, Inc., *An Evaluation of the Special Impact Program: Interim Report,* vol. 3, prepared for the Office of Economic Opportunity,

March 1973, pp. 2-1 to 2-28. The following discussion is based on the three-volume Abt evaluation.

14. Raymond Williams and Lloyd Biser, *Analysis of Emerging Cooperatives* (Washington: Department of Agriculture, Farmer Cooperative Service, 1972), pp. 15, 21.

15. Abt Associates, Inc., *A Study of Rural Cooperatives: Final Report,* prepared for the Office of Economic Opportunity, 1973, pp. 62, 130.

15. CONSIDERING BLACK INTERESTS IN FEDERAL POLICYMAKING

1. Peter Henle, "The Dilemma of Low-Wage Jobs" (Washington: Brookings Institution, 1972), unpublished paper, table 1.

2. U.S. Bureau of the Census, *Employment Profiles of Selected Low-Income Areas: United States Summary—Urban Areas,* Series PHC(3)-1, January 1972, table E.

3. U.S. Bureau of the Census, *Employment Profiles of Selected Low-Income Areas: Selected Rural Counties in Alabama,* Series PHC(3)-69, April 1972; *Selected Rural Counties in North Carolina,* Series PHC(3)-74, May 1972; and *Selected Rural Counties in Arkansas,* Series PHC(3)-71, April-May 1972, table E.

4. Vera C. Perrella, *Young Workers and Their Earnings, October 1969,* Special Labor Force Report 132, U.S. Bureau of Labor Statistics, 1971, table B.

5. Yale Brozen, "The Effect of Statutory Minimum Wage Increases on Teen-age Unemployment," *Journal of Law and Economics* (April 1969), pp. 109–122.

6. Finis Welch, "Statement on Minimum Wage Legislation," National Bureau of Economic Research, 1971 (mimeographed).

7. *Employment and Earnings,* January 1973, table 1.

8. *Employment and Earnings,* January 1973, table 37.

9. U.S. Army, Office of the Surgeon General, *Supplement to the Health of the Army,* September 1972, table 1.

10. *Racial and Ethnic Composition of the Male Enlisted Force,* Manpower Research Note 72–19, prepared by the Directorate for Manpower Research, Office of the Assistant Secretary for Defense (M&RA), October 1972.

11. Robert J. McIntire, "Project One Hundred Thousand: Update and Critique," Fall 1971, Department of Defense, unpublished.

12. Office of the Assistant Secretary of Defense, *Racial and Ethnic Group Composition of the Male Enlisted Force,* October 1972, table IX.

13. Eli S. Flyer, *Promotion Opportunities for First-Term Enlisted Personnel by Race, Aptitudes, Educational Level of Military Occupation,* Manpower Research Note 71-4, Office of the Assistant Secretary of Defense, April 1971, table 8; and *The Negro in the Armed Forces: A Statistical Fact Book,* September 15, 1971, pp. 10–13.

14. Office of the Assistant Secretary of Defense, *Analysis of Disciplinary Action Affecting First-Term Negro and Caucasian Servicemen,* Manpower Research Note 71-1 (M&RA), April 1971.

15. Flyer, *Promotion Opportunities for First-Term Enlisted Personnel,* table 8.

16. Martin Binkin and John D. Johnston, *All-Volunteer Armed Forces: Progress, Problems, and Prospects,* Report to Senate Committee on Armed Services, 93d Cong., 1st Sess. (Washington: Government Printing Office, June 1973), p. 18.

17. U.S. Bureau of the Census, *Statistical Abstract of the United States, 1970* (Washington: Government Printing Office, 1970), table 243.

18. The following discussion is based on Robert Taggart, *The Prison of Unemployment* (Baltimore: Johns Hopkins University Press, 1972).

19. Federal Bureau of Investigation, *Uniform Crime Reports for the United States, 1969* (Washington: Government Printing Office, 1970), p. 38.

INDEX